The Mahab

by Krishna-Dwaipayana Vyasa

Translated by Kisari Mohan Ganguli

[1883-1896]

SECTION I

(Sabhakriya Parva)

Om! After having bowed down to Narayana, and Nara, the most exalted male being, and also to the goddess Saraswati, must the word Jaya be uttered.

Vaisampayana said,--"Then, in the presence of Vasudeva, Maya Danava, having worshipped Arjuna, repeatedly spoke unto him with joined hands and in amiable words,--'O son of Kunti, saved have I been by thee from this Krishna in spate and from Pavaka (fire) desirous of consuming me. Tell me what I have to do for thee.'

"Arjuna said,--'O great Asura, everything hath already been done by thee (even by this offer of thine). Blest be thou. Go whithersoever thou likest. Be kind and well-disposed towards me, as we are even kind to and well- pleased with thee!'

"Maya said,--'O bull amongst men, what thou hast said is worthy of thee, O exalted one. But O Bharata, I desire to do something for thee cheerfully. I am a great artist, a Viswakarma among the Danavas. O son of Pandu, being what I am, I desire to do something for thee.'

"Arjuna said,--'O sinless one, thou regardest thyself as saved (by me) from imminent death. Even if it hath been so, I cannot make thee do anything for me. At the same time, O Danava, I do not wish to frustrate thy intentions. Do thou something for Krishna. That will be a sufficient requital for my services to thee.'"

Vaisampayana said,--"Then, O bull of the Bharata race, urged by Maya, Vasudeva reflected for a moment as to what he should ask Maya to accomplish. Krishna, the Lord of the universe and the Creator of every object, having reflected in his mind, thus commanded Maya,--'Let a palatial sabha (meeting hall) as thou choosest, be built (by thee), if thou, O son of

Diti, who art the foremost of all artists, desirest to do good to Yudhishthira the just. Indeed, build thou such a palace that persons belonging to the world of men may not be able to imitate it even after examining it with care, while seated within. And, O Maya, build thou a mansion in which we may behold a combination of godly, asuric and human designs.'"

Vaisampayana continued,--"Having heard those words, Maya became exceedingly glad. And he forthwith built a magnificent palace for the son of Pandu like unto the palace of the celestials themselves. Then Krishna and Partha (Arjuna) after having narrated everything unto king Yudhishthira the just, introduced Maya unto him. Yudhishthira received Maya with respect, offering him the honour he deserved. And, O Bharata, Maya accepted that honour thinking highly of it. O monarch of the Bharata race, that great son of Diti then recited unto the sons of Pandu the history of the Danava Vrisha-parva, and that foremost of artists then, having rested awhile, set himself after much thoughtful planning to build a palace for the illustrious sons of Pandu. Agreeably to the wishes of both Krishna and the sons of Pritha, the illustrious Danava of great prowess, having performed on an auspicious day the initial propitiatory rites of foundation and having also gratified thousands of well-versed Brahmanas with sweetened milk and rice and with rich presents of various kinds, measured out a plot of land five thousand cubits square, which was delightful and exceedingly handsome to behold and which was favourable for construction of a building well-suited to the exigencies of every season."

SECTION II

Vaisampayana said,--"Janardana deserving the worship of all, having lived happily at Khandavaprastha for some time, and having been treated all the while with respectful love and affection by the sons of Pritha, became desirous one day of leaving Khandavaprastha to behold his father. That possessor of large eyes, unto whom was due the obeisance of the universe, then saluted both Yudhishthira and Pritha and made obeisance with his head unto the feet of Kunti, his father's sister. Thus revered by Kesava, Pritha smelt his head and embraced him. The illustrious Hrishikesa approached his own sister Subhadra affectionately, with his eyes filled with tears, and spoke unto her words of excellent import and truth, terse proper, unanswerable and fraught with good. The sweet-speeched Subhadra also, saluting him in return and worshipping him repeatedly with bent head, told him all that she wished to be conveyed to her relatives on the paternal side. And bidding her farewell and uttering benedictions on his handsome sister, he of the Vrishni race, next saw Draupadi and Dhaumya. That best of men duly made obeisance unto Dhaumya, and consoling Draupadi obtained leave from her. Then the learned and mighty Krishna, accompanied by Partha, went to his cousins. And surrounded by the five brothers, Krishna shone like Sakra in the midst of the celestials. He whose banner bore the figure of Garuda, desirous of performing the rites preparatory to the commencement of a journey, purified himself by a bath and adorned his person with ornaments. The bull of the Yadu race then worshipped the gods and Brahmanas with floral wreaths, mantras, bows of the head, and excellent perfumes. Having finished all these rites, that foremost of steady and virtuous persons then thought of setting out. The chief of the Yadu race then came out of the inner to the outer apartment, and issuing thence he made unto Brahmanas, deserving of worship, offerings of vessel- fulls of curd and fruits, and parched-grain and caused them to pronounce benedictions upon him. And making unto them presents also of wealth, he went round them. Then ascending his excellent car of gold endued with great speed and adorned with banner bearing the figure of Tarkhya (Garuda) and furnished also with mace, discus, sword, his bow Sharnga and other weapons, and yoking thereunto his horses Saivya and Sugriva, he of eyes like lotuses set out at an excellent moment of a lunar day of auspicious stellar conjunction. And Yudhishthira, the king of the Kurus, from affection, ascended the chariot after Krishna, and causing that best charioteer Daruka to stand aside, himself took the reins. And Arjuna also, of long arms, riding on that car, walked round Krishna and fanned him with a white chamara furnished with a handle of gold. And the mighty Bhimasena accompanied by the twin brothers Nakula and Sahadeva and the priests and citizens all followed Krishna from behind. And Kesava, that slayer of hostile heroes, followed by all the brothers, shone like a preceptor followed by his favourite pupils. Then Govinda spoke unto Arjuna and clasped him firmly, and worshipping Yudhisthira and Bhima, embraced the twins. And embraced in return by the three elder Pandavas, he was reverentially saluted by the twins. After having gone about half a Yojana (two miles), Krishna, that subjugator of hostile towns, respectfully addressed Yudhishthira and requested him, O Bharata, to stop following him further. And Govinda, conversant with every duty, then reverentially saluted Yudhishthira and took hold of his feet. But Yudhishthira soon raised Kesava and smelt his head. King Yudhishthira the just, the son of Pandu, having raised Krishna endued with eyes like lotus-petals and the foremost of the Yadava race, gave him leave, saying,--'Good bye!' Then the slayer of Madhu, making an appointment with them (about his return) in words that were proper, and preventing with difficulty the Pandavas from following him further on foot, gladly proceeded towards his own city, like Indra going towards Amravati. Out of the love and affection they bore him, the Pandavas gazed on Krishna as long as he was within sight, and their minds also followed him when he got out of sight. And Kesava of agreeable person soon disappeared from their sight, unsatiated though their minds were with looking at him. Those bulls among men, the sons of Pritha, with minds fixed on Govinda, desisted (from following him further) and unwillingly returned to their own city in haste. And Krishna in his car soon reached Dwaraka followed by that hero Satyaki. Then Sauri, the son of Devaki, accompanied by his charioteer Daruka reached Dwaraka with the speed of Garuda."

Vaisampayana continued,--"Meanwhile king Yudhishthira of unfading glory, accompanied by his brothers and surrounded by friends, entered his excellent capital. And that tiger among men, dismissing all his relatives, brothers, and sons, sought to make himself happy in the company of Draupadi. And Kesava also, worshipped by the principal Yadavas including Ugrasena, entered with a happy heart his own excellent city. And worshipping his old father and his illustrious mother, and saluting (his brother) Valadeva, he of eyes like lotus-petals took his seat. Embracing Pradyumna, Shamva, Nishatha, Charudeshna, Gada, Aniruddha and Bhanu, and obtaining the leave of all the elderly men, Janardana entered the apartments of Rukmini."

SECTION III

Vaisampayana said,--"Then Maya Danava addressed Arjuna, that foremost of successful warriors, saying,--'I now go with thy leave, but shall come back soon. On the north of the Kailasa peak near the mountains of Mainaka, while the Danavas were engaged in a sacrifice on the banks of Vindu lake, I gathered a huge quantity of delightful and variegated vanda (a kind of rough materials) composed of jewels and gems. This was placed in the mansion of Vrishaparva ever devoted to truth. If it be yet existing, I shall come back, O Bharata, with it. I shall then commence the construction of the delightful palace of the Pandavas, which is to be adorned with every kind of gems and celebrated all over the world. There is also, I think, O thou of the Kuru race, a fierce club placed in the lake Vindu by the King (of the Danavas) after slaughtering therewith all his foes in battle. Besides being heavy and strong and variegated with golden knobs, it is capable of bearing great weight, and of slaying all foes, and is equal in strength unto an hundred thousand clubs. It is a fit weapon for Bhima, even as the Gandiva is for thee. There is also (in that lake) a large conch-shell called Devadatta of loud sound, that came from Varuna. I shall no doubt give all these to thee.' Having spoken thus unto Partha, the Asura went away in a north-easterly direction. On the north of Kailasa in the mountains of Mainaka, there is a huge peak of gems and jewels called Hiranya-sringa. Near that peak is a delightful lake of the name of Vindu. There, on its banks, previously dwelt king Bhagiratha for many years, desiring to behold the goddess Ganga, since called Bhagirathee after that king's name. And there, on its banks, O thou best of the Bharatas, Indra the illustrious lord of every created thing, performed one hundred great sacrifices. There, for the sake of beauty, though not according to the dictates of the ordinance, were placed sacrificial stakes made of gems and altars of gold. There, after performing those sacrifices, the thousand-eyed lord of Sachi became crowned with success. There the fierce Mahadeva, the eternal lord of every creature, has taken up his abode after having created all the worlds and there he dwelleth, worshipped with reverence by thousands of spirits. There Nara and Narayana, Brahma and Yama and Sthanu the fifth, perform their sacrifices at the expiration of a thousand yugas. There, for the establishment of virtue and religion, Vasudeva, with pious devotion, performed his sacrifices extending for many, many long years. There were placed by Keshava thousands and tens of thousands of sacrificial stakes adorned with golden garlands and altars of great splendour. Going thither, O Bharata, Maya brought back the club and the conch-shell and the various crystalline articles that had belonged to king Vrishaparva. And the great Asura, Maya, having gone thither, possessed himself of the whole of the great wealth which was guarded by Yakshas and Rakshasas. Bringing them, the Asura constructed therewith a peerless palace, which was of great beauty and of celestial make, composed entirely of gems and precious stones, and celebrated throughout the three worlds. He gave unto Bhimasena that best of clubs, and unto Arjuna the most excellent conch-shell at whose sound all creatures trembled in awe. And the palace that Maya built consisted of columns of gold, and occupied, O monarch, an area of five thousand cubits. The palace, possessing an exceedingly beautiful form, like unto that of Agni or Suryya, or Soma, shone in great splendour, and by its brilliance seemed to darken even the bright rays of the sun. And with the effulgence it exhibited, which was a mixture of both celestial and terrestrial light, it looked as if it was on fire. Like unto a mass of new clouds conspicuous in the sky, the palace rose up coming into view of all. Indeed, the palace that the dexterous Maya built was so wide, delightful, and refreshing, and composed of such excellent materials, and furnished with such golden walls and archways, and adorned with so many varied pictures, and was withal so rich and well-built, that in beauty it far surpassed Sudharma of the Dasarha race, or the mansion of Brahma himself. And eight thousand Rakshasas called Kinkaras, fierce, huge-bodied and endued with great strength, of red coppery eyes and arrowy ears, well-armed and capable of ranging through the air, used to guard and protect that palace. Within that palace Maya placed a peerless tank, and in that tank were lotuses with leaves of dark-coloured gems and stalks of bright jewels, and other flowers also of golden leaves. And aquatic fowls of various species sported on its bosom. Itself variegated with full-blown lotuses and stocked with fishes and tortoises of golden hue, its bottom was without mud and its water transparent. There was a flight of crystal stairs leading from the banks to the edge of the water. The gentle breezes that swept along its bosom softly shook the flowers that studded it. The banks of that tank were overlaid with slabs of costly marble set with pearls. And beholding that tank thus adorned all around with jewels and precious stones, many kings that came there mistook it for land and fell into it with eyes open. Many tall trees of various kinds were planted all around the palace. Of green foliage and cool shade, and ever blossoming, they were all very charming to behold. Artificial woods were laid around, always emitting a delicious fragrance. And there were many tanks also that were adorned with swans and Karandavas and Chakravakas (Brahminy ducks) in the grounds lying about the mansion. And the breeze bearing the fragrance of lotuses growing in water and (of those growing on land) ministered unto the pleasure and happiness of the Pandavas. And Maya having constructed such a palatial hall within fourteen months, reported its completion unto Yudhishthira."

SECTION IV

Vaisampayana said,--"Then that chief of men, king Yudhishthira, entered that palatial sabha having first fed ten thousand Brahmanas with preparations of milk and rice mixed with clarified butter and honey with fruits and roots, and with pork and venison. The king gratified those superior Brahmanas, who had come from various countries with food seasoned with seasamum and prepared with vegetables called jibanti, with rice mixed with clarified butter, with different preparations of meat--with indeed various kinds of other food, as also numberless viands that are fit to be sucked and innumerable kinds of drinks, with new and unused robes and clothes, and with excellent floral wreaths. The king also gave unto each of those Brahmanas a thousand kine. And, O Bharata, the voice of the gratified Brahmanas uttering,--'What an auspicious day is this!' became so loud that it seemed to reach heaven itself. And when the Kuru king entered the palatial sabha having also worshipped the gods with various kinds of music and numerous species of excellent and costly perfumes, the athletes and mimes and prize-fighters and bards and encomiasts began to gratify that illustrious son of Dharma by exhibiting their skill. And thus celebrating his entry into the palace, Yudhishthira with his brothers sported within that palace like Sakra himself in heaven. Upon the seats in that palace sat, along with the Pandavas, Rishis and kings that came from various countries, viz., Asita and Devala, Satya, Sarpamali and Mahasira; Arvavasu, Sumitra, Maitreya, Sunaka and Vali; Vaka, Dalvya, Sthulasira, Krishna-Dwaipayana, and Suka Sumanta, Jaimini, Paila, and the disciples of Vyasa, viz., ourselves; Tittiri, Yajanavalkya, and Lomaharshana with his son; Apsuhomya, Dhaumya, Animandavya; and Kausika; Damoshnisha and Traivali, Parnada, and Varayanuka, Maunjayana, Vayubhaksha, Parasarya, and Sarika; Valivaka, Silivaka, Satyapala, and Krita-srama; Jatukarna, and Sikhavat. Alamva and Parijataka; the exalted Parvata, and the great Muni Markandeya; Pavitrapani, Savarna, Bhaluki, and Galava. Janghabandhu, Raibhya, Kopavega, and Bhrigu: Harivabhru, Kaundinya, Vabhrumali, and Sanatana, Kakshivat, and Ashija, Nachiketa, and Aushija, Nachiketa, and Gautama; Painga, Varaha, Sunaka, and Sandilya of great ascetic merit: Kukkura, Venujangha, Kalapa and Katha;--these virtuous and learned Munis with senses and souls under complete control, and many others as numerous, all well-skilled in the Vedas and Vedangas and conversant with (rules of) morality and pure and spotless in behaviour, waited on the illustrious Yudhishthira, and gladdened him by their sacred discourses. And so also numerous principal Kshatriyas, such as the illustrious and virtuous Mujaketu, Vivarddhana, Sangramjit, Durmukha, the powerful Ugrasena; Kakshasena, the lord of the Earth, Kshemaka the invincible; Kamatha, the king of Kamvoja, and the mighty Kampana who alone made the Yavanas to ever tremble at his name just as the god that wieldeth the thunder-bolt maketh those Asuras, the Kalakeyas, tremble before him; Jatasura, and the king of the Madrakas, Kunti, Pulinda the king of the Kiratas, and the kings of Anga and Vanga, and Pandrya, and the king of Udhara, and Andhaka; Sumitra, and Saivya that slayer of foes; Sumanas, the king of the Kiratas, and Chanur the King of the Yavanas, Devarata, Bhoja, and the so called Bhimaratha, Srutayudha--the king of Kalinga, Jayasena the king of Magadha; and Sukarman, and Chekitana, and Puru that slayer of foes; Ketumata, Vasudana, and Vaideha and Kritakshana:

Sudharman, Aniruddha, Srutayu endued with great strength; the invincible Anuparaja, the handsome Karmajit; Sisupala with his son, the king of Karusha; and the invincible youths of the Vrishni race, all equal in beauty unto the celestials, viz., Ahuka, Viprithu, Sada, Sarana, Akrura, Kritavarman, and Satyaka, the son of Sini; and Bhismaka, Ankriti, and the powerful Dyumatsena, those chief of bowmen viz., the Kaikeyas and Yajnasena of the Somaka race; these Kshatriyas endued with great might, all well-armed and wealthy, and many others also regarded as the foremost, all waited upon Yudhishthira, the son of Kunti, in that Sabha, desirous of ministering to his happiness. And those princes also, endued with great strength, who dressing themselves in deer-skins learnt the science of weapons under Arjuna, waited upon Yudhishthira. And O king, the princes also of the Vrishni race, viz., Pradyumna (the son of Rukmini) and Samva, and Yuyudhana the son of Satyaki and Sudharman and Aniruddha and Saivya that foremost of men who had learnt the science of arms under Arjuna these and many other kings, O lord of the Earth, used to wait on Yudhishthira on that occasion. And that friend of Dhananjaya, Tumvuru, and the Gandharva Chittasena with his ministers, any many other Gandharvas and Apsaras, well-skilled in vocal and instrumental music and in cadence and Kinnaras also well-versed in (musical) measures and motions singing celestial tunes in proper and charming voices, waited upon and gladdened the sons of Pandu and the Rishis who sat in that Sabha. And seated in that Sabha, those bull among men, of rigid vows and devoted to truth, all waited upon Yudhishthira like the celestials in heaven waiting upon Brahma."

SECTION V

(Lokapala Sabhakhayana Parva)

Vaisampayana said,--"While the illustrious Pandavas were seated in that Sabha along with the principal Gandharvas, there came, O Bharata, unto that assembly the celestial Rishi Narada, conversant with the Vedas and Upanishadas, worshipped by the celestials acquainted with histories and Puranas, well-versed in all that occurred in ancient kalpas (cycles), conversant with Nyaya (logic) and the truth of moral science, possessing a complete knowledge of the six Angas (viz., pronunciation, grammar, prosody, explanation of basic terms, description of religious rites, and astronomy). He was a perfect master in reconciling contradictory texts and differentiating in applying general principles to particular cases, as also in interpreting contraries by reference to differences in situation, eloquent, resolute, intelligent, possessed of powerful memory. He was acquainted with the science of morals and politics, learned, proficient in distinguishing inferior things from superior ones, skilled in drawing inference from evidence, competent to judge of the correctness or incorrectness of syllogistic statements consisting of five propositions. He was capable of answering successively Vrihaspati himself while arguing, with definite conclusions properly framed about religion, wealth, pleasure and salvation, of great soul and beholding this whole universe, above, below, and around, as if it were present before his eyes. He was master of both the Sankhya and Yoga systems of philosophy, ever desirous of humbling the celestials and Asuras by fomenting quarrels among them, conversant with the sciences of war and treaty, proficient in drawing conclusions by judging of things not within direct ken, as also in the six sciences of treaty, war, military campaigns, maintenance of posts against the enemy and stratagems by ambuscades and reserves. He was a thorough master of every branch of learning, fond of war and music, incapable of being repulsed by any science or any course of action, and possessed of these and numberless other accomplishments. The Rishi, having wandered over the different worlds, came into that Sabha. And the celestial Rishi of immeasurable splendour, endued with great energy was accompanied, O monarch, by Parijata and the intelligent Raivata and Saumya and Sumukha. Possessing the speed of the mind, the Rishi came thither and was filled with gladness upon beholding the Pandavas. The Brahmana, on arriving there, paid homage unto Yudhishthira by uttering blessings on him and wishing him victory. Beholding the learned Rishi arrive, the eldest of the Pandavas, conversant with all rules of duty, quickly stood up with his younger brothers. Bending low with humility, the monarch cheerfully saluted the Rishi, and gave with due ceremonies a befitting seat unto him. The king also gave him kine and the usual offerings of the Arghya including honey and the other ingredients. Conversant with every duty the monarch also worshipped the Rishi with gems and jewels with a whole heart. Receiving that worship from Yudhishthira in proper form, the Rishi became gratified. Thus worshipped by the Pandavas and the great Rishis, Narada possessing a complete mastery over the Vedas, said unto Yudhishthira the following words bearing upon religion, wealth, pleasures and salvation.

"Narada said--'Is the wealth thou art earning being spent on proper objects? Doth thy mind take pleasure in virtue? Art thou enjoying the pleasures of life? Doth not thy mind sink under their weight? O chief of men, continuest thou in the noble conduct consistent with religion and wealth practised by thy ancestors towards the three classes of subjects, (viz., good, indifferent, and bad)? Never injurest thou religion for the sake of wealth, or both religion and wealth for the sake of pleasure that easily seduces? O thou foremost of victorious men ever devoted to the good of all, conversant as thou art with the timeliness of everything, followest thou religion, wealth, pleasure and salvation dividing thy time judiciously? O sinless one, with the six attributes of kings (viz., cleverness of speech, readiness in providing means, intelligence in dealing with the foe, memory, and acquaintance with morals and politics), dost thou attend to the seven means (viz., sowing dissensions, chastisement, conciliation, gifts, incantations, medicine and magic)? Examinest thou also, after a survey of thy own strength and weakness, the fourteen possessions of thy foes? These are the country, forts, cars, elephants, cavalry, foot-soldiers, the principal officials of state, the zenana, food supply, computations of the army and income, the religious treatises in force, the accounts of state, the revenue, wine-shops and other secret enemies. Attendest thou to the eight occupations (of agriculture, trade, &c), having examined, O thou foremost of victorious monarchs, thy own and thy enemy's means, and having made peace with thy enemies? O bull of the Bharata race, thy seven principal officers of state (viz., the governor of the citadel, the commander of forces, the chief judge, the general in interior command, the chief priest, the chief physician, and the chief astrologer), have not, I hope, succumbed to the influence of thy foes, nor have they, I hope, become idle in consequence of the wealth they have earned? They are, I hope, all obedient to thee. Thy counsels, I hope, are never divulged by thy trusted spies in disguise, by thyself or by thy ministers? Thou ascertainest, I hope, what thy friends, foes and strangers are about? Makest thou peace and makest thou war at proper times? Observest thou neutrality towards strangers and persons that are neutral towards thee? And, O hero, hast thou made persons like thyself, persons that are old, continent in behaviour, capable of understanding what should be done and what should not, pure as regards birth and blood, and devoted to thee, thy ministers? O Bharata, the victories of kings can be attributed to good counsels. O child, is thy kingdom protected by ministers learned in Sastras, keeping their counsels close? Are thy foes unable to injure it? Thou hast not become the slave of sleep? Wakest thou at the proper time? Conversant with pursuits yielding profit, thinkest thou, during the small hours of night, as to what thou shouldst do and what thou shouldst not do the next day? Thou settlest nothing alone, nor takest counsels with many? The counsels thou hast resolved upon, do not become known all over thy kingdom? Commencest thou soon to accomplish measures of great utility that are easy of accomplishment? Such measures are never obstructed? Keepest thou the agriculturists not out of thy sight? They do not fear to approach thee? Achievest thou thy measures through persons that are trusted incorruptible, and possessed of practical experience? And, O brave king, I hope, people only know the measures already accomplished by thee and those that have been partially accomplished and are awaiting completion, but not those that are only in contemplation and uncommenced? Have experienced teachers capable of explaining the causes of things and learned in the science of morals and every branch of learning, been appointed to instruct the princes and the chiefs of the army? Buyest thou a single learned man by giving in exchange a thousand ignorant individuals? The man that is learned conferreth the greatest benefit in seasons of distress. Are thy forts always filled with treasure, food, weapons, water, engines and instruments, as also with engineers and bowmen? Even a single minister that is intelligent, brave, with his passions under complete control, and possessed of wisdom and judgment, is capable of conferring the highest prosperity on a king or a king's son. I ask thee, therefore, whether there is even one such minister with thee? Seekest thou to know everything about the eighteen Tirthas of the foe and fifteen of thy own by means of three and three spies all unacquainted with one another? O slayer of all foes, watchest thou all thy enemies with care and attention, and unknown to them? Is the priest thou honourest, possessed of humility, and purity of blood, and renown, and without jealousy and illiberality? Hath any well- behaved, intelligent, and guileless Brahmana, well-up in the ordinance, been employed by thee in the performance of thy daily rites before the sacred fire, and doth he remind thee in proper time as to when thy homa should be performed? Is the astrologer thou hast employed skilled in reading physiognomy, capable of interpreting omens, and competent to neutralise the effect of the disturbances of nature? Have respectable servants been employed by thee in offices that are respectable, indifferent ones in indifferent offices, and low ones in offices that are low? Hast thou appointed to high offices ministers that are guileless and of well conduct for generations and above the common run? Oppressest thou not thy people with cruel and severe punishment? And, O bull of the Bharata race, do thy ministers rule thy kingdom under thy orders? Do thy ministers ever slight thee like sacrificial priests slighting men that are fallen (and incapable of performing any more sacrifices) or like wives slighting husbands that are proud and incontinent in their behaviour? Is the commander of thy forces possessed of sufficient confidence, brave, intelligent, patient, well-conducted, of good birth, devoted to thee, and competent? Treatest thou with consideration and regard the chief officers of thy army that are skilled in every kind of welfare, are forward, well- behaved, and endued with prowess? Givest thou to thy troops their sanctioned rations and pay in the appointed time? Thou dost not oppress them by withholding these? Knowest thou that the misery caused by arrears of pay and irregularity in the distribution of rations driveth the troops to mutiny, and that is called by the learned to be one of the greatest of mischiefs? Are all the principal high-born men devoted to thee, and ready with cheerfulness to lay down their lives in battle for thy sake? I hope no single individual of passions uncontrolled is ever permitted by thee to rule as he likes a number of concerns at the same time appertaining to the army? Is any servant of thine, who hath accomplished well a particular business by the employment of special ability, disappointed in obtaining from thee a little more regard, and an increase of food and pay? I hope thou rewardest persons of learning and humility, and skill in every kind of knowledge with gifts of wealth and honour proportionate to their qualifications. Dost thou support, O bull in the Bharata race, the wives and children of men that have given their lives for thee and have been distressed on thy account? Cherishest thou, O son of Pritha, with paternal affection the foe that hath been weakened, or him also that hath sought thy shelter, having been vanquished in battle? O lord of Earth, art thou equal unto all men, and can every one approach thee without fear, as if thou wert their mother and father? And O bull of the Bharata race, marchest thou, without loss of time, and reflecting well upon three kinds of forces, against thy foe when thou hearest that he is in distress? O subjugator of all foes beginnest thou thy march when the time cometh, having taken into consideration all the omens you might see, the resolutions thou hast made, and that the ultimate victory depends upon the twelve mandalas (such as reserves, ambuscades, &c, and payment of pay to the troops in advance)? And, O persecutor of all foes, givest thou gems and jewels, unto the principal officers of enemy, as they deserve, without thy enemy's knowledge? O son of Pritha, seekest thou to conquer thy incensed foes that are slaves to their passions, having first conquered thy own soul and obtained the mastery over thy own senses? Before thou marchest out against thy foes, dost thou properly employ the four arts of reconciliation, gift (of wealth) producing disunion, and application of force? O monarch, goest thou out against thy enemies, having first strengthened thy own kingdom? And having gone out against them, exertest thou to the utmost to obtain victory over them? And having conquered them, seekest thou to protect them with care? Are thy army consisting of four kinds of forces, viz., the regular troops, the allies, the mercenaries, and the irregulars, each furnished with the eight ingredients, viz., cars, elephants, horses, offices, infantry, camp-followers, spies possessing a thorough knowledge of the country, and ensigns led out against thy enemies after having been well trained by superior officers? O oppressor of all foes, O great king, I hope thou slayest thy foes without regarding their seasons of reaping and of famine? O king, I hope thy servants and agents in thy own kingdom and in the kingdoms of thy foes continue to look after their respective duties and to protect one another. O monarch, I hope trusted servants have been employed by thee to look after thy food, the robes thou wearest and the perfumes thou usest. I hope, O king, thy treasury, barns, stables arsenals, and women's apartments, are all protected by servants devoted to thee and ever seeking thy welfare. I hope, O monarch, thou protectest first thyself from thy domestic and public servants, then from those servants of thy relatives and from one another. Do thy servants, O king, ever speak to thee in the forenoon regarding thy extravagant expenditure in respect of thy drinks, sports, and women? Is thy expenditure always covered by a fourth, a third or a half of thy income? Cherishest thou always, with food and wealth, relatives, superiors, merchants, the aged, and other proteges, and the distressed? Do the accountants and clerks employed by thee in looking after thy income and expenditure, always appraise thee every day in the forenoon of thy income and expenditure? Dismissest thou without fault servants accomplished in business and popular and devoted to thy welfare? O Bharata, dost thou employ superior, indifferent, and low men, after examining them well in offices they deserve? O monarch, employest thou in thy business persons that are thievish or open to temptation, or hostile, or minors? Persecutest thou thy kingdom by the help of thievish or covetous men, or minors, or women? Are the agriculturists in thy kingdom contented. Are large tanks and lakes constructed all over thy kingdom at proper distances, without agriculture being in thy realm entirely dependent on the showers of heaven? Are the agriculturists in thy kingdom wanting in either seed or food? Grantest thou with kindness loans (of seed-grains) unto the tillers, taking only a fourth in excess of every measure by the hundred? O child, are the four professions of agriculture, trade, cattle-rearing, and lending at interest, carried on by honest men? Upon these O monarch, depends the happiness of thy people. O king, do the five brave and wise men, employed in the five offices of protecting the city, the citadel, the merchants, and the agriculturists, and punishing the criminals, always benefit thy kingdom by working in union with one another? For the protection of thy city, have the villages been made like towns, and the hamlets and outskirts of villages like villages? Are all these entirely under thy supervision and sway? Are thieves and robbers that sack thy town pursued by thy police over the even and uneven parts of thy kingdom? Consolest thou women and are they protected in thy realm? I hope thou placest not any confidence in them, nor divulgest any secret before any of them? O monarch, having heard of any danger and having reflected on it also, liest thou in the inner apartments enjoying every agreeable object? Having slept during the second and the third divisions of the night, thinkest thou of religion and profit in the fourth division wakefully. O son of Pandu, rising from bed at the proper time and dressing thyself well, showest thou thyself to thy people, accompanied by ministers conversant with the auspiciousness or otherwise of moments? O represser of all foes, do men dressed in red and armed with swords and adorned with ornaments stand by thy side to protect thy person? O monarch! behavest thou like the god of justice himself unto those that deserve punishment and those that deserve worship, unto those that are dear to thee and those that thou likest not? O son of Pritha, seekest thou to cure bodily diseases by medicines and fasts, and mental illness with the advice of the aged? I hope that the physicians engaged in looking after thy health are well conversant with the eight kinds of treatment and are all attached and devoted to thee. Happeneth it ever, O monarch, that from covetousness or folly or pride thou failest to decide between the plaintiff and the defendant who have come to thee? Deprivest thou, through covetousness or folly, of their pensions the proteges who have sought thy shelter from trustfulness or love? Do the people that inhabit thy realm, bought by thy foes, ever seek to raise disputes with thee, uniting themselves with one another? Are those amongst thy foes that are feeble always repressed by the help of troops that are strong, by the help of both counsels and troops? Are all the principal chieftains (of thy empire) all devoted to thee? Are they ready to lay down their lives for thy sake, commanded by thee? Dost thou worship Brahmanas and wise men according to their merits in respect of various branches of learning? I tell thee, such worship is without doubt, highly beneficial to thee. Hast thou faith in the religion based on the three Vedas and practised by men who have gone before thee? Dost thou carefully follow the practices that were followed by them? Are accomplished Brahmanas entertained in thy house and in thy presence with nutritive and excellent food, and do they also obtain pecuniary gifts at the conclusion of those feasts? Dost thou, with passions under complete control and with singleness of mind, strive to perform the sacrifices called Vajapeya and Pundarika with their full complement of rites? Bowest thou unto thy relatives and superiors, the aged, the gods, the ascetics, the Brahmanas, and the tall trees (banian) in villages, that are of so much benefit to people? O sinless one, causest thou ever grief or anger in any one? Do priests capable of granting thee auspicious fruits ever stand by thy side? O sinless one, are thy inclinations and practices such as I have described them, and as always enhance the duration of life and spread one's renown and as always help the cause of religion, pleasure, and profit? He who conducteth himself according to this way, never findeth his kingdom distressed or afflicted; and that monarch, subjugating the whole earth, enjoyeth a high degree of felicity. O monarch, I hope, no well-behaved, pure-souled, and respected person is ever ruined and his life taken, on a false charge or theft, by thy ministers ignorant of Sastras and acting from greed? And, O bull among men, I hope thy ministers never from covetousness set free a real thief, knowing him to be such and having apprehended him with the booty about him? O Bharata, I hope, thy ministers are never won over by bribes, nor do they wrongly decide the disputes that arise between the rich and the poor. Dost thou keep thyself free from the fourteen vices of kings, viz., atheism, untruthfulness, anger, incautiousness, procrastination, non-visit to the wise, idleness, restlessness of mind, taking counsels with only one man, consultation with persons unacquainted with the science of profit, abandonment of a settled plan, divulgence of counsels, non-accomplishment of beneficial projects, and undertaking everything without reflection? By these, O king, even monarchs firmly seated on their thrones are ruined. Hath thy study of the Vedas, thy wealth and knowledge of the Sastras and marriage been fruitful?'"

Vaisampayana continued,--"After the Rishi had finished, Yudhishthira asked,--'How, O Rishi, do the Vedas, wealth, wife, and knowledge of the Sastras bear fruit?'

"The Rishi answered,--'The Vedas are said to bear fruit when he that hath studied them performeth the Agnihotra and other sacrifices. Wealth is said to bear fruit when he that hath it enjoyeth it himself and giveth it away in charity. A wife is said to bear fruit when she is useful and when she beareth children. Knowledge of the Sastras is said to bear fruit when it resulteth in humility and good behaviour.'"

Vaisampayana continued,--"The great ascetic Narada, having answered Yudhishthira thus, again asked that just ruler,--'Do the officers of thy government, O king, that are paid from the taxes levied on the community, take only their just dues from the merchants that come to thy territories from distant lands impelled by the desire of gain? Are the merchants, O king, treated with consideration in thy capital and kingdom, capable of bringing their goods thither without being deceived by the false pretexts of (both the buyers and the officers of government)?

"'Listenest thou always, O monarch, to the words, fraught with instructions in religion and wealth, of old men acquainted with economic doctrines? Are gifts of honey and clarified butter made to the Brahmanas intended for the increase of agricultural produce, of kine, of fruits and flowers, and for the sake of virtue? Givest thou always, O king, regularly unto all the artisans and artists employed by thee the materials of their works and their wages for periods not more than four months? Examinest thou the works executed by those that are employed by thee, and applaudest thou them before good men, and rewardest thou them, having shewn them proper respect? O bull of the Bharata race, followest thou the aphorisms (of the sage) in respect of every concern particularly those relating to elephants, horses, and cars? O bull of the Bharata race, are the aphorisms relating to the science of arms, as also those that relate to the practice of engines in warfare--so useful to towns and fortified places, studied in thy court? O sinless one, art thou acquainted with all mysterious incantations, and with the secrets of poisons destructive of all foes? Protectest thou thy kingdom from the fear of fire, of snakes and other animals destructive of life, of disease, and Rakshasas? As acquainted thou art with every duty, cherishest thou like a father, the blind, the dumb, the lame, the deformed, the friendless, and ascetics that have no homes. Hast thou banished these six evils, O monarch, viz., sleep, idleness, fear, anger, weakness of mind, and procrastination?'"

Vaisampayana continued,--"The illustrious bull among the Kurus, having heard these words of that best of Brahmanas, bowed down unto him and worshipped his feet. And gratified with everything he heard, the monarch said unto Narada of celestial form,--'I shall do all that thou hast directed, for my knowledge hath expanded under thy advice!' Having said this the king acted conformably to that advice, and gained in time the whole Earth bounded by her belt of seas. Narada again spoke, saying,-- 'That king who is thus employed in the protection of four orders, Brahmanas, Kshatriyas, Vaishyas, and Sudras, passeth his days here happily and attaineth hereafter to the region of Sakra (heaven).'"

SECTION VI

Vaisampayana said,--"At the conclusion of Narada's words, king Yudhishthira the just worshipped him duly; and commanded by him the monarch began to reply succinctly to the questions the Rishi had asked.

"Yudhishthira said--'O holy one, the truths of religion and morality thou hast indicated one after another, are just and proper. As regards myself, I duly observe those ordinances to the best of my power. Indeed, the acts that were properly performed by monarchs of yore are, without doubt, to be regarded as bearing proper fruit, and undertaken from solid reasons for the attainment of proper objects. O master, we desire to walk in the virtuous path of those rulers that had, besides, their souls under complete control.'"

Vaisampayana continued,--"Yudhishthira, the son of Pandu, possessed of great glory, having received with reverence the words of Narada and having also answered the Rishi thus, reflected for a moment. And perceiving a proper opportunity, the monarch, seated beside the Rishi, asked Narada sitting at his ease and capable of going into every world at will, in the presence of that assembly of kings, saying,--'Possessed of the speed of mind, thou wanderest over various and many worlds created in days of yore by Brahma, beholding everything. Tell me, I ask thee, if thou hast, O Brahmana, ever beheld before anywhere an assembly room like this of mine or superior to it!' Hearing these words of Yudhishthira the just, Narada smilingly answered the son of Pandu in these sweet accents,--

"Narada said,--'O child, O king I did neither see nor hear of ever before amongst men, any assembly room built of gems and precious stones like this of thine, O Bharata. I shall, however, describe unto thee the rooms of the king of the departed (Yama), of Varuna (Neptune) of great intelligence, of Indra, the King of Gods and also of him who hath his home in Kailasha (Kuvera). I shall also describe unto thee the celestial Sabha of Brahma that dispelleth every kind of uneasiness. All these assembly rooms exhibit in their structure both celestial and human designs and present every kind of form that exists in the universe. And they are ever worshipped by the gods and the Pitris, the Sadhyas, (under-deities called Gana), by ascetics offering sacrifices, with souls under complete command, by peaceful Munis engaged without intermission in Vedic sacrifices with presents to Brahmanas. I shall describe all these to you if, O bull of the Bharata race, thou hast any inclinations to listen to me!'"

Vaisampayana continued,--"Thus addressed by Narada, the high-souled king Yudhishthira the just, with his brothers and all those foremost of Brahmanas (seated around him), joined his hands (in entreaty). And the monarch then asked Narada, saying,--'Describe unto us all those assembly rooms. We desire to listen to thee. O Brahmana, what are the articles with which each of the Sabhas are made of? What is the area of each, and what is the length and breadth of each? Who wait upon the Grandsire in that assembly room? And who also upon Vasava, the Lord of the celestials and upon Yama, the son of Vivaswana? Who wait upon Varuna and upon Kuvera in their respective assembly rooms. O Brahmana Rishi, tell us all about these. We all together desire to hear thee describe them. Indeed, our curiosity is great.'" Thus addressed by the son of Pandu, Narada replied, saying,--"O monarch, hear ye all about those celestial assembly rooms one after another."

SECTION VII

"Narada said,--'the celestial assembly room of Sakra is full of lustre. He hath obtained it as the fruit of his own acts. Possessed of the splendour of the sun, it was built, O scion of the Kuru race, by Sakra himself. Capable of going everywhere at will, this celestial assembly house is full one hundred and fifty yojanas in length, and hundred yojanas in breadth, and five yojanas in height. Dispelling weakness of age, grief, fatigue, and fear, auspicious and bestowing good fortune, furnished with rooms and seats and adorned with celestial trees, it is delightful in the extreme. There sitteth in that assembly room, O son of Pritha, on an excellent seat, the Lord of celestials, with his wife Sachi endowed with beauty and affluence. Assuming a form incapable of description for its vagueness, with a crown on his head and bright bracelets on the upper arms, attired in robes of pure white and decked with floral wreaths of many hues, there he sitteth with beauty, fame, and glory by his side. And the illustrious deity of a hundred sacrifices is daily waited upon, O monarch, in that assembly by the Marutas in a body, each leading the life of a householder in the bosom of his family. And the Siddhyas, celestial Rishis, the Sadhyas in all, the gods, and Marutas of brilliant complexion and adorned with golden garlands,--all of them in celestial form and decked in ornaments, always wait upon and worship the illustrious chief of the immortals, that mighty represser of all foes. And O son of Pritha, the celestial Rishis also, all of pure souls, with sins completely washed off and resplendent as the fire, and possessed of energy, and without sorrow of any kind, and freed from the fever of anxiety, and all performers of the Soma sacrifice, also wait upon and worship Indra. And Parasara and Parvata and Savarni and Galava; and Sankha, and the Muni, Gaursiras, and Durvasa, and Krodhana and Swena and the Muni Dhirghatamas; and Pavitrapani, Savarni, Yajnavalkya and Bhaluki; and Udyalaka, Swetaketu, and Tandya, and also Bhandayani; and Havishmat, and Garishta, and king Harischandra; and Hridya, Udarshandilya. Parasarya, Krishivala; Vataskandha, Visakha, Vidhatas and Kala. Karaladanta, Tastri, and Vishwakarman, and Tumuru;

and other Rishis, some born of women and others living upon air, and others again living upon fire, these all worship Indra, the wielder of the thunderbolt, the lord of all the worlds. And Sahadeva, and Sunitha, and Valmiki of great ascetic merit; and Samika of truthful speech, and Prachetas ever fulfilling their promises, and Medhatithi, and Vamadeva, and Pulastya, Pulaha and Kratu; and Maruta and Marichi, and Sthanu of great ascetic merit; and Kakshivat, and Gautama, and Tarkhya, and also the Muni Vaishwanara; and the Muni Kalakavrikhiya and Asravya, and also Hiranmaya, and Samvartta, and Dehavya, and Viswaksena of great energy; and Kanwa, and Katyayana, O king, and Gargya, and Kaushika;--all are present there along with the celestial waters and plants; and faith, and intelligence, and the goddess of learning, and wealth, religion, and pleasure; and lightning, O son of Pandu; and the rain-charged clouds, and the winds, and all the loud-sounding forces of heaven; the eastern point, the twenty seven fires conveying the sacrificial butter, Agni and Soma, and the fire of Indra, and Mitra, and Savitri, and Aryaman; Bhaga, Viswa the Sadhyas, the preceptor (Vrihaspati), and also Sukra; and Vishwavasu and Chitrasena, and Sumanas, and also Taruna; the Sacrifices, the gifts to Brahmanas, the planets, and the stars, O Bharata, and the mantras that are uttered in sacrifices--all these are present there. And, O King, many Apsaras and Gandharvas, by various kinds of dances and music both instrumental and vocal, and by the practice of auspicious rites, and by the exhibition of many feats of skill, gratify the lord of the celestials-- Satakratu--the illustrious slayer of Vala and Vritra. Besides these, many other Brahmanas and royal and celestial Rishis, all resplendent as the fire, decked in floral wreaths and ornaments, frequently come to and leave that assembly, riding on celestial cars of various kinds. And Vrihaspati and Sukra are present there on all occasions. These and many other illustrious ascetics of rigid vows, and Bhrigu and the seven Rishis who are equal, O king, unto Brahma himself, come to and leave that assembly house, riding on cars beautiful as the car of Soma, and themselves looking as bright therein as Soma himself. This, O mighty armed monarch, is the assembly house, called Pushkaramalini, of Indra of a hundred sacrifices that I have seen. Listen now to the account of Yama's assembly house.'

SECTION VIII

"Narada said,--'O Yudhisthira, I shall now describe the assembly house of
Yama, the son of Vivaswat, which, O son of Pritha, was built by
Viswakarma. Listen now to me. Bright as burnished gold, that assembly
house, O monarch, covers an area of much more than a hundred yojanas.
Possessed of the splendour of the sun, it yieldeth everything that one may
desire. Neither very cool nor very hot, it delighteth the heart. In that
assembly house there is neither grief nor weakness of age, neither hunger
nor thirst. Nothing disagreeable findeth a place there, nor any kind of evil
feelings there. Every object of desire, celestial or human, is to be found in
that mansion. And all kinds of enjoyable articles, as also of sweet, juicy,
agreeable, and delicious edibles in profusion that are licked, sucked, and
drunk, are there, O chastiser of all enemies. The floral wreaths in that
mansion are of the most delicious fragrance, and the trees that stand around
it yield fruits that are desired of them. There are both cold and hot waters
and these are sweet and agreeable. In that mansion many royal sages of great
sanctity and Brahmana sages also of great purity, cheerfully wait upon, O
child, and worship Yama, the son of Vivaswat. And Yayati, Nahusha, Puru,
Mandhatri, Somaka, Nriga; the royal sage Trasadasyu, Kritavirya,
Sautasravas; Arishtanemi, Siddha, Kritavega, Kriti, Nimi, Pratarddana, Sivi,
Matsya, Prithulaksha, Vrihadratha, Vartta, Marutta, Kusika, Sankasya,
Sankriti, Dhruva, Chaturaswa, Sadaswormi and king Kartavirya; Bharata
and Suratha, Sunitha, Nisatha, Nala, Divodasa, and Sumanas, Amvarisha,
Bhagiratha; Vyaswa, Vadhraswa, Prithuvega, Prithusravas, Prishadaswa,
Vasumanas, Kshupa, and Sumahavala, Vrishadgu, and Vrishasena,
Purukutsa, Dhwajin and Rathin; Arshtisena, Dwilipa, and the high-souled
Ushinara; Ausinari, Pundarika, Saryati, Sarava, and Suchi; Anga, Rishta,
Vena, Dushmanta, Srinjaya and Jaya; Bhangasuri, Sunitha, and Nishada, and
Bahinara; Karandhama, Valhika, Sudymna, and the mighty Madhu; Aila and
the mighty king of earth Maruta; Kapota, Trinaka, and Shadeva, and Arjuna
also. Vysawa; Saswa and Krishaswa, and king Sasavindu; Rama the son of
Dasaratha, and Lakshmana, and Pratarddana; Alarka, and Kakshasena, Gaya,
and Gauraswa; Rama the son of Jamadagnya, Nabhaga, and Sagara;

Bhuridyumna and Mahaswa, Prithaswa, and also Janaka; king Vainya, Varisena, Purujit, and Janamejaya; Brahmadatta, and Trigarta, and king Uparichara also; Indradyumna, Bhimajanu, Gauraprishta, Nala, Gaya; Padma and Machukunda, Bhuridyumna, Prasenajit; Aristanemi, Sudymna, Prithulauswa, and Ashtaka also; a hundred kings of the Matsya race and hundred of the Vipa and a hundred of the Haya races; a hundred kings of the name of Dhritarashtra, eighty kings of the name of Janamejaya; a hundred monarchs called Brahmadatta, and a hundred kings of the name of Iri; more than two hundred Bhishmas, and also a hundred Bhimas; a hundred Prativindhyas, a hundred Nagas, and a hundred Palasas, and a hundred called Kasa and Kusa; that king of kings Santanu, and thy father Pandu, Usangava, Sata-ratha, Devaraja, Jayadratha; the intelligent royal sage Vrishadarva with his ministers; and a thousand other kings known by the name of Sasa-vindu, and who have died, having performed many grand horse-sacrifices with large presents to the Brahmanas--these holy royal sages of grand achievements and great knowledge of the Sastras, wait upon, O King, and worship the son of Vivaswat in that assembly house. And Agastya and Matanga, and Kala, and Mrityu (Death), performers of sacrifices, the Siddhas, and many Yogins; the Prtris (belonging to the classes--called Agniswattas, Fenapa, Ushampa, Swadhavat, and Verhishada), as also those others that have forms; the wheel of time, and the illustrious conveyer himself of the sacrificial butter; all sinners among human beings, as also those that have died during the winter solstice; these officers of Yama who have been appointed to count the allotted days of everybody and everything; the Singsapa, Palasa, Kasa, and Kusa trees and plants, in their embodied forms, these all, O king, wait upon and worship the god of justice in that assembly house of his. These and many others are present at the Sabha of the king of the Pitris (manes). So numerous are they that I am incapable of describing them either by mentioning their names or deeds. O son of Pritha, the delightful assembly house, moving everywhere at the will of its owner, is of wide extent. It was built by Viswakarma after a long course of ascetic penances. And, O Bharata, resplendent with his own effulgence, it stands glorified in all its beauty. Sannyasis of severe ascetic penance, of excellent vows, and of truthful speech, peaceful and pure and sanctified by holy deeds, of shining bodies and attired in spotless robes, decked with bracelets and floral garlands, with ear-rings of burnished gold, and adorned with their own holy acts as with the marks of their order (painted over their bodies), constantly visit that Sabha (Assembly). Many illustrious Gandharvas, and many Apsaras fill every part of that mansion with music; both instrumental and vocal and with sounds of laughter and dance. And, O son of Pritha, excellent perfumes, and sweet sounds and garlands of celestial flowers always contribute towards making that mansion supremely blest. And hundreds of thousands of virtuous persons, of celestial beauty and great wisdom, always wait upon and worship the illustrious Yama, the lord of created beings in that assembly house. Such, O monarch, is the Sabha, of the illustrious king of the Pitris! I shall now describe unto the assembly house of Varuna also called Pushkaramalini!'

SECTION IX

"Narada said--'O Yudhishthira, the celestial Sabha of Varuna is unparalleled in splendour. In dimensions it is similar to that of Yama. Its walls and arches are all of pure white. It hath been built by Viswakarma (the celestial architect) within the waters. It is surrounded on all sides by many celestial trees made of gems and jewels and yielding excellent fruits and flowers. And many plants with their weight of blossoms, blue and yellow, and black and darkish, and white and red, that stand there, or excellent bowers around. Within those bowers hundreds and thousands of birds of diverse species, beautiful and variegated, always pour forth their melodies. The atmosphere of that mansion is extremely delightful, neither cold nor hot. Owned by Varuna, that delightful assembly house of pure white consists of many rooms and is furnished with many seats. There sitteth Varuna attired in celestial robe, decked in celestial ornaments and jewels, with his queen, adorned with celestial scents and besmeared with paste of celestial fragrance. The Adityas wait upon and worship the illustrious Varuna, the lord of the waters. And Vasuki and Takshaka, and the Naga called Airavana; Krishna and Lohita; Padma and Chitra endued with great energy; the Nagas called Kamvala and Aswatara; and Dhritarashtra and Valahaka; Matimat and

Kundadhara and Karkotaka and Dhananjaya; Panimat and the mighty Kundaka, O lord of the Earth; and Prahlada and Mushikada, and Janamejaya,--all having auspicious marks and mandalas and extended hoods;--these and many other snakes, O Yudhishthira, without anxiety of any kind, wait upon and worship the illustrious Varuna. And, O king, Vali the son of Virochana, and Naraka the subjugator of the whole Earth; Sanghraha and Viprachitti, and those Danavas called Kalakanja; and Suhanu and Durmukha and Sankha and Sumanas and also Sumati; and Ghatodara, and Mahaparswa, and Karthana and also Pithara and Viswarupa, Swarupa and Virupa, Mahasiras; and Dasagriva, Vali, and Meghavasas and Dasavara; Tittiva, and Vitabhuta, and Sanghrada, and Indratapana--these Daityas and Danavas, all bedecked with ear-rings and floral wreaths and crowns, and attired in the celestial robes, all blessed with boons and possessed of great bravery, and enjoying immortality, and all well of conduct and of excellent vows, wait upon and worship in that mansion the illustrious Varuna, the deity bearing the noose as his weapon. And, O king, there are also the four oceans, the river Bhagirathee, the Kalindi, the Vidisa, the Venwa, the Narmada of rapid current; the Vipasa, the Satadu, the Chandrabhaga, the Saraswati; the Iravati, the Vitasta, the Sindhu, the Devanadi; the Godavari, the Krishnavenwa and that queen of rivers the Kaveri; the Kimpuna, the Visalya and the river Vaitarani also; the Tritiya, the Jeshthila, and the great Sone (Soane); the Charmanwati and the great river Parnasa; the Sarayu, the Varavatya, and that queen of rivers the Langali, the Karatoya, the Atreyi, the red Mahanada, the Laghanti, the Gomati, the Sandhya, and also the Trisrotasi--these and other rivers which are all sacred and are world-renowned places of pilgrimage, as also other rivers and sacred waters and lakes and wells and springs, and tanks, large or small, in their personified form, O Bharata, wait upon and worship the lord Varuna. The points of the heavens, the Earth, and all the Mountains, as also every species of aquatic animals, all worship Varuna there. And various tribes of Gandharvas and Apsaras, devoted to music, both vocal and instrumental, wait upon Varuna, singing eulogistic hymns unto him. And all those mountains that are noted for being both delightful and rich in jewels, wait (in their personified forms) in that Sabha, enjoying sweet converse with one another. And the chief minister of Varuna, Sunabha by name, surrounded by his sons and grandsons, also attend upon his master, along with (the personified form) of a sacred water called go. These all, in their personified forms, worship the deity. O bull of the Bharata race, such is the assembly room of Varuna seen by me before, in the course of my wanderings. Listen now to the account I give of the assembly room of Kuvera.'

SECTION X

"Narada said,--'Possessed of great splendour, the assembly house of Vaisravana, O king, is a hundred yojanas in length and seventy yojanas in breadth. It was built, O king, by Vaisravana himself using his ascetic power. Possessing the splendour of the peaks of Kailasa, that mansion eclipses by its own the brilliance of the Moon himself. Supported by Guhyakas, that mansion seems to be attached to the firmament. Of celestial make, it is rendered extremely handsome with high chambers of gold. Extremely delightful and rendered fragrant with celestial perfumes, it is variegated with numberless costly jewels. Resembling the peaks of a mass of white clouds, it seems to be floating in the air. Painted with colours of celestial gold, it seems to be decked with streaks of lightning. Within that mansion sitteth on an excellent seat bright as the sun and covered with celestial carpets and furnished with a handsome footstool, king Vaisravana of agreeable person, attired in excellent robes and adorned with costly ornaments and ear-rings of great brilliance, surrounded by his thousand wives. Delicious and cooling breezes murmuring through forests of tall Mandaras, and bearing fragrance of extensive plantations of jasmine, as also of the lotuses on the bosom of the river Alaka and of the Nandana- gardens, always minister to the pleasure of the King of the Yakshas. There the deities with the Gandharvas surrounded by various tribes of Apsaras, sing in chorus, O king, notes of celestial sweetness. Misrakesi and Rambha, and Chitrasena, and Suchismita; and Charunetra, and Gritachi and Menaka, and Punjikasthala; and Viswachi Sahajanya, and Pramlocha and Urvasi and Ira, and Varga and Sauraveyi, and Samichi, and Vududa, and Lata--these and a thousand other Apsaras and Gandharvas, all well-skilled in music and dance, attend upon Kuvera, the lord of treasures. And that mansion, always filled with the notes of instrumental and vocal music, as also with the sounds of dance of various tribes of Gandharvas, and Apsaras hath become extremely charming and delicious. The Gandharvas called Kinnaras, and others called Naras, and Manibhadra, and Dhanada, and Swetabhadra and Guhyaka; Kaseraka, Gandakandu, and the mighty Pradyota; Kustumvuru, Pisacha, Gajakarna, and Visalaka, Varaha-Karna, Tamraushtica, Falkaksha, and Falodaka; Hansachuda, Sikhavarta, Vibhishana, Pushpanana, Pingalaka, Sonitoda and Pravalaka; Vrikshavaspa-niketa, and Chiravasas--these O Bharata, and many other Yakshas by hundred and thousands always wait upon Kuvera. The goddess Lakshmi always stayeth there, also Kuvera's son Nalakuvera. Myself and many others like myself often repair thither. Many Brahmana Rishis and celestial Rishis also repair there often. Many Rakshasas, and many Gandharvas, besides those that have been named, wait upon the worship, in that mansion, the illustrious lord of all treasures. And, O tiger among kings, the illustrious husband of Uma and lord of created things, the three-eyed Mahadeva, the wielder of the trident and the slayer of the Asura called Bhaga-netra, the mighty god of the fierce bow, surrounded by multitudes of spirits in their hundreds and thousands, some of dwarfish stature, some of fierce visage, some hunch-backed, some of blood-red eyes, some of frightful yells, some feeding upon fat and flesh, and some terrible to behold, but all armed with various weapons and endued with the speed of wind, with the goddess (Parvati) ever cheerful and knowing no fatigue, always waiteth here upon their friend Kuvera, the lord of treasures. And hundreds of Gandharva chiefs, with cheerful hearts and attired in their respective robes and Viswavasu, and Haha and Huhu; and Tumvuru and Parvatta, and Sailusha; and Chitrasena skilled in music and also Chitraratha,--these and innumerable Gandharvas worship the lord of treasures. And Chakradhaman, the chief of the Vidyadharas, with his followers, waiteth in that mansion upon the lord of treasures. And Kinnaras by hundreds and innumerable kings with Bhagadatta as their chief, and Druma, the chief of the Kimpurushas, and Mahendra, the chief of the Rakshasas, and Gandhamadana accompanied by many Yakshas and Gandharvas and many Rakshasas wait upon the lord of treasures. The virtuous Vibhishana also worshippeth there his elder brother the lord Kuvera (Croesus). The mountains of Himavat, Paripatra, Vindhya, Kailasa, Mandara, Malaya, Durdura, Mahendra, Gandhamadana, Indrakila, Sunava, and Eastern and the Western hills--these and many other mountains, in their personified forms, with Meru standing before all, wait upon and worship the illustrious lord of treasures. The illustrious Nandiswaras, and Mahakala, and many spirits with arrowy ears and sharp-pointed mouths, Kaksha, Kuthimukha, Danti, and Vijaya of great ascetic merit, and the mighty white bull of Siva roaring deep, all wait in that mansion. Besides these many other Rakshasas and Pisachas (devils) worship Kuvera in that assembly house. The son of Pulastya (Kuvera) formerly used always to worship in all the modes and sit, with permission obtained, beside the god of gods, Siva, the creator of the three worlds, that supreme Deity surrounded by his attendants. One day the exalted Bhava (Siva) made friendship with Kuvera. From that time, O king, Mahadeva always sitteth on the mansion of his friend, the lord of treasures. Those best of all jewels, those princes of all gems in the three worlds, viz., Sankha and Padma, in their personified forms, accompanied by all the jewels of the earth (also in their personified forms) worship Kuvera.'

"'This delightful assembly house of Kuvera that I have seen, attached to the firmament and capable of moving along it, is such, O king. Listen now to the Sabha I describe unto thee, belonging to Brahma the Grandsire.'

SECTION XI

"Narada said,--'Listen to me, O child, as I tell thee of the assembly house of the Grandsire, that house which none can describe, saying it is such. In the Krita (golden) age of old, O king, the exalted deity Aditya (once) came down from heaven into the world of men. Having seen before the assembly-house of Brahma the Self-created, Aditya was cheerfully wandering over the Earth in human form, desirous of beholding what could be seen here. It was on that occasion, O son of Pandu, that the god of day spoke unto me, O bull of the Bharata race, of that celestial Sabha (assembly) of the Grandsire, immeasurable and immaterial and indescribable, as regards form and shape, and capable of delighting the heart of every creature by its splendour. Hearing, O bull of the Bharata race, of the merits of that Sabha, I became, O king, desirous of beholding it. I then asked Aditya, saying,--"O exalted one, I desire to behold the sacred Sabha of the Grandsire. O lord of light, tell me, O exalted one, by what ascetic penances, or by what acts, or by what charms or by what rites, I may be enabled to behold that excellent sin-cleaning Sabha."--Hearing these words of mine, Aditya the god of day, the deity of a thousand rays, answered me, "O chief of the Bharata race, thus: Observe thou, with mind rapt in meditation, the Brahma vow extending for a thousand years." Repairing then to the breast of the Himavat, I commenced that great vow, and after I had completed it the exalted and sinless deity Surya endued with great energy, and knowing no fatigue, took me with him to the Sabha of the Grandsire. O king, it is impossible to describe that Sabha, saying--it is such, for within a moment it assumes a different form that language fails to paint. O Bharata, it is impossible to indicate its dimensions or shape. I never saw anything like it before. Ever contributing to the happiness of those within it, its atmosphere is neither cold nor warm. Hunger and thirst or any kind of uneasiness disappear as soon as one goeth thither. It seems to be made up of brilliant gems of many kinds. It doth not seem to be supported on columns, it knoweth no deterioration, being eternal. That self effulgent mansion, by its numerous blazing, celestial indications of unrivalled splendour, seems to surpass the moon, the sun and the fire in splendour. Stationed in heaven, it blazes forth, censuring as it were the maker of the day. In that mansion O king, the Supreme Deity, the Grand-sire of all created things, having himself created everything by virtue of his creative illusion, stayeth ever. And Daksha, Prachetas, Pulaha, Marichi, the master Kasyapa, Bhrigu, Atri, and Vasistha and Gautama, and also Angiras, and Pulastya, Kraut, Prahlada, and Kardama, these Prajapatis, and Angirasa of the Atharvan Veda, the Valikhilyas, the Marichipas; Intelligence, Space, Knowledge, Air, Heat, Water, Earth, Sound, Touch, Form, Taste, Scent; Nature, and the Modes (of Nature), and the elemental and prime causes of the world,--all stay in that mansion beside the lord Brahma. And Agastya of great energy, and Markandeya, of great ascetic power, and Jamadagni and Bharadwaja, and Samvarta, and Chyavana, and exalted Durvasa, and the virtuous Rishyasringa, the illustrious Sanatkumara of great ascetic merit and the preceptor in all matters affecting Yoga; Asita and Devala, and Jaigishavya acquainted with truth; Rishava, Ajitasatru, and Mani of great energy; and the Science of healing with its eight branches--all in their personified forms, O Bharata; the moon with all the stars and the stellar conjunctions; Aditya with all his rays; the winds; the Sacrifices, the Declarations of purpose (in sacrifices), the Vital principles,--these illustrious and vow-observing beings in their personified forms, and many others too numerous to mention, attend all upon Brahma in that mansion. Wealth and Religion and Desire, and Joy, and Aversion, and Asceticism and Tranquillity--all wait together upon the Supreme Deity in that palace. The twenty tribes of the Gandharvas and Apsaras, as also their seven other tribes, and all the Lokapalas (chief protectors of several regions), and Sukra, and Vrihaspati, and Vudha, and Angaraka (Mangala), Sani, Rahu, and the other planets; the Mantras (of the Sama Veda), the special Mantras (of the same Veda); (the rites of) Harimat and Vasumat, the Adityas with Indra, the two Agnis mentioned by name (viz. Agnisoma and Indragni), the Marutas, Viswakarman, and the Vasus, O Bharata; the Pitris, and all kinds of sacrificial libations, the four Vedas. viz., Rig, Sama, Yajuh, and Atharva; all Sciences and branches of learning; Histories and all minor branches of learning; the several branches of the Vedas; the planets, the Sacrifices, the Soma, all the deities; Savitri (Gayatri), the seven kinds of rhyme; Understanding, Patience, Memory, Wisdom, Intelligence, Fame, Forgiveness; the Hymns of the Sama Veda; the Science of hymns in general, and various kinds of Verses and Songs; various Commentaries with arguments;--all in their personified forms, O king, and various Dramas and Poems and Stories and abridged Glosses--these also, and many others wait upon the Supreme Deity in that Sabha, Kshanas, Lavas, Muhurtas, Day, Night, Fortnights, Months, the six Seasons, O Bharata, Years, Yugas, the four kinds of Days and Nights (viz., appearing to man, to the Pitris, to the gods, and to Brahma) and that eternal, indestructible, undeteriorating, excellent Wheel of Time and also the Wheel of Virtue,--these always wait there, O Yudhishthira; and Aditi, Diti, Danu, Surasa, Vinata, Ira, Kalika, Suravi, Devi, Sarama, Gautami and the goddesses Pradha, and Kadru;--these mothers of the celestials, and Rudrani, Sree, Lakshmi, Bhadra, Shashthi, the Earth, Ganga, Hri, Swaha, Kriti, the goddess Sura, Sachi Pushti, Arundhati, Samvritti, Asa, Niyati, Srishti, Rati,--these and many other goddesses wait upon the Creator of all. The Adityas, Vasus, Rudras, Marutas, Aswinas, the Viswadevas Sadhyas, and the Pitris gifted with the speed of the mind; these all wait there upon the Grandsire. And, O bull amongst men, know thou that there are seven classes of Pitris, of which four classes have embodied forms and the remaining three without embodied forms. It is well known that the illustrious Vairajas and Agniswattas and Garhapattyas (three classes of Pitris) range in heaven. And those amongst the Pitris that are called the Somapas, the Ekasringras, the Chaturvedas, and the Kalas, are ever worshipped amongst the four orders of men. Gratified with the Soma (juice), first, these gratify Soma afterwards. All these tribes of Pitris wait upon the Lord of the creation and cheerfully worship the Supreme Deity of immeasurable energy. And Rakshasas, Pisachas, the Danavas and Guhyakas; Nagas, Birds, and various animals; and all mobile and immobile great beings;--all worship the Grandsire. And Purandara the chief of the celestials, and Varuna and Kuvera and Yama, and Mahadeva accompanied by Uma, always repair thither. And, O king of kings, Mahasena (Kartikeya) also adoreth there the Grandsire. Narayana himself, and the celestial Rishis, and those Rishis called Valakhillyas, and all beings born of females and all those not born of females, and whatever else is seen in the three worlds--both mobile and immobile, were all seen by me there, know O king. And eighty thousand Rishis with vital seed drawn up, and O Pandu, fifty thousand Rishis having sons, were all seen by me there. And all the dwellers in heaven repairing thither behold the Supreme Deity when they please, and worshipping him with a bow of their head return whence they came. And, O king of men, the Grandsire of all created beings, the Soul of the universe, the Self create Brahma of immeasurable intelligence and glory, equally kind unto all creatures, honoureth as they deserve, and gratifieth with sweet speech and gift of wealth and other enjoyable articles, the gods, the Daityas, the Nagas, the Brahmanas, the Yakshas, the Birds, the Kaleyas, the Gandharvas, the Apsaras, and all other exalted beings that came to him as his guests. And that delicious Sabha, O child, is always crowded with persons coming and going. Filled with every kind of energy, and worshipped by Brahmarshis, that celestial Sabha blazes forth with the graceful possessions of Brahma and looks extremely handsome, O tiger among kings as this Sabha of yours is unrivalled in the world of men, so is that Sabha of Brahma, seen by me unrivalled in all the worlds. I have seen these Sabhas, O Bharata, in regions of the celestials. This thy Sabha is unquestionably the foremost in the world of men!'

SECTION XII

"Yudhishthira said,--'O thou foremost of eloquent men, as thou hast described the different Sabhas unto me, it appeareth that almost all the monarchs of the earth are to be found in the Sabha of Yama. And, O master, almost all the Nagas, and principal Daityas, and rivers, and oceans, are to be found in the Sabha of Varuna. And so the Yakshas, the Guhyakas, the Rakshasas, the Gandharvas and Apsaras and the Deity (Yama) having the bull for his vehicle, are to be found in the Sabha of the lord of treasures. Thou hast said that in the Sabha of the Grandsire are to be seen all the great Rishis, all the gods, all the branches of learning. As regards the Sabha of Sakra, however, thou hast named, O Muni, all the gods, the Gandharvas, and various Rishis. But, O great Muni, thou hast mentioned one and only one king, viz., the royal Rishi Harishchandra as living in the Sabha of the illustrious chief of the gods. What act was performed by that celebrated king, or what ascetic penances with steady vows, in consequence of which he hath been equal to Indra himself? O Brahmana, how didst thou also meet with my father, the exalted Pandu, now a guest in the region of the Pitris? O exalted one of excellent vows hath he told thee anything? O tell me all as I am exceedingly curious to hear all this from thee.'

"Narada said,--'O king of kings, I shall tell thee all that thou askest me about Harischandra, I shall presently tell thee of his high excellence. He was a powerful king, in fact, an emperor over all the kings of the earth. Indeed, all the kings of the earth obeyed his sway. O monarch, mounted alone upon a victorious car adorned with gold, that king by the prowess of his weapons brought the whole earth with her seven islands under his sway. And, O monarch, having subjugated the whole earth with her mountains, forests, and woods, he made preparations for the great sacrifice called the Rajasuya. And all the kings of the earth brought at his command wealth unto that sacrifice. All of them consented to become distributors of food and gifts unto the Brahmanas that were fed on the occasion. At that sacrifice king Harishchandra gave away unto all who asked, wealth that was five times what each had solicited. At the conclusion of the sacrifice, the king gratified the Brahmanas that came from various countries with large presents of various kinds of wealth. The Brahmanas gratified with various kinds of food and enjoyable articles, given away unto them to the extent of their desires, and with the heaps of jewels distributed amongst them, began to say,--"King Harischandra is superior to all kings in energy and renown."--And know, O monarch, O bull of the Bharata race, it was for this reason that Harischandra shone more brightly than thousands of other kings. The powerful Harischandra having concluded his great sacrifice, became installed, O king, in the sovereignty of the earth and looked resplendent on his throne. O bull of the Bharata race, all those monarchs that perform the sacrifice of Rajasuya, (attaining to the region of Indra) pass their time in felicity in Indra's company. And, O bull of the Bharata race, those kings also that yield up their lives without turning their backs on the field of battle attain to the mansion of Indra and live in joy with him. Those again that yield up their bodies after severe ascetic penances also attain to the same region and shine brightly there for ages. O king of the Kuru race, O son of Kunti, thy father Pandu, beholding the good fortune of Harischandra and wondering much thereat, hath told thee something. Knowing that I was coming to the world of men, he bowed unto me and said,--"Thou shouldst tell Yudhishthira, O Rishi, that he can subjugate the whole Earth inasmuch as his brothers are all obedient to him. And having done this let him commence the grand sacrifice called Rajasuya. He is my son; if he performeth that sacrifice, I may, like Harischandra, soon attain to the region of Indra, and there in his Sabha pass countless years in continuous joy." I told him in reply,--"O King, I shall tell thy son all this, if I go to the world of man." I have now told thee what he said, O tiger among men. Accomplish then, O son of Pandu, the desires of thy father. If thou performest that sacrifice, thou shall then be able to go, along with thy deceased ancestors, into the same region that is inhabited by the chief of the immortals. It hath been said,--O king, that the performance of this great sacrifice is attended with many obstacles. A class of Rakshasas called Brahma Rakshasas, employed in obstructing all sacrifices, always search for loop-holes when this great sacrifice is commenced. On the commencement of such a sacrifice a war may take place destroying the Kshatriyas and even furnishing occasion for the destruction of the whole Earth. A slight obstacle may involve the whole Earth in ruin. Reflecting upon all this, O king of kings do what is for thy good. Be thou watchful and ready in protecting the four orders of thy subjects. Grow, thou in prosperity, and enjoy thou felicity. Gratify thou the Brahmanas with gifts of wealth. I have now answered in detail all that thou hast asked me. With thy leave I will now go to the city (Dwaravati) of that Dasarhas.'"

Vaisampayana said,--"O Janamejaya, having said this unto the son of Pritha, Narada went away, accompanied by those Rishis with whom he had come. And after Narada had gone away, king Yudhishthira, O thou of the Kuru race, began to think, along with his brothers, of that foremost of sacrifices called Rajasuya."

SECTION XIII

Vaisampayana said,--"Yudhishthira, having heard these words of Narada, began to sigh heavily. And, O Bharata, engaged in his thoughts about the Rajasuya, the king had no peace of mind. Having heard of this glory of the illustrious monarchs (of old) and being certain about the acquisition of regions of felicity by performers of sacrifices in consequence of their sacred deeds, and thinking especially of that royal sage Harischandra who had performed the great sacrifice king Yudhishthira desired to make preparations for the Rajasuya sacrifice. Then worshipping his counsellors and others present at his Sabha, and worshipped by them in return, he began to discuss with them about that sacrifice. Having reflected much, that king of kings, that bull amongst the Kurus, inclined his mind towards making preparations for the Rajasuya. That prince of wonderful energy and prowess, however, reflecting upon virtue and righteousness, again set his heart to find out what would be for the good of all his people. For Yudhishthira, that foremost of all virtuous men, always kind unto his subjects, worked for the good of all without making any distinctions. Indeed, shaking off both anger and arrogance, Yudhishthira always said,-- 'Give unto each what is due to each,'--and the only sounds that he could hear were,--'Blessed be Dharma! Blessed be Dharma!' Yudhishthira conducting himself thus and giving paternal assurance to everybody, there was none in the kingdom who entertained any hostile feelings towards him. He therefore came to be called Ajatasatru (one with no enemy at all). The king cherished every one as belonging to his family, and Bhima ruled over all justly. Arjuna, used to employing both his hands with equal skill, protected the people from (external) enemies. And the wise Sahadeva administered justice impartially. And Nakula behaved towards all with humility that was natural to him. Owing to all this, the kingdom became free from disputes and fear of every kind. And all the people became attentive to their respective occupations. The rain became so abundant as to leave no room for desiring more; and the kingdom grew in prosperity. And in consequence of the virtues of the king, money-lenders, the articles required for sacrifices, cattle-rearing, tillage, and traders, all and everything grew in prosperity. Indeed, during the reign of Yudhishthira who was ever devoted to truth, there was no extortion, no stringent realisation of arrears of rent, no fear of disease, of fire, or of death by poisoning and incantations, in the kingdom. It was never heard at that time that thieves or cheats or royal favourites ever behaved wrongfully towards the king or towards one another amongst themselves. Kings conquered on the six occasions (of war, treaty, &c) were wont to wait upon him in order to do good unto the monarch and worship him ever, while the traders of different classes came to pay him the taxes leviable on their respective occupations. And accordingly during the reign of Yudhishthira who was ever devoted to virtue, his dominion grew in prosperity. Indeed, the prosperity of the kingdom was increased not by these alone but even by persons wedded to voluptuousness and indulging in all luxuries to their fill. And the king of kings, Yudhishthira, whose sway extended over all, was possessed of every accomplishment and bore everything with patience. And, O king, whatever countries the celebrated and illustrious monarch conquered, the people everywhere, from Brahmanas to swains, were all more attached to him than to their own fathers and mothers."

Vaisampayana said,--"King Yudhishthira, then, that foremost of speakers, summoning together his counsellors and brothers, asked them repeatedly about the Rajasuya sacrifice. Those ministers in a body, thus asked by the wise Yudhishthira desirous of performing the sacrifice, then told him these words of grave import,--'One already in possession of a kingdom desireth all the attributes of an emperor by means of that sacrifice which aideth a king in acquiring the attributes of Varuna. O prince of Kuru race, thy friends think that as thou art worthy of the attributes of an emperor, the time is even come for thee for the performance of the Rajasuya sacrifice. The time for the performance of that sacrifice in which Rishis of austere vows kindle six fires with mantras of the Sama Veda, is come for thee in consequence of thy Kshatriya possessions. At the conclusion of the Rajasuya sacrifice when the performer is installed in the sovereignty of the empire, he is rewarded with the fruits of all sacrifices including the Agnihotra. It is for this that he is called the conqueror of all. Thou art quite able, O strong-armed one, to perform this sacrifice. All of us are obedient to thee. Soon will you be able, O great king, to perform the Rajasuya sacrifice. Therefore, O great king, let thy resolution be taken to perform this sacrifice without further discussion.' Thus spoke unto the king all his friends and counsellors separately and jointly. And, O king, Yudhishthira that slayer of all enemies, having heard these virtuous, bold, agreeable and weighty words of theirs, accepted them mentally. And having heard those words of his friends and counsellors, and knowing his own strength also, the king, O Bharata, repeatedly thought over the matter. After this the intelligent and virtuous Yudhishthira, wise in counsel, again consulted with his brothers, with the illustrious Ritwijas about him, with his ministers and with Dhaumya and Dwaipayana and others."

"Yudhishthira said,--'How may this wish that I entertain of performing the excellent sacrifice of Rajasuya that is worthy of an emperor, bear fruit, in consequence of my faith and speech alone.'"

Vaisampayana said,--"O thou of eyes like lotus-petals, thus asked by the king, they replied at that time unto Yudhishthira the just in these words,-- 'Being conversant with the dictates of morality, thou art, O king, worthy to perform the grand sacrifice of Rajasuya.' After the Ritwijas and the Rishis had told these words unto the king, his ministers and brothers highly approved of the speech. The king, however, possessed of great wisdom, and with mind under complete control, actuated by the desire of doing good unto the world, again resolved the matter in his mind, thinking of his own strength and means, the circumstances of time and place and his income and expenditure. For he knew that the wise never come to grief owing to their always acting after full deliberation. Thinking that the sacrifice should not be commenced, pursuant to his own resolution only, Yudhishthira, carefully bearing upon his shoulder the weight of affairs thought of Krishna that persecutor of all sinners as the fittest person to decide the matter, in as much as he knew him to be the foremost of all persons, possessed of immeasurable energy, strong-armed, without birth but born amongst men from Will alone. Reflecting upon his god-like feats the son of Pandu concluded that there was nothing that was unknown to him, nothing that he could not achieve, and nothing that he could not bear, and Yudhishthira, the son of Pritha, having come to this settled resolution soon sent a messenger unto that master of all beings, conveying through him blessings and speeches such as one senior in age might send to one that is younger. And that messenger riding in a swift car arrived amongst the Yadavas and approached Krishna who was then residing in Dwaravati. And Achyuta (Krishna) hearing that the son of Pritha had become desirous of seeing him, desired to see his cousin. And quickly passing over many regions, being drawn by his own swift horses, Krishna arrived at Indraprastha, accompanied by Indrasena. And having arrived at Indraprastha, Janardana approached Yudhisthira without loss of time. And Yudhisthira received Krishna with paternal-affection, and Bhima also received him likewise. And Janardana then went with a cheerful heart to his father's sister (Kunti). And worshipped then with reverence by the twins, he began to converse cheerfully with his friend Arjuna who was overjoyed at seeing him. And after he had rested awhile in a pleasant apartment and had been fully refreshed, Yudhishthira approached him at his leisure and informed him all about the Rajasuya sacrifice.

"Yudhishthira said,--'I have wished to perform the Rajasuya sacrifice. That sacrifice, however, cannot be performed by one's wishing alone to perform it. Thou knowest, O Krishna, even thing about the means by which it may be accomplished. He alone can achieve this sacrifice in whom everything is possible, who is worshipped everywhere and who is the king of kings. My friends and counsellors approaching me have said that I should perform that sacrifice. But, O Krishna, in respect of that matter, thy words shall be my guide. Of counsellors some from friendship do not notice the difficulties; others from motives of self-interest say only what is agreeable. Some again regard that which is beneficial to themselves as worthy of adoption. Men are seen to counsel thus on matters awaiting decision. But thou, O Krishna, art above such motives. Thou hast conquered both desire and anger. It behoveth thee to tell me what is most beneficial to the world.'

SECTION XIV

(Rajasuyarambha Parva)

"Krishna said,--'O great king, thou art a worthy possessor of all the qualities essential for the performance of the Rajasuya sacrifice. Thou knowest everything, O Bharata. I shall, however, still tell thee something. Those persons in the world that now go by the name of Kshatriyas are inferior (in everything) to those Kshatriyas that Rama, the son of Jamadagnya, exterminated. O lord of the earth, O bull of the Bharata race, thou knowest what form of rule these Kshatriyas, guided by the instructions traditionally handed down from generation to generation, have established amongst their own order, and how far they are competent to perform the Rajasuya sacrifice. The numerous royal lines and other ordinary Kshatriyas all represent themselves to be the descendants of Aila and Ikshwaku. The descendants of Aila, O king, as, indeed, the kings of Ikshwaku's race, are, know O bull of the Bharata race, each divided into a hundred separate dynasties. The descendants of Yayati and the Bhojas are great, both in extent (number) and accomplishments. O king, these last are to-day scattered all over the earth. And all the Kshatriyas worship the prosperity of those monarchs. At present, however, O monarch, king Jarasandha, overcoming that prosperity enjoyed by their whole order, and overpowering them by his energy hath set himself over the heads of all these kings. And Jarasandha, enjoying the sovereignty over the middle portion of the earth (Mathura), resolved to create a disunion amongst ourselves. O monarch, the king who is the lord paramount of all kings, and in whom alone the dominion of the universe is centered, properly deserves to be called an emperor. And, O monarch, king Sisupala endued with great energy, hath placed himself under his protection and hath become the generalissimo of his forces. And, O great king, the mighty Vaka, the king of the Karushas, capable of fighting by putting forth his powers of illusion, waiteth, upon Jarasandha, as his disciple. There are two others, Hansa and Dimvaka, of great energy and great soul, who have sought the shelter of the mighty Jarasandha. There are others also viz., Dantavakra, Karusha, Karava, Meghavahana, that wait upon Jarasandha. He also that beareth on his head that gem which is known as the most wonderful on earth, that king of the Yavanas, who hath chastised Muru and Naraka, whose power is unlimited, and who ruleth the west like another Varuna, who is called Bhagadatta, and who is the old friend of thy father, hath bowed his head before Jarasandha, by speech and specially by act. In his heart, however, tied as he is by affection to thee, he regardeth thee as a father regardeth his child. O king, that lord of the earth who hath his dominions on the west and the south, who is thy maternal uncle and who is called Purujit, that brave perpetuator of the Kunti race, that slayer of all foes, is the single king that regardeth thee from affection. He whom I did not formerly slay, that wicked wretch amongst the Chedis, who represented himself in this world as a divine personage and who hath become known also as such, and who always beareth, from foolishness, the signs that distinguish me that king of Vanga Pundra and the Kiratas, endowed with great strength, and who is known on earth by the names of Paundraka and Vasudeva hath also espoused the side of Jarasandha. And, O king of kings,

Bhishmaka, the mighty king of the Bhojas--the friend of Indra--the slayer of hostile heroes--who governs a fourth part of the world, who by his learning conquered the Pandyas and the Kratha-Kausikas, whose brother the brave Akriti was like Rama, the son of Jamdagni, hath become a servitor to the king of Magadha. We are his relatives and are, therefore, engaged everyday in doing what is agreeable unto him. But although we regard him much, still he regardeth us not and is engaged in doing us ill. And, O king, without knowing his own strength and the dignity of the race to which he belongeth, he hath placed himself under Jarasandha's shelter at sight of the latter's blazing fame alone. And, O exalted one, the eighteen tribes of the Bhojas, from fear of Jarasandha, have all fled towards the west; so also have the Surasenas, the Bhadrakas, the Vodhas, the Salwas, the Patachchavas, the Susthalas, the Mukuttas, and the Kulindas, along with the Kuntis. And the king of the Salwayana tribe with their brethren and followers; and the southern Panchalas and the eastern Kosalas have all fled to the country of the Kuntis. So also the Matsyas and the Sannyastapadas, overcome with fear, leaving their dominions in the north, have fled into the southern country. And so all the Panchalas, alarmed at the power of Jarasandha, have left their own kingdom and fled in all directions. Some time before, the foolish Kansa, having persecuted the Yadavas, married two of the daughters of Jarasandha. They are called Asti and Prapti and are the sister of Sahadeva. Strengthened by such an alliance, the fool persecuting his relatives gained an ascendency over them all. But by this conduct he earned great obloquy. The wretch also began to oppress the old kings of the Bhoja tribe, but they, to protect themselves from the persecution of their relative, sought our help. Having bestowed upon Akrura the handsome daughter of Ahuka, with Sankarshana as my second I did a service to my relatives, for both Kansa and Sunaman were slain by me assisted by Rama. But after the immediate cause of fear was removed (by the death of Kansa), Jarasandha, his father-in-law, took up arms. Ourselves consisting of the eighteen younger branches of the Yadavas arrived at the conclusion that even if we struck our enemies continually with excellent weapons capable of taking the lives of the foes, we should still be unable to do anything unto him even in three hundred years. He hath two friends that are like unto the immortals, and in point of strength the foremost of all men endued with might. They are called Hansa and Dimvaka who are both incapable of being slain by weapons. The mighty Jarasandha, being united with them, becomes incapable, I think, of being vanquished by even the three worlds. O thou foremost of all intelligent men, this is not our opinion alone but all other kings also are of the same mind. There lived, O monarch, a king of the name of Hansa, who was slain by Rama (Valadeva) after a battle of eighteen days. But, O Bharata, hearing people say that Hansa had been killed, Dimvaka, O king, thought that he could not live without Hansa. He accordingly jumped into the waters of the Yamuna and killed himself. Afterwards when Hansa, the subjugator of hostile heroes, heard that Dimvaka, had killed himself, he went to the Yamuna and jumped into its waters. Then, O bull of the Bharata race, king Jarasandha, hearing that both Hansa and Dimvaka had been killed, returned to his kingdom with an empty heart. After Jarasandha had returned, O slayer of all foes, we were filled with pleasure and continued to live at Mathura. Then the widow of Hansa and the daughter of Jarasandha, that handsome woman with eyes like lotus-petals, grieved at the death of her lord, went unto her father, and repeatedly urged, O Monarch, the king of Magadha, saying,--O slayer of all foes, kill thou the slayer of my husband.--Then, O great king, remembering the conclusion to which we had come of old we became exceedingly cheerless and fled from Mathura. Dividing our large wealth into small portions so as to make each portion easily portable, we fled from fear of Jarasandha, with our cousins and relatives. Reflecting upon everything, we fled towards the west. There is a delightful town towards the west called Kusasthali, adorned by the mountains of Raivata. In that city, O monarch, we took up our abode. We rebuilt its fort and made it so strong that it has become impregnable even to the Gods. And from within it even the women might fight the foe, what to speak of the Yadava heroes without fear of any kind? O slayer of all foes, we are now living in that city. And, O tiger of the Kuru race, considering the inaccessibility of that first of mountains and regarding themselves as having already crossed the fear of Jarasandha, the descendants of Madhu have become exceedingly glad. Thus, O king, though possessed of strength and energy, yet from the oppressions of Jarasandha we have been obliged to repair to the mountains of Gomanta, measuring three Yojanas in length.

Within each yojana have been established one and twenty posts of armed men. And at intervals of each yojana are hundred gates with arches which are defended by valourous heroes engaged in guarding them. And innumerable Kshatriyas invincible in war, belonging to the eighteen younger branches of the Yadavas, are employed in defending these works. In our race, O king, there are full eighteen thousand brothers and cousins. Ahuka hath had a hundred sons, each of whom is almost like a god (in prowess), Charudeshna with his brother Chakradeva, Satyaki, myself, Valadeva the son of Rohini, and my son Samva who is equal unto me in battle--these seven, O king are Atirathas. Besides these, there are others, O king, whom I shall presently name. They are Kritavarman, Anadhrishti, Samika, Samitinjaya, Kanka, Sanku and Kunti. These seven are Maharathas. There are also two sons of Andhakabhoja, and the old king himself. Endued with great energy these are all heroes, each mighty as the thunderbolt. These Maharathas, choosing the middle country, are now living amongst the Vrishnis. O thou best of the Bharata line, thou alone art worthy of being an emperor. It behoveth thee, O Bharata, to establish thy empire over all the Kshatriyas. But this is my judgment, O king, that thou wilt not be able to celebrate the Rajasuya sacrifice as long as the mighty Jarasandha liveth. By him have been immured in his hillfort numerous monarchs, like a lion that hath deposited the slain bodies of mighty elephants within a cave of the king of mountains. O slayer of all enemies, king Jarasandha, desirous of offering in sacrifice hundred monarchs, adored for his fierce ascetic penances the illustrious god of gods, the lord of Uma. It is by this means that the kings of the earth have been vanquished by Jarasandha. And, O best of monarchs, he hath by that means been able to fulfil the vow he had made relative to his sacrifice. By defeating the kings with their troops and bringing all of them as captives into this city, he had swelled its crowds enormously. We also, O king, from fear of Jarasandha, at one time had to leave Mathura and fly to the city of Dwaravati. If, O great king, thou desirest to perform this sacrifice, strive to release the kings confined by Jarasandha, as also to compass his death, O son of the Kuru race, otherwise this undertaking of thine can never be completed. O thou foremost of intelligent men if the Rajasuya is to be performed by thee, you must do this in this way and not otherwise. This, O king, is my view (on the matter). Do, O sinless one, as thou thinkest. Under these circumstances, O king, having reflected upon everything, taking note of causes, tell us what thou thyself thinkest proper."

SECTION XV

"Yudhishthira said,--'Intelligent as thou art, thou hast said what none else is capable of saying. There is none else on earth who is settler of all doubts. Behold, there are kings in every province employed in benefiting their respective selves. But no one amongst them hath been able to achieve the imperial dignity. Indeed, the title emperor is difficult of acquisition. He that knoweth the valour and strength of others never applaudeth himself. He, indeed, is really worthy of applause (worship) who, engaged in encounters with his enemies, beareth himself commendably. O thou supporter of the dignity of the Vrishni race, man's desires and propensities, like the wide earth itself adorned with many jewels, are varied and extensive. As experience can seldom be gained but by travelling in regions remote from one's home, so salvation can never be attained except by acting according to principles that are very high, compared with the ordinary level of our desire and propensities. I regard peace of mind as the highest object here, for from that quality may proceed my prosperity. In my judgment, if I undertake to celebrate this sacrifice, I shall never win the highest reward. O Janardana, endued with energy and intelligence, these that have been born in our race think that some one amongst them will at one time become the foremost amongst all Kshatriyas. But, O exalted one, we also were all frightened by the fear of Jarasandha and, O sinless one, by the wickedness of that monarch. O thou invincible in battle, the might of thy arm is my refuge. When, therefore, thou taken fright at Jarasandha's might, how should I regard myself strong in comparison with him? Madhava, O thou of the Vrishni race, I am repeatedly depressed by the thought whether Jarasandha is capable or not of being slain by thee, by Rama, by Bhimasena, or by Arjuna. But what shall I say, O Keshava? Thou art my highest authority on everything.'

"On hearing these words, Bhima well-skilled in speech said,--'That king who is without exertion, or who being weak and without resources entereth into hostility with one that is strong, perisheth like an ant-hill. It may be generally seen, however, that even a king that is weak may vanquish an enemy that is strong and obtain the fruition of all his wishes, by wakefulness and by the application of policy. In Krishna is policy, in myself strength, in Arjuna triumphs. So like the three (sacrificial) fires that accomplish a sacrifice, we shall accomplish the death of the king of Magadha.'

"Krishna then said,--'One that is immature in understanding seeketh the fruition of his desire without an eye to what may happen to him in future. It is seen that no one forgiveth for that reason a foe that is of immature understanding and inclined to serve his own interests. It hath been heard by us that in the krita age, having brought every one under their subjection, Yauvanaswin by the abolition of all taxes, Bhagiratha by his kind treatment to his subjects, Kartavirya by the energy of his asceticism, the lord Bharata by his strength and valour, and Maruta by his prosperity, all these five became emperors. But, O Yudhishthira, thou who covetest the imperial dignity deserves it, not by one but by all these qualities, viz., victory, protection afforded to thy people, virtue, prosperity, and policy. Know, O bull of the Kuru race, that Jarasandha, the son of Vrihadratha, is even such (i.e., a candidate for the imperial dignity). A hundred dynasties of kings have become unable to oppose Jarasandha. He, therefore, may be regarded to be an emperor for his strength. Kings that are wearers of jewels worship Jarasandha (with presents of jewels). But, wicked from his childhood, he is scarcely satisfied with such worship. Having become the foremost among all, he attacketh yet with violence kings with crowns on their heads. Nor is there seen any king from whom he taketh not tribute. Thus hath he brought under his sway nearly a hundred kings. How can, O son of Pritha, any weak monarch approach him with hostile intentions? Confined in the temple of Shiva and offered as sacrifice unto him like so many animals, do not these monarchs dedicated unto that god feel the most poignant misery, O bull of the Bharata race? A Kshatriya that dieth in battle is ever regarded with respect. Why shall we not, therefore, meet together and oppose Jarsandha in battle? He hath already brought eighty- six kings; fourteen only are wanting to complete one hundred. As soon as he obtaineth those fourteen, he will begin his cruel act. He that shall be to obstruct that act will surely win blazing renown. And he that will vanquish Jarasandha will surely become the emperor of all the Kshatriyas.'

SECTION XVI

"Yudhishthira said,--'Desirous of the imperial dignity but acting from selfish motives and relying upon courage alone, how, O Krishna, can I despatch ye (unto Jarasandha)? Both Bhima and Arjuna, I regard as my eyes, and thee, O Janardana as my mind. How shall I live, deprived of my eyes and mind. Yama himself cannot vanquish in battle the mighty host of Jarasandha that is endued, besides, with terrible valour. What valour can ye exhibit against it. This affair that promises to terminate otherwise may lead to great mischief. It is my opinion, therefore, that the proposed task should not be undertaken. Listen, O Krishna, to what I for one think. O Janardana, desisting from this act seemeth to me to be beneficial. My heart to-day is afflicted. The Rajasuya appeareth to me difficult of accomplishment.'"

Vaisampayana said,--"Arjuna who had obtained that excellent of bows and that couple of inexhaustible quivers, and that car with that banner, as also that assembly room, now addressed Yudhishthira and said,--'I have obtained, O king, a bow and weapons and arrows and energy and allies and dominions and fame and strength. Those are always difficult of acquisition, however much they may be desired. Learned men of repute always praise in good society nobleness of descent. But nothing is equal to might. Indeed, O monarch, there is nothing I like more than prowess. Born in a race noted for its valour, one that is without valour is scarcely worthy of regard. One, however, possessed of valour, that is born in a race not noted for it, is much superior to the former. He, O king, is a Kshatriya in every thing who increaseth his fame and possessions by the subjugation of his enemies. And he that is possessed of valour, though destitute of all (other) merits, will vanquish his foes. One, however, that is destitute of valour, though possessed of every (other) merit, can scarcely accomplish anything. Every merit exists by the side of valour in an incipient state. Concentration of attention, exertion and destiny exist as the three causes of victory. One, however, that is possessed of valour doth not yet deserve success if he acts carelessly. It is for this that an enemy endued with strength sometimes suffers death at the hands of his foes. As meanness overtakes the weak, so folly sometimes overtakes the strong. A king, therefore, that is desirous of victory, should avoid both these causes of destruction. If, for the purpose of our sacrifice, we endeavour to slay Jarasandha and rescue the kings kept by him for a cruel purpose, there is no higher act which we could employ ourselves in. If, however, we do not undertake the task, the world will always think us incompetent. We have certainly the competence, O king! Why should you, therefore, regard us as incompetent? Those that have become Munis desirous of achieving tranquillity of souls, obtain yellow robes with ease. So if we vanquish the foe, the imperial dignity will easily be ours. We shall, therefore fight the foe.'

SECTION XVII

"Vasudeva said,--'Arjuna hath indicated what the inclination should be of one that is born in the Bharata race, especially of one who is the son of Kunti. We know not when death will overtake us, in the night or in the day. Nor have we ever heard that immortality hath been achieved by desisting from fight. This, therefore, is the duty of men, viz., to attack all enemies in accordance with the principles laid down in the ordinance. This always gives satisfaction to the heart. Aided by good policy, if not frustrated by Destiny, an undertaking becomes crowned with success. If both parties aided by such means encounter each other, one must obtain ascendency over the other, for both cannot win or lose. A battle however, if directed by bad policy which again is destitute of the well-known arts, ends in defeat or destruction. If, again, both parties are equally circumstanced, the result becomes doubtful. Both, however, cannot win. When such is the case, why should we not, aided by good policy, directly approach the foe; and destroy him, like the current of the river uprooting a tree? If, disguising our own faults, we attack the enemy taking advantage of his loopholes, why should we not succeed?

Indeed, the policy of intelligent men, is that one should not fight openly with foes that are exceedingly powerful and are at the head of their well-arrayed forces. This too is my opinion. If, however, we accomplish our purpose secretly entering the abode of our foe and attacking his person, we shall never earn obloquy. That bull among men--Jarasandha--alone enjoyeth unfaded glory, like unto him who is the self in the heart of every created being. But I see his destruction before me. Desirous of protecting our relatives we will either slay him in battle or shall ascend to heaven being ourselves slain in the end by him.'

"Yudhishthira said--'O Krishna, who is this Jarasandha? What is his energy and what is his prowess, that having touched thee he hath not been burnt like an insect at the touch of fire?'

"Krishna said,--'Hear, O monarch, who Jarasandha is; what his energy; and what is his prowess; and why also he hath been spared by us, even though he hath repeatedly offended us. There was a mighty king of the name of Vrihadratha, the lord of the Magadhas. Proud in battle, he had three Akshauhinis of troops. Handsome and endued with energy, possessed of affluence and prowess beyond measure, and always bearing on his person marks indicating installation at sacrifices. He was like a second Indra. In glory he was like unto Suryya, in forgiveness like unto the Earth, in wrath like unto the destroyer Yama and in wealth like unto Vaisravana. And O thou foremost of the Bharata race, the whole earth was covered by his qualities that descended upon him from a long line of ancestors, like the rays emerging from the sun. And, O bull of the Bharata race, endued with great energy that monarch married two twin daughters of the king of Kasi, both endued with the wealth of beauty. And that bull among men made an engagement in secret with his wives that he would love them equally and would never show a preference for either. And the lord of the earth in the company of his two dearly loved wives, both of whom suited him well, passed his days in joy like a mighty elephant in the company of two cow-elephants, or like the ocean in his personified form between Ganga and Yamuna (also in their personified forms). The monarch's youth however, passed away in the enjoyment of his possessions, without any son being born unto him to perpetuate his line. The best of monarch failed to obtain a son to perpetuate his race, even by means of various auspicious rites, and homas, and sacrifices performed with the desire for having an offspring. One day the king heard that the high-souled Chanda-kausika, the son of Kakshivat of the illustrious Gautama race, having desisted from ascetic penances had come in course of his wanderings to his capital and had taken his seat under the shade of a mango tree. The king went unto that Muni accompanied by his two wives, and worshipping him with jewels and valuable presents gratified him highly. That best of Rishis truthful in speech and firmly attached to truth, then told the king,--"O king of kings, I have been pleased with thee. O thou of excellent vows, solicit thou a boon." King Vrihadratha then, with his wives, bending low unto that Rishi, spoke these words choked with tears in consequence of his despair of obtaining a child.-- "O holy one forsaking my kingdom I am about to go into the woods to practise ascetic penances. I am very unfortunate for I have no son. What shall I do, therefore, with my kingdom or with a boon?"'

"Krishna continued,--'Hearing these words (of the king), the Muni controlling his outer senses entered into meditation, sitting in the shade of that very mango tree where he was. And there fell upon the lap of the seated Muni a mango that was juicy and untouched by the beak of a parrot or any other bird. That best of Munis, taking up the fruit and mentally pronouncing certain mantras over it, gave it unto the king as the means of his obtaining an incomparable offspring. And the great Muni, possessed also of extraordinary wisdom, addressing the monarch, said,--"Return, O king, thy wish is fulfilled. Desist, O king, from going (into the woods)".--Hearing these words of the Muni and worshipping his feet, the monarch possessed of great wisdom, returned to his own abode. And recollecting his former promise (unto them) the king gave, O bull of the Bharata race, unto his two wives that one fruit. His beautiful queens, dividing that single fruit into two parts, ate it up. In consequence of the certainty of the realisation of the Muni's words and his truthfulness, both of them conceived, as an effect of their having eaten that fruit. And the king beholding them in that state became filled with great joy. Then, O wise monarch, some time after, when the time came, each of the queens brought forth a fragmentary body. And each fragment had one eye, one arm, one leg, half a stomach, half a face, and half an anus. Beholding the fragmentary bodies, both the mothers trembled much. The helpless sisters then anxiously consulted each other, and sorrowfully abandoned those fragments endued with life. The two midwives (that waited upon the queens) then carefully wrapping up the still-born (?) fragments went out of the inner apartments (of the palace) by the back door and throwing away the bodies, returned in haste. A little while after, O tiger among men, a Rakshasa woman of the name of Jara living upon flesh and blood, took up the fragments that lay on a crossing. And impelled by force of fate, the female cannibal united the fragments for facility of carrying them away. And, O bull among men, as soon as the fragments were united they formed a sturdy child of one body (endued with life). Then, O king, the female cannibal, with eyes expanded in wonder, found herself unable to carry away that child having a body as hard and strong as the thunder-bolt. That infant then closing his fists red as copper and inserting them into its mouth, began to roar terribly as rain-charged clouds. Alarmed at the sound, the inmates of the palace, O tiger among men, suddenly came out with the king, O slayer of all foes. The helpless and disappointed and sad queens also, with breasts full of milk, also came out suddenly to recover their child. The female cannibal beholding the queens in that condition and the king too so desirous of an offspring, and the child was possessed of such strength thought within herself--I live within dominions of the king who is so desirous of an offspring. It behoveth not me, therefore, to kill the infant child of such an illustrious and virtuous monarch. The Rakshasa woman then, holding the child in her arms like the clouds enveloping the sun, and assuming a human form, told the king these words,--"O Vrihadratha, this is thy child. Given to thee by me, O, take it. It hath been born of both thy wives by virtue of the command of the great Brahmana. Cast away by the midwives, it hath been protected by me!'"

"Krishna continued,--'O thou foremost of the Bharata race, the handsome daughters of the king of Kasi, having obtained the child, soon drenched it with their lacteal streams. The king ascertaining everything, was filled with joy, and addressing that female cannibal disguised as a human being possessing the complexion of gold, asked,--O thou of the complexion of the filament of the lotus, who art thou that givest me this child? O auspicious one, thou seemest to me as a goddess roaming at thy pleasure!'

SECTION XVIII

"Krishna continued,--'Hearing these words of the king, the Rakshasa woman answered--"Blessed be thou, O king of kings. Capable of assuming any form at will, I am a Rakshasa woman called Jara. I am living, O king, happily in thy house, worshipped by all. Every day I wander from house to house of men. Indeed, I was created of old by the Self-create and was named Grihadevi (the household goddess). Of celestial beauty I was placed (in the world) for the destruction of the Danavas. He that with devotion painteth on the walls (of his house) a likeness of myself endued with youth and in the midst of children, must have prosperity in his abode; otherwise a household must sustain decay and destruction. O lord, painted on the walls of thy house is a likeness of myself surrounded by numerous children. Stationed there I am daily worshipped with scents and flowers, with incense and edibles and various objects of enjoyment. Thus worshipped in thy house, I daily think of doing thee some good in return. It chanced, O virtuous king, that I beheld the fragmentary bodies of thy son. When these happened to be united by me, a living child was formed of them. O great king, it hath been so owing to thy good fortune alone. I have been only the instrument, I am capable of swallowing the mountain of Meru itself, what shall I say of the child? I have, however, been gratified with thee in consequence of the worship I receive in thy house. It is, therefore, O king, that I have bestowed this child on thee."'

"Krishna continued,--'Having spoken these words, O king, Jara disappeared there and then. The king having obtained the child then entered the palace. And the king then caused all the rites of infancy to be performed on that child, and ordered a festival to be observed by his people in honour of that Rakshasa woman. And the monarch equal unto Brahma himself then bestowed a name on his child. And he said that because the child had been united by Jara, he should be called (Jarasandha i.e., united by Jara). And the son of the king of Magadha endued with great energy, began to grow up in bulk and strength like a fire into which hath been poured libation of clarified butter. And increasing day by day like the moon in the bright fortnight, the child began to enhance the joy of his parents.'

SECTION XIX

"Krishna said,--'some time after this, the great ascetic, the exalted Chandakausika, again came into the country of the Magadhas. Filled with joy at the advent of the Rishi, king Vrihadratha, accompanied by his ministers and priest and wives and son, went out to receive him. And, O Bharata, worshipping the Rishi with water to wash his feet and face, and with the offerings of Arghya the king then offered his whole kingdom along with his son for the acceptance of the Rishi. The adorable Rishi accepting that worship offered by the king, addressing the ruler of Magadha, O monarch, said with well-pleased heart,--"O king, I knew all this by spiritual insight. But hear, O king of kings, what this son of thine will be in future, as also what his beauty, excellence, strength, and valour will be. Without doubt this son of thine, growing in prosperity and endued with prowess, will obtain all these. Like other birds that can never imitate the speed of Vinata's son (Garuda), the other monarchs of the earth will not be able to equal in energy this thy son, who will be endued with great valour. And all those that will stand in his way will certainly be destroyed. Like the force of the current that can never make the slightest impression upon the rocky breast of a mountain, weapons hurled at him even by the celestials will fail to produce the least pain in him. He will blaze forth above the heads of all that wear crowns on their brows. Like the sun that dims the lustre of all luminous bodies, this son of thine will rob all monarchs of their splendour. Even kings that are powerful and own large armies and numberless vehicles and animals, upon approaching this son of thine, will all perish as insects upon fire. This child will seize the growing prosperity of all kings like the ocean receiving the rivers swollen with the water of the rainy season. Like the huge earth that bears all kinds of produce, supporting things that are both good and evil, this child endued with great strength will support all the four orders of men. And all the kings of the earth will live in obedience to the commands of this child just as every creature endued with body live in dependence upon Vayu that is dear as self unto beings. This prince of Magadha--the mightiest of all men in the world--will behold with his physical eyes the god of gods called Rudra or Hara, the slayer of Tripura." O thou slayer of all foes, saying this, the Rishi, thinking of his own business, dismissed king Vrihadratha. The lord of the Magadhas then, re-entering his capital, and calling together his friends and relations, installed Jarasandha, on the throne. King Vrihadratha then came to feel a great distaste for worldly pleasures. And after the installation of Jarasandha king Vrihadratha followed by his two wives became an inmate of an ascetic asylum in the woods. And, O king, after his father and mothers had retired into the woods, Jarasandha by his valour brought numerous kings under his sway.'"

Vaisampayana continued,--"King Vrihadratha, having lived for some time in the woods and practised ascetic penances, ascended to heaven at last with his wives. King Jarasandha, also, as uttered by Kausika, having received those numerous boons ruled his kingdom like a father. Some time after when king Kansa was slain by Vasudeva, an enmity arose between him and Krishna. Then, O Bharata, the mighty king of Magadha from his city of Girivraja, whirling a mace ninety-nine times, hurled it towards Mathura. At that time Krishna of wonderful deeds was residing at Mathura. The handsome mace hurled by Jarasandha fell near Mathura at a distance of ninety-nine yojanas from Gririvraja. The citizens beholding the circumstance well, went unto Krishna and informed him of the fall of the mace. The place where the mace fell is adjacent to Mathura and is called Gadavasan. Jarasandha had two supporters called Hansa and Dimvaka, both of whom were incapable of being slain by weapons. Well-conversant with the science of politics and morality, in counsel they were the foremost of all intelligent men. I have already told thee everything about that mighty pair. They two and Jarasandha, I believe, are more than a match for three worlds. O brave king, it was for this reason that the powerful Kukkura, Andhaka and Vrishni tribes, acting from motives of policy, did not deem it proper to fight with him.

SECTION XX

(Jarasandhta-badha Parva)

"Krishna said,--'both Hansa and Dimvaka have fallen; Kansa also with all his followers has been slain. The time hath, therefore come for the destruction of Jarasandha. He is incapable of being vanquished in battle even by all the celestials and the Asuras (fighting together). We think, however, that he should be vanquished in a personal struggle with bare arms. In me is policy, in Bhima is strength and in Arjuna is triumph; and therefore, as prelude to performing the Rajasuya, we will certainly achieve the destruction of the ruler of Magadha. When we three approach that monarch in secret, and he will, without doubt, be engaged in an encounter with one of us. From fear of disgrace, from covetousness, and from pride of strength he will certainly summon Bhima to the encounter. Like death himself that slays a person however swollen with pride, the long-armed and mighty Bhimasena will effect the destruction of the king. If thou knowest my heart, if thou hast any faith in me, then make over to me, as a pledge, Bhima and Arjuna without loss of time!'"

Vaisampayana continued,--"Thus addressed by the exalted one, Yudhishthira, beholding both Bhima and Arjuna standing with cheerful faces, replied, saying--'O Achyuta, O Achyuta, thou slayer of all enemies, say not so. Thou art the lord of the Pandavas! We are dependent on thee. What thou sayest, O Govinda, is consistent with wise counsels. Thou never leadest those upon whom Prosperity hath turned her back. I who stay under thy command regard that Jarasandha is already slain, that the monarchs confined by him have already been set free, that the Rajasuya hath already been accomplished by me. O lord of the universe, O thou best of persons, watchfully act thou so that this task may be accomplished. Without ye then I dare not live, like a sorrowful man afflicted with disease, and bereft of the three attributes of morality, pleasure and wealth. Partha cannot live without Sauri (Krishna), nor can Sauri live without Partha. Nor is there anything in the world that is unconquerable by these two, viz., Krishna and Arjuna. This handsome Bhima also is the foremost of all persons endued with might. Of great renown, what can he not achieve when with ye two? Troops, when properly led, always do excellent service. A force without a leader hath been called inert by the wise. Forces, therefore, should always be led by experienced commanders. Into places that are low, the wise always conduct the water. Even fishermen cause the water (of tank) to run out through holes. (Experienced leaders always lead their forces noting the loopholes and assailable points of the foe). We shall, therefore, strive to accomplish our purpose following the leadership of Govinda conversant with the science of politics, that personage whose fame hath spread all over the world. For the successful accomplishment of one's purposes one should ever place Krishna in the van, that foremost of personages whose strength consists in wisdom and policy and who possesseth a knowledge of both method and means. For the accomplishment of one's purpose let, therefore, Arjuna, the son of Pritha, follow Krishna the foremost of the Yadavas and let Bhima follow Arjuna. Policy and good fortune and might will (then) bring about success in a matter requiring valour.'" Vaisampayana said,--"Thus addressed by Yudhishthira, the trio Krishna, Arjuna and Bhima, all possessed of great energy, set out for Magadha attired in the garb of Snataka Brahmanas of resplendent bodies, and blessed by the agreeable speeches of friends and relatives. Possessed of superior energy and of bodies already like the Sun, the Moon, and the Fire, inflamed with wrath at the sad lot of their relative kings, those bodies of theirs became much more blazing. And the people, beholding Krishna and Arjuna, both of whom had never before been vanquished in battle, with Bhima in the van, all ready to achieve the same task, regarded Jarasandha as already slain. For the illustrious pair (Krishna and Arjuna) were masters that directed every operation (in the universe), as also all acts relating to the morality, wealth, and pleasure of every being. Having set out from the country of the Kurus, they passed through Kuru-jangala and arrived at the charming lake of lotuses. Passing over the hills of Kalakuta, they then went on crossing the Gandaki, the Sadanira (Karatoya), and the Sarkaravarta and the other rivers taking their rise in the same mountains. They then crossed the delightful Sarayu and saw the country of Eastern Kosala. Passing over that country they went to Mithila and then crossing the Mala and Charamanwati, the three heroes crossed the Ganges and the Sone and went on towards the east. At last those heroes of unfaded glory arrived at Magadha in the heart of (the country of) Kushamva. Reaching then the hills of Goratha, they saw the city of Magadha that was always filled with kine and wealth and water and rendered handsome with the innumerable trees standing there.

SECTION XXI

"Vasudeva said,--'behold, O Partha, the great capital of Magadha, standing in all its beauty. Filled with flocks and herds and its stock of water never exhausted, and adorned also with fine mansions standing in excellent array, it is free from every kind of calamity. The five large hills of Vaihara, Varaha, Vrishava, Rishigiri, and the delightful Chaitya, all of high peaks and overgrown with tall trees of cool shade and connected with one another, seem to be jointly protecting the city of Girivraja. The breasts of the hills are concealed by forests of delightful and fragrant Lodhras having the ends of their branches covered with flowers. It was here that the illustrious Gautama of rigid vows begat on the Sudra woman Ausinari (the daughter of Usinara) Kakshivat and other celebrated sons. That the race sprung from Gautama doth yet live under the sway of an ordinary human race (of monarchs) is only evidence of Gautama's kindness to kings. And, O Arjuna, it was here that in olden times the mighty monarchs of Anga, and Vanga and other countries, came to the abode of Gautama, and passed their days in joy and happiness. Behold, O Partha, those forests of delightful Pippalas and beautiful Lodhras standing near the side of Gautama's abode. There dwelt in old days those Nagas, Arvuda and Sakravapin, those persecutors of all enemies, as also the Naga Swastika and that other excellent Naga called Manu. Manu himself had ordered the country of the Magadhas to be never afflicted with drought, and Kaushika and Manimat also have favoured the country. Owning such a delightful and impregnable city, Jarasandha is ever bent on seeking the fruition of his purposes unlike other monarchs. We shall, however, by slaying him to-day humble his pride.'"

Vaisampayana said,--"Thus saying those brothers of abundant energy, viz., he of the Vrishni race and the two Pandavas entered the city of Magadha. They then approached towards the impregnable city of Girivraja that was full of cheerful and well-fed inhabitants belonging to all the four orders, and where festivities were perennial. On arriving then at the gate of the city, the brothers (instead of passing through it) began to pierce (with their shafts) the heart of the high Chaityaka peak that was worshipped by the race of Vrihadratha, as also by the citizens and which delighted the hearts of all the Magadhas. There Vrihadratha had slain a cannibal called Rishava and having slain the monster made of his hide three drums which he placed in his own city. And those drums were such that once beaten their sound lasted one full month. And the brothers broke down the Chaityaka peak that was delightful to all the Magadhas, at that point where those drums covered with celestial flowers used to yield their continuous sound. And desirous of slaying Jarasandha they seemed by that act of theirs to place their feet upon the head of their foe. And attacking with their mighty arms that immovable and huge and high and old and celebrated peak always worshipped with perfumes and floral wreaths, those heroes broke it down. And with joyful hearts they then entered the city. And it so happened that the learned Brahmanas residing within the city saw many evil omens which they reported to Jarasandha. And the priest making the king mount an elephant whirled lighted brands about him. And king Jarasandha also, possessed of great prowess, with a view to warding of those evils, entered upon the celebration of a sacrifice, with proper vows and fasts. Meanwhile, O Bharata, the brothers unarmed, or rather with their bare arms as their only weapons, desirous of fighting with Jarasandha, entered the capital in the guise of Brahmanas. They beheld the extraordinary beauty of the shops full of various edibles and floral wreaths, and supplied with articles of every variety of various qualities that man can desire. Those best of men, Krishna, Bhima, and Dhananjaya, beholding in those shops their affluence, passed along the public road. And endued with great strength they snatched forcibly from the flower-vendors the garlands they had exposed for sale. And attired in robes of various colours and decked in garlands and ear-rings the heroes entered the abode of Jarasandha possessed of great intelligence, like Himalayan lions eyeing cattle-folds. And the arms of those warriors, O king, besmeared with sandal paste, looked like the trunks of sala trees. The people of Magadha, beholding those heroes looking like elephants, with necks broad like those of trees and wide chests, began to wonder much. Those bull among men, passing through three gates that were crowded with men, proudly and cheerfully approached the king. And Jarasandha rising up in haste received them with water to wash their feet with, and honey and the other ingredients of the Arghya--with gifts of kine, and with other forms of respect. The great king addressing them said,--'Ye are welcome'! And, O Janamejaya, both Partha and Bhima remained silent at this. And addressing the monarch Krishna said,--'O king of kings these two are now in the observance of a vow. Therefore they will not speak. Silent they will remain till midnight. After that hour they will speak with thee!' The king then quartering his guests in the sacrificial apartments retired into his private chambers. And when midnight arrived, the monarch arrived at the place where his guests attired as Brahmanas were. For, O King, that ever victorious monarch observed this vow which was known throughout the Worlds that as soon as he should hear of the arrival of Snataka Brahmanas at his place, should it be even at midnight, he would immediately, O Bharata, come out and grant them an audience. Beholding the strange attire of his guests that best of kings wondered much. For all that, however, he waited on them respectfully. Those bulls among men, those slayers of all foes, on the other hand, O thou best of the Bharata race, beholding king Jarasandha, said,--'Let salvation be attained by thee, O king, without difficulty.' And, O tiger among kings, having said this unto the monarch, they stood looking at each other. And, O king of kings, Jarasandha then said unto those sons of Pandu and him of the Yadu race, all disguised as Brahmanas-- 'Take your seats.' And those bulls among men sat themselves down, and like the three priests of a great sacrifice blazed forth in their beauty. And king Jarasandha, O thou of the Kuru race, firmly devoted to truth, censuring the disguised guests, said unto them,--'It is well known to me that in the whole world Brahmanas in the observance of Snataka vow never deck their persons with garlands and fragrant paste unseasonably. Who are ye, therefore, thus decked with flowers, and with hands bearing the marks of the bow-string? Attired in coloured robes and decked unseasonably with flowers and paste, ye give me to understand that ye are Brahmanas, although ye bear Kshatriya energy. Tell me truly who ye are. Truth decks even kings. Breaking down the peak of the Chaityaka hill, why have ye, in disguise, entered (the city) by an improper gate without fear of the royal wrath? The energy of a Brahmana dwelleth in his speech, (not in act). This your feat is not suited to the order to which ye profess to belong. Tell us therefore, the end ye have in view. Arrived here by such an improper way, why accept ye not the worship I offer? What is your motive for coming to me?' Thus addressed by the king, the high-souled Krishna, well-skilled in speech, thus replied unto the monarch in a calm and grave voice.

"Krishna said,--'O king, know us for Snataka Brahmanas. Brahmanas and Kshatriyas and Vaishyas are all, O monarch, competent to observe the vow of Snataka. This vow, besides, hath (many) especial and general rules. A Kshatriya observing this vow with especial rules always achieve prosperity. Therefore, have we decked ourselves with flowers. Kshatriyas again, O king, exhibit their energy by their arms and not in speech. It is, therefore, O son of Vrihadratha, that the speeches uttered by a Kshatriya are never audacious. O monarch, the creator hath planted his own energy in the aim of the Kshatriya. If thou wishest to behold it, thou shalt certainly behold it today. These are the rules of the ordinance, viz., that an enemy's abode should be entered through a wrong gate and a friend's abode through the right one. And know, O monarch, that this also is our eternal vow that having entered the foe's abode for the accomplishment of our purpose, we accept not the worship offered to us!'

SECTION XXII

"Jarasandha said,--'I do not recollect if I ever acted injuriously towards ye! Even upon a careful mental scrutiny I fail to see the injury I did unto ye.

When I have never done ye an injury, why, ye Brahmanas do ye regard me, who am innocent, as your foe? O, answer me truly, for this, indeed, is the rule followed by the honest. The mind is pained at the injury to one's pleasure and morality. That Kshatriya who injures an innocent man's (sources of) pleasure and morality even if he be otherwise a great warrior and well-versed in all rules of morality, obtains, without any doubt the fate of sinners (hereafter) and falls off from prosperity. The practices of the Kshatriyas are the best of those that are honest in the three worlds. Indeed, those that are acquainted with morality applaud the Kshatriya practices. Adhering to those practices of my order with steady soul, I never injure those that are under me. In bringing this charge, therefore, against me, it appears that ye speak erroneously!'

"Krishna said,--'O thou of mighty arms, there is a certain person of the head of a (royal) line who upholdeth the dignity of his race. At his command have we come against thee. Thou hast brought, O king, many of the Kshatriyas of the world as captives (to thy city.) Having perpetrated that wicked wrong how dost thou regard thyself as innocent? O best of monarchs, how can a king act wrongfully towards other virtuous kings? But thou, O king, treating other kings with cruelty, seekest to offer them as sacrifice unto the god Rudra! O son of Vrihadratha, this sin committed by thee may touch even us, for as we are virtuous in our practices, we are capable of protecting virtue. The slaughter of human being as sacrifice unto the gods is never seen. Why dost thou, therefore, seek to perform a sacrifice unto god Sankara by slaughtering human beings? Thou art addressing persons belonging to thy own order as animals (fit for sacrifice)! Fool as thou art, who else, O Jarasandha, is capable of behaving in this way? One always obtaineth the fruits of whatever acts one performeth under whatever circumstances. Therefore, desirous as we are of helping all distressed people, we have, for the prosperity of our race, come hither to slay thee, the slaughterer of our relatives. Thou thinkest that there is no man among the Kshatriyas (equal to thee). This, O king, is a great error of judgment on thy part. What Kshatriya is there, O king, who endued with greatness of soul and recollecting the dignity of his own parentage, would not ascend to eternal heaven that hath not its like anywhere, falling in open fight? Know O bull among men, that Kshatriyas engage themselves in battle, as persons installed in sacrifices, with heaven in view, and vanquish the whole world! Study of the Vedas, great fame, ascetic penances, and death in battle, are all acts that lead to heaven. The attainment of heaven by the three other acts may be uncertain, but death in battle hath that for its certain consequence. Death in battle is the sure cause of triumph like Indra's. It is graced by numerous merits. It is for this reason that he of a hundred sacrifices (Indra) hath become what he is, and by vanquishing the Asuras he ruleth the universe. Hostility with whom else than thee is so sure of leading to heaven, proud as thou art of the excessive strength of thy vast Magadha host? Don't disregard others, O king. Valour dwelleth in every man. O king of men, there are many men whose valour may be equal or superior to thine. As long as these are not known, so long only art thou noted for thy valour. Thy prowess, O king, can be borne by us. It is, therefore, that I say so. O king of Magadha, cast off thy superiority and pride in the presence of those that are thy equals. Go not, O king, with thy children and ministers and army, into the regions of Yama. Damvodhava, Kartavirya, Uttara, and Vrihadratha, were kings that met with destruction, along with all their forces, for having disregarded their superiors. Desirous of liberating the captive monarchs from thee, know that we are certainly not Brahmanas. I am Hrishesha otherwise called Sauri, and these two heroes among men are the sons of Pandu. O king of Magadha, we challenge thee. Fight standing before us. Either set free all the monarchs, or go thou to the abode of Yama.'

"Jarasandha said,--'I never make a captive of a king without first vanquishing him. Who hath been kept here that hath not been defeated in war? This, O Krishna, it hath been said, is the duty that should be followed by the Kshatriyas, viz., to bring others under sway by the exhibition of prowess and then to treat them as slaves. Having gathered these monarchs with the intention of offering them as sacrifices unto the god, how shall I, O Krishna, from fear liberate them to-day, when I recollect also the duty I have recited of a Kshatriya? With troops against troops arrayed in order of battle, or alone against one, or against two, or against three, at the same time or separately, I am ready to fight.'"

Vaisampayana said,--"Having spoken thus, and desiring to fight with those heroes of terrible achievements, king Jarasandha ordered (his son) Sahadeva to be installed on the throne. Then, O bull of the Bharata race, the king, on the eve of battle, thought of his two generals Kausika and Chitrasena. These two, O king, were formerly called by everybody in the world of men by the respectful appellations of Hansa and Dimvaka. And, O monarch, that tiger among men, the lord Sauri ever devoted to truth, the slayer of Madhu, the younger brother of Haladhara, the foremost of all persons having their senses under complete control, keeping in view the command of Brahma and remembering that the ruler of Magadha was destined to be slain in battle by Bhima and not by the descendant of Madhu (Yadavas), desired not to slay himself king Jarasandha, that foremost of all men endued with strength, that hero possessed of the prowess of a tiger, that warrior of terrible valour."

SECTION XXIII

Vaisampayana said,--"then that foremost of all speakers, Krishna of the Yadava race, addressing king Jarasandha who was resolved upon fighting, said,--'O king, with whom amongst us three dost thou desire to fight? Who amongst us shall prepare himself for battle (with thee)?' Thus addressed, the ruler of Magadha, king Jarasandha of great splendour, expressed his desire for fighting with Bhima. The priest then, bringing with him the yellow pigment obtained from the cow and garlands of flowers and other auspicious articles, as also various excellent medicines for restoring lost consciousness and alleviating pain, approached Jarasandha, panting for battle. The king Jarasandha, on whose behalf propitiatory ceremonies with benedictions were performed by a renowned Brahmana, remembering the duty of a Kshatriya dressed himself for battle. Taking off his crown and binding his hair properly, Jarasandha stood up like an ocean bursting its continents. Then the monarch possessed of terrible prowess, addressing Bhima, said, 'I will fight with thee. It is better to be vanquished by a superior person.' And saying this, Jarasandha, that represser of all foes endued, rushed with great energy at

Bhimasena like the Asura Vala of old who rushed at the chief of the celestials. And the mighty Bhimasena, on whose behalf the gods had been invoked by Krishna, that cousin of his, having consulted with advanced towards Jarasandha, impelled by the desire of fight. Then those tigers among men, those heroes of great prowess, with their bare arms as their only weapons, cheerfully engaged themselves in the encounter, each desirous of vanquishing the other. And seizing each other's arms and twining each other's legs, (at times) they slapped their arm-pits, causing the enclosure to tremble at the sound. And frequently seizing each other's necks with their hands and dragging and pushing it with violence, and each pressing every limb of his body against every limb of the other, they continued, O exalted one, to slap their arm-pits (at time). And sometimes stretching their arms and sometimes drawing them close, and now raising them up and now dropping them down, they began to seize each other. And striking neck against neck and forehead against forehead, they caused fiery sparks to come out like flashes of lightning. And grasping each other in various ways by means of their arms, and kicking each other with such violence as to affect the innermost nerves, they struck at each other's breasts with clenched fists. With bare arms as their only weapons roaring like clouds they grasped and struck each other like two mad elephants encountering each other with their trunks. Incensed at each other's blow, they fought on dragging and pushing each other and fiercely looking at each other like two wrathful lions. And each striking every limb of the other with his own and using his arms also against the other, and catching hold of each other's waist, they hurled each other to a distance. Accomplished in wrestling, the two heroes clasping each other with their arms and each dragging the other unto himself, began to press each other with great violence. The heroes then performed those grandest of all feats in wrestling called Prishtabhanga, which consisted in throwing each other down with face towards the earth and maintaining the one knocked down in that position as long as possible. And employing his arms, each also performed the feats called Sampurna-murchcha and Purna-kumbha. At times they twisted each other's arms and other limbs as if these were vegetable fibres that were to be twisted into chords. And with clenched fists they struck each other at times, pretending to aim at particular limbs while the blows descended upon other parts of the body. It was thus that those heroes fought with each other. The citizens consisting of thousands, of Brahmanas, Kshatriyas and Vaisyas and Sudras, and even women and the aged, O tiger among men, came out and gathered there to behold the fight. And the crowd became so great that it was one solid mass of humanity with no space between body and body. The sound the wrestlers made by the slapping of their arms, the seizing of each other's necks for bringing each other down, and the grasping of each other's legs for dashing each other to the ground, became so loud that it resembled the roar of thunder or of falling cliffs. Both of them were foremost of mighty men, and both took great delight in such encounter. Desirous of vanquishing the other, each was on the alert for taking advantage of the slightest lapse of the other. And, O monarch, the mighty Bhima and Jarasandha fought terribly on in those lists, driving the crowd at times by the motions of their hands like Vritra and Vasava of old. Thus two heroes, dragging each other forward and pressing each other backward and with sudden jerks throwing each other face downward and sideways, mangled each other dreadfully. And at times they struck each other with their knee-joints. And addressing each other loudly in stinging speeches, they struck each other with clenched fists, the blows descending like a mass of stone upon each other. With broad shoulders and long arms and both well-skilled in wrestling encounters, they struck each other with those long arms of theirs that were like maces of iron. That encounter of the heroes commenced on the first (lunar) day of the month of Kartic (October) and the illustrious heroes fought on without intermission and food, day and night, till the thirteenth lunar day. It was on the night of the fourteenth of the lunar fortnight that the monarch of Magadha desisted from fatigue. And O king, Janardana beholding the monarch tired, addressed Bhima of terrible deeds, and as if to stimulate him said,--'O son of Kunti, a foe that is fatigued cannot be pressed for if pressed at such a time he may even die. Therefore, O son of Kunti, this king should not be oppressed by thee. On the other hand, O bull of the Bharata race, fight with him with thy arms, putting forth as much strength only as thy antagonist hath now left!' Then that slayer of hostile heroes, the son of Pandu, thus addressed by Krishna, understood the plight of Jarasandha and forthwith resolved upon taking his life. And that foremost of all men endued with strength, that prince of the Kuru race, desirous of vanquishing the hitherto unvanquished Jarasandha, mustered all his strength and courage."

SECTION XXIV

Vaisampayana said,--"thus addressed, Bhima firmly resolved upon slaying Jarasandha, replied unto Krishna of the Yadu race, saying,--'O tiger of the Yadu race, O Krishna, this wretch that yet stayeth before me with sufficient strength and bent upon fight, should not be forgiven by me.' Hearing these words of Vrikodara (Bhima), that tiger among men, Krishna, desiring to encourage that hero to accomplish the death of Jarasandha without any delay, answered,--'O Bhima, exhibit today upon Jarasandha the strength thou hast luckily derived, the might thou hast obtained from (thy father), the god Maruta.' Thus addressed by Krishna, Bhima, that slayer of foes, holding up in the air the powerful Jarasandha, began to whirl him on high. And, O bull of the Bharata race, having so whirled him in the air full hundred times, Bhima pressed his knee against Jarasandha's backbone and broke his body in twain. And having killed him thus, the mighty Vrikodara uttered a terrible roar. And the roar of the Pandava mingling with that death knell of Jarasandha, while he was being broken on Bhima's knee, caused a loud uproar that struck fear into the heart of every creature. And all the citizens of Magadha became dumb with terror and many women were even prematurely delivered. And hearing those roars, the people of Magadha thought that either the Himavat was tumbling down or the earth itself was being rent asunder. And those oppressors of all foes then, leaving the lifeless body of the king at the palace gate where he lay as one asleep, went out of the town. And Krishna, causing Jarasandha's car furnished with an excellent flagstaff to be made ready and making the brothers (Bhima and Arjuna) ride in it, went in and released his (imprisoned) relatives. And those kings rescued from terrible fate, rich in the possession of jewels, approaching Krishna made presents unto him of jewels and gems. And having vanquished his foe, Krishna furnished with weapons and unwounded and accompanied by the kings (he had released), came out of Girivraja riding in that celestial car (of

Jarasandha). And he also who could wield the bow with both hands (Arjuna), who was incapable of being vanquished by any of the monarchs on earth, who was exceedingly handsome in person and well-skilled in the destruction of the foe, accompanied by the possessor of great strength (Bhima), came out of that fort with Krishna driving the car whereon he rode. And that best of cars, incapable of being vanquished by any king, ridden in by those warriors Bhima and Arjuna, and driven by Krishna, looked exceedingly handsome. Indeed, it was upon that car that Indra and Vishnu had fought of old in the battle (with the Asuras) in which Taraka (the wife of Vrihaspati) had become the immediate cause of much slaughter. And riding upon that car Krishna now came out of the hill-fort. Possessed of the splendour of heated gold, and decked with rows of jingling bells and furnished with wheels whose clatter was like the roar of clouds, and ever victorious in battle, and always slaughtering the foe against whom it was driven, it was that very car riding upon which Indra had slain ninety-nine Asuras of old. And those bulls among men (the three cousins) having obtained that car became exceedingly glad. The people of Magadha, behold the long-armed Krishna along with the two brothers, seated in that car (of Jarasandha) wondered much. O Bharata, that car, whereunto were yoked celestial horses and which possessed the speed of the wind, thus ridden upon by Krishna, looked exceedingly beautiful. And upon that best of cars was a flag-staff without being visibly attached thereto, and which was the product of celestial skill. And the handsome flag-staff, possessed of the splendour of the rainbow, could be seen from the distance of a yojana. And Krishna while coming out, thought of Garuda. And Garuda, thought of by his master, came thither in no time, like a tree of vast proportions standing in a village worshipped by all. Garuda of immense weight of body and living upon snakes sat upon that excellent car along with the numberless open- mouthed and frightfully-roaring creatures on its flag-staff. And thereupon that best of cars became still more dazzling with its splendour and was as incapable of being looked at by created being as the midday sun surrounded by a thousand rays. And, O king, such was that best of flag-staffs of celestial make that it never struck against any tree nor could any weapon injure it at all even though visible to men's eyes. And Achyuta, that tiger among men, riding with the two sons of

Pandu upon that celestial car, the clatter of whose wheels was like the roar of the clouds, came out of Girivraja. The car upon which Krishna rode had been obtained by king Vasu from Vasava, and from Vasu by Vrihadratha, and from the latter in due course by king Jarasandha. And he of long arms and eyes like lotus-petals and possessed of illustrious reputation, coming out of Girivraja, stopped (for some time) on a level plain outside the town. And, O king, all the citizens then, with the Brahmanas at their head, hastened thither to adore him with due religious rites. And the kings who had been released from confinement worshipped the slayer of Madhu with reverence, and addressing him with eulogies said,--'O thou of long arms, thou hast to-day rescued us, sunk in the deep mire of sorrow in the hand of Jarasandha. Such an act of virtue by thee, O son of Devaki, assisted by the might of Bhima and Arjuna, is most extraordinary. O Vishnu, languishing as we all were in the terrible hill-fort of Jarasandha, it was verily from sheer good fortune alone that thou hast rescued us, O son of the Yadu race, and achieved thereby a remarkable reputation. O tiger among men, we bow down to thee. O, command us what we shall do. However difficult of accomplishment, thy command being made known to us, O lord (Krishna), it will at once be accomplished by us.' Thus addressed by the monarchs, the high-souled Hrishikesa gave them every assurance and said,--'Yudhishthira is desirous of performing the sacrifice of Rajasuya. That monarch, ever guided by virtue, is solicitous of acquiring the imperial dignity. Having known this from me assist ye him in his endeavours.' Then, O king, all those monarchs with joyous hearts accepted the words of Krishna, saying,--'So be it!' And saying this, those lords of earth made presents of jewels unto him of the Dasarha race. And Govinda, moved by kindness towards them, took a portion of those presents.

"Then the son of Jarasandha, the high-souled Sahadeva, accompanied by his relatives and the principal officers of state, and with his priest in front came thither. And the prince, bending himself low and making large presents of jewels and precious stones, worshipped Vasudeva, that god among men. Then that best of men, Krishna, giving every assurance unto the prince afflicted with fear, accepted those presents of his of great value. And

Krishna joyfully installed the prince there and then in the sovereignty of Magadha. And the strong-armed and illustrious son of Jarasandha, thus installed on the throne by those most exalted of men and having obtained the friendship of Krishna and treated with respect and kindness by the two sons of Pritha, re-entered the city of his father. And that bull amongst men, Krishna, accompanied by the sons of Pritha and graced with great good fortune, left the city of Magadha, laden with numerous jewels. Accompanied by the two sons of Pandu, Achyuta (Krishna) arrived at Indraprastha, and approaching Yudhishthira joyfully addressing that monarch said,--'O best of kings, from good fortune, the mighty Jarasandha hath been slain by Bhima, and the kings confined (at Girivraja) have been all set free. From good fortune also, these two, Bhima and Dhananjaya, are well and arrived, O Bharata, at their own city unwounded.' Then Yudhishthira worshipped Krishna as he deserved and embraced Bhima and Arjuna in joy. And the monarch who had no enemy, having obtained victory through the agency of his brothers in consequence of the death of Jarasandha, gave himself up to pleasure and merriment with all his brothers. And the oldest son of Pandu (Yudhisthira) together with his brothers approached the kings who had come to Indraprastha and entertaining and worshipping them, each according to his age, dismissed them all. Commanded by Yudhishthira those kings with joyful hearts, set out for their respective countries without loss of time, riding upon excellent vehicles. Thus, O king, did that tiger among men, Janardana of great intelligence, caused his foe Jarasandha to be slain through the instrumentality of the Pandavas. And, O Bharata, that chastiser of all foes having thus caused Jarasandha to be slain, took leave of Yudhishthira and Pritha, and Draupadi and Subhadra, and Bhimasena and Arjuna and the twins Nakula and Sahadeva. After taking leave of Dhananjaya also, he set out for his own city (of Dwarka), riding upon that best of cars of celestial make, possessed of the speed of the mind and given unto him by Yudhishthira, filling the ten points of the horizon with the deep rattle of its wheels. And, O bull of the Bharata race, just as Krishna was on the point of setting out, the Pandavas with Yudhishthira at their head walked round that tiger among men who was never fatigued with exertion.

"And after the illustrious Krishna, the son of Devaki, had departed (from Indraprastha) having acquired that great victory and having also dispelled the fears of the kings, that feat, O Bharata, swelled the fame of the Pandavas. And, O king, the Pandavas passed their days, continuing to gladden the heart of Draupadi. And at that time, whatever was proper and consistent with virtue, pleasure, and profit, continued to be properly executed by king Yudhishthira in the exercise of his duties of protecting his subjects."

SECTION XXV

(Digvijaya Parva)

Vaisampayana said,--"Arjuna, having obtained that best of bows and that couple of inexhaustible quivers and that car and flag-staff, as also that assembly-house, addressing Yudhisthira said,--'Bow, weapons, great energy, allies, territory, fame, army--those, O king, difficult of acquisition however desirable, have all been obtained by me. I think, therefore, that what should now be done is for the swelling up of our treasury. I desire, O best of monarchs, to make the kings (of the earth) pay tributes to us. I desire to set out, in an auspicious moment of a holy day of the moon under a favourable constellation for the conquest of the direction that is presided over by the Lord of treasures (viz. the North).'"

Vaisampayana continued,--"King Yudhisthira the just, hearing these words of Dhananjaya, replied unto him in a grave and collected tone, saying,--'O bull of the Bharata race, set thou out, having made holy Brahmanas utter benedictions on thee, to plunge thy enemies in sorrow and to fill thy friend with joy. Victory, O son of Pritha, will surely be thine, and thou wilt surely obtain thy desires fulfilled.'

"Thus addressed, Arjuna, surrounded by a large host, set out in that celestial car of wonderful achievements he had obtained from Agni. And Bhimasena also, and those bull among men, the twins, dismissed with affection by Yudhishthira the just set out, each at the head of a large army.

And Arjuna, the son of the chastiser of Paka then brought under subjugation that direction (the North) which was presided over by the Lord of treasures. And Bhimasena overcome by force the East and Sahadeva the South, and Nakula, O king, acquainted with all the weapons, conquered the West. Thus while his brothers were so employed, the exalted king Yudishthira the just stayed within Khandavaprastha in the enjoyment of great affluence in the midst of friends and relatives."

"Bhagadatta, hearing this, said,--'O thou who hast Kunto for thy mother, as thou art to me, so is Yudhishthira also. I shall do all this. Tell me, what else I may do for thee.'"

SECTION XXVI

Vaisampayana continued,--"thus addressed, Dhananjaya replied unto Bhagadatta, saying,--'If thou wilt give thy promise to do this, thou hast done all I desire.' And having thus subjugated the king of Pragjyotisha, Dhananjaya of long arms, the son of Kunti, then marched towards the north- - the direction presided over by the lord of treasures. That bull amongst men, that son of Kunti, then conquered the mountainous tracts and their outskirts, as also the hilly regions. And having conquered all the mountains and the kings that reigned there, and bringing them under his sway, he exacted tributes from all. And winning the affections of those kings and uniting himself with them, he next marched, O king, against Vrihanta, the king of Uluka, making this earth tremble with the sound of his drums, the clatter of his chariot-wheels, and the roar of the elephants in his train. Vrihanta, however, quickly coming out of his city followed by his army consisting of four kinds of troops, gave battle to Falguna (Arjuna). And the fight that took place between Vrihanta and Dhananjaya was terrible. It so happened that Vrihanta was unable to bear the prowess of the son of Pandu. Then that invincible king of the mountainous region regarding the son of Kunti irresistible, approached him with all his wealth. Arjuna snatched out the kingdom from Vrihanta, but having made peace with him marched, accompanied by that king, against Senavindu whom he soon expelled from his kingdom. After this he subjugated Modapura, Vamadeva, Sudaman, Susankula, the Northern Ulukas, and the kings of those countries and peoples. Hereafter at the command of Yudhishthira, O monarch, Arjuna did not move from the city of Senavindu but sent his troops only and brought under his sway those five countries and peoples. For Arjuna, having arrived at Devaprastha, the city of Senavindu, took up his quarters there with his army consisting of four kinds of forces. Thence, surrounded by the kings and the peoples he had subjugated, the hero marched against king Viswagaswa-- that bull of Puru's race. Having vanquished in battle the brave mountaineers, who were all great warriors, the son of Pandu, O king, then occupied with the help of his troops, the town protected by the Puru king. Having vanquished in battle the Puru king, as also the robber tribes of the mountains, the son of Pandu brought under his sway the seven tribes called Utsava-sanketa. That bull of the Kshatriya race then defeated the brave Kshatriyas of Kashmira and also king Lohita along with ten minor chiefs. Then the Trigartas, the Daravas, the Kokonadas, and various other Kshatriyas, O king, advanced against the son of Pandu. That Prince of the Kuru race then took the delightful town of Avisari, and then brought under his sway Rochamana ruling in Uraga. Then the son of Indra (Arjuna), putting forth his might, pressed the delightful town of Singhapura that was well-protected with various weapons. Then Arjuna, that bull amongst the son of Pandu, at the head of all his troops, fiercely attacked the regions called Suhma and Sumala. Then the son of Indra, endued with great prowess, after pressing them with great force, brought the Valhikas always difficult of being vanquished, under his sway. Then Falguna, the son of Pandu, taking with him a select force, defeated the Daradas along with the Kambojas. Then the exalted son of Indra vanquished the robber tribes that dwelt in the north-eastern frontier and those also that dwelt in the woods. And, O great king, the son of Indra also subjugated the allied tribes of the Lohas, the eastern Kambojas, and northern Rishikas. And the battle with the Rishikas was fierce in the extreme. Indeed, the fight that took place between them and the son of Pritha was equal to that between the gods and the Asuras in which Taraka (the wife of Vrihaspati) had become the cause of so much slaughter. And defeating, O king, the Rishikas in the field of battle, Arjuna took from them as tribute eight horses that were of the colour of the parrot's breast, as also other horses of the hues of the peacock, born in northern and other climes and endued with high speed. At last having conquered all the Himalayas and the Nishkuta mountains, that bull among men, arriving at the White mountains, encamped on its breast."

SECTION XXVII

Vaisampayana said,--"that heroic and foremost of the Pandavas endued with great energy, crossing the White mountains, subjugated the country of the Limpurushas ruled by Durmaputra, after a collision involving a great slaughter of Kshatriyas, and brought the region under his complete sway. Having reduced that country, the son of Indra (Arjuna) with a collected mind marched at the head of his troops to the country called Harataka, ruled by the Guhakas. Subjugating them by a policy of conciliation, the Kuru prince beheld (in that region) that excellent of lakes called Manasa and various other lakes and tanks sacred to the Rishis. And the exalted prince having arrived at the lake Manasa conquered the regions ruled by the Gandharvas that lay around the Harataka territories. Here the conqueror took, as tribute from the country, numerous excellent horses called Tittiri, Kalmasha, Manduka. At last the son of the slayer of Paka, arriving in the country of North Harivarsha desired to conquer it. Thereupon certain frontier-guards of huge bodies and endued with great strength and energy, coming to him with gallant hearts, said, 'O son of Pritha, this country can be never conquered by thee. If thou seekest thy good, return hence. He that entereth this region, if human, is sure to perish. We have been gratified with thee; O hero, thy conquests have been enough. Nor is anything to be seen here, O Arjuna, that may be conquered by thee. The Northern Kurus live here. There cannot be war here. Even if thou enterest it, thou will not be able to behold anything, for with human eyes nothing can be seen here. If, however thou seekest anything else, O Bharata tell us, O tiger among men, so that we may do thy bidding.' Thus addressed by them, Arjuna smilingly addressing them, said,-- 'I desire the acquisition of the imperial dignity by Yudhishthira the just, of great intelligence. If your land is shut against human beings, I shall not enter it. Let something be paid unto Yudhishthira by ye as tribute.' Hearing these words of Arjuna, they gave him as tribute many cloths and ornaments of celestial make, silks of celestial texture and skins of celestial origin.

"It was thus that tiger among men subjugated the countries that lay to the North, having fought numberless battles with both Kshatriya and robber tribes. And having vanquished the chiefs and brought them under his sway he exacted from them much wealth, various gems and jewels, the horses of the species called Tittiri and Kalmasha, as also those of the colour of the parrot's wings and those that were like the peacocks in hue and all endued with the speed of the wind. And surrounded, O king, by a large army consisting of the four kinds of forces, the hero came back to the excellent city of Sakraprastha. And Partha offered the whole of that wealth, together with the animals he had brought, unto Yudhishthira the just. And commanded by the monarch, the hero retired to a chamber of the palace for rest."

SECTION XXVIII

Vaisampayana said,--"in the meantime, Bhimasena also endued with great energy, having obtained the assent of Yudhishthira the just marched towards the eastern direction. And the tiger among the Bharatas, possessed of great valour and ever increasing the sorrows of his foes, was accompanied by a mighty host with the full complement of elephants and horses and cars, well-armed and capable of crushing all hostile kingdoms. That tiger among men, the son of Pandu, going first into the great country of the Panchalas, began by various means to conciliate that tribe. Then that hero, that bull of the Bharata race, within a short time, vanquished the Gandakas and the Videhas. That exalted one then subjugated the Dasarnas. There in the country of the Dasarnas, the king called Sudharman with his bare arms fought a fierce battle with Bhimasena. And Bhimasena, beholding that feat of the illustrious king, appointed the mighty Sudharman as the first in command of his forces. Then Bhima of terrible prowess marched towards the east, causing the earth itself to tremble with the tread of the mighty host that followed him. Then that hero who in strength was the foremost of all strong men defeated in battle Rochamana, the king of Aswamedha, at the head of all his troops. And the son of Kunti, having vanquished that monarch by performing feats that excelled in fierceness, subjugated the eastern region. Then that prince of the Kuru race, endued with great prowess going into the country of Pulinda in the south, brought Sukumara and the king Sumitra under his sway. Then, O Janamejaya, that bull in the Bharata race, at the command of Yudhishthira the just marched against Sisupala of great energy. The king of Chedi, hearing of the intentions of the son of Pandu, came out of his city. And that chastiser of all foes then received the son of Pritha with respect. Then, O king, those bulls of the Chedi and the Kuru lines, thus met together, enquired after each other's welfare. Then, O monarch, the king of Chedi offered his kingdom unto Bhima and said smilingly,--'O sinless one, upon what art thou bent?' And Bhima thereupon represented unto him the intentions of king Yudhishthira. And Bhima dwelt there, O king, for thirty nights, duly entertained by Sisupala. And after this he set out from Chedi with his troops and vehicles."

SECTION XXIX

Vaisampayana said,--"that chastiser of all foes then vanquished king Srenimat of the country of Kumara, and then Vrihadvala, the king of Kosala. Then the foremost of the sons of Pandu, by performing feats excelling in fierceness, defeated the virtuous and mighty king Dirghayaghna of Ayodhya. And the exalted one then subjugated the country of Gopalakaksha and the northern Kosalas and also the king of Mallas. And the mighty one, arriving then in the moist region at the foot of the Himalayas soon brought the whole country under his sway. And that bull of Bharata race brought under control in this way diverse countries. And endued with great energy and in strength the foremost of all strong men, the son of Pandu next conquered the country of Bhallata, as also the mountain of Suktimanta that was by the side of Bhallata. Then Bhima of terrible prowess and long arms, vanquishing in battle the unretreating Suvahu the king of Kasi, brought him under complete sway. Then that bull among the sons of Pandu overcame in battle, by sheer force, the great king Kratha reigning in the region lying about Suparsa. Then the hero of great energy vanquished the Matsya and the powerful Maladas and the country called Pasubhumi that was without fear or oppression of any kind. And the long-armed hero then, coming from that land, conquered Madahara, Mahidara, and the Somadheyas, and turned his steps towards the north. And the mighty son of Kunti then subjugated, by sheer force, the country called Vatsabhumi, and the king of the Bhargas, as also the ruler of the Nishadas and Manimat and numerous other kings. Then Bhima, with scarcely any degree of exertion and very soon, vanquished the southern Mallas and the Bhagauanta mountains. And the hero next vanquished, by policy alone, the Sarmakas and the Varmakas. And that tiger among men then defeated with comparative ease that lord of earth, Janaka the king of the Videhas. And the hero then subjugated strategically the Sakas and the barbarians living in that part of the country. And the son of Pandu, sending forth expeditions from Videha, conquered the seven kings of the Kiratas living about the Indra mountain. The mighty hero then, endued with abundant energy, vanquished in battle the Submas and the Prasuhmas. And winning them over to his side, the son of Kunti, possessed of great strength, marched against Magadha. On his way he subjugated the monarchs known by the names of Danda and Dandadhara. And accompanied by those monarchs, the son of Pandu marched against Girivraja. After bringing the son of Jarasandha under his sway by conciliation and making him pay tribute, the hero then accompanied by the monarchs he had vanquished, marched against Kansa. And making the earth tremble by means of his troops consisting of the four kinds of forces, the foremost of the Pandavas then encountered Karna that slayer of foes. And, O Bharata, having subjugated Karna and brought him under his sway, the mighty hero then vanquished the powerful king of the mountainous regions. And the son of Pandu then slew in a fierce encounter, by the strength of his arms, the mighty king who dwelt in Madagiri. And the Pandava then, O king, subjugated in battle those strong and brave heroes of fierce prowess, viz., the heroic and mighty Vasudeva, the king of Pundra and king Mahaujah who reigned in Kausika-kachchha, and then attacked the king of Vanga. And having vanquished Samudrasena and king Chandrasena and Tamralipta, and also the king of the Karvatas and the ruler of the Suhmas, as also the kings that dwelt on the sea-shore, that bull among the Bharatas then conquered all Mlechchha tribes. The mighty son of the wind-god having thus conquered various countries, and exacting tributes from them all advanced towards Lohity. And the son of Pandu then made all the Mlechchha kings dwelling in the marshy regions on the sea-coast, pay tributes and various kinds of wealth, and sandal wood and aloes, and clothes and gems, and pearls and blankets and gold and silver and valuable corals. The Mlechchha kings showered upon the illustrious son of Kunti a thick downpour of wealth consisting of coins and gems counted by hundreds of millions. Then returning to Indraprastha, Bhima of terrible prowess offered the whole of that wealth unto king Yudhisthira the just."

SECTION XXX

Vaisampayana said,--"thus also Sahadeva, dismissed with affection by king Yudhisthira the just, marched towards the southern direction accompanied by a mighty host. Strong in strength, that mighty prince of the Kuru race, vanquishing completely at the outset the Surasenas, brought the king of Matsya under his sway. And the hero then, defeating Dantavakra, the mighty king of the Adhirajas and making him pay tribute, re-established him on his throne. The prince then brought under his sway Sukumara and then king Sumitra, and he next vanquished the other Matsyas and then the Patacharas. Endued with great intelligence, the Kuru warrior then conquered soon enough the country of the Nishadas and also the high hill called Gosringa, and that lord of earth called Srenimat. And subjugating next the country called Navarashtra, the hero marched against Kuntibhoja, who with great willingness accepted the sway of the conquering hero. And marching thence to the banks of the Charmanwati, the Kuru warrior met the son of king Jamvaka, who had, on account of old hostilities, been defeated before by Vasudeva. O Bharata, the son of Jamvaka gave battle to Sahadeva. And Sahadeva defeating the prince marched towards the south. The mighty warrior then vanquished the Sekas and others, and exacted tributes from them and also various kinds of gems and wealth. Allying himself with the vanquished tribes the prince then marched towards the countries that lay on the banks of the Narmada. And defeating there in battle the two heroic kings of Avanti, called Vinda and Anuvinda, supported by a mighty host, the mighty son of the twin gods exacted much wealth from them. After this the hero marched towards the town of Bhojakata, and there, O king of unfading glory, a fierce encounter took place between him and the king of that city for two whole days. But the son of Madri, vanquishing the invincible Bhismaka, then defeated in battle the king of Kosala and the ruler of the territories lying on the banks of the Venwa, as also the Kantarakas and the kings of the eastern Kosalas. The hero then defeating both the Natakeyas and the Heramvaks in battle, and subjugating the country of Marudha, reduced Munjagrama by sheer strength. And the son of Pandu then vanquished the mighty monarchs of the Nachinas and the Arvukas and the various forest king of that part of the country. Endued with great strength the hero then reduced to subjection king Vatadhipa. And defeating in battle the Pulindas, the hero then marched southward. And the younger brother of Nakula then fought for one whole day with the king of Pandrya. The long-armed hero having vanquished that monarch marched further to the south. And then he beheld the celebrated caves of Kishkindhya and in that region fought for seven days with the monkey-kings Mainda and Dwivida. Those illustrious kings however, without being tired in the encounter, were gratified with Sahadeva. And joyfully addressing the Kuru prince, they said,--'O tiger among the sons of Pandu, go hence, taking with the tribute from us all. Let the mission of the king Yudhishthira the just possessed of great intelligence, be accomplished without hindrance.' And taking jewels and gems from them all, the hero marched towards the city of Mahishmati, and there that bull of men did battle with king Nila. The battle that took place between king Nila and the mighty Sahadeva the son of Pandu, that slayer of hostile heroes, was fierce and terrible. And the encounter was an exceedingly bloody one, and the life of the hero himself was exposed to great risk, for the god Agni himself assisted king Nila in that fight. Then the cars, heroes, elephants, and the soldiers in their coats of mail of Sahadeva's army all appeared to be on fire. And beholding this the prince of the Kuru race became exceedingly anxious. And, O Janamejaya, at sight of this the hero could not resolve upon what he should do."

Janamejaya said,--"O regenerate one, why was it that the god Agni become hostile in battle unto Sahadeva, who was fighting simply for the accomplishment of a sacrifice (and therefore, for the gratification of Agni himself)?"

Vaisampayana said,--"It is said, O Janamejaya, that the god Agni while residing in Mahishmati, earned the reputation of a lover. King Nila had a daughter who was exceedingly beautiful. She used always to stay near the sacred fire of her father, causing it to blaze up with vigour. And it so happened that king Nila's fire, even if fanned, would not blaze up till agitated by the gentle breath of that girl's fair lips. And it was said in King Nila's palace and in the house of all his subjects that the god Agni desired that beautiful girl for his bride. And it so happened that he was accepted by the girl herself. One day the deity assuming the form of a Brahmana, was happily enjoying the society of the fair one, when he was discovered by the king. And the virtuous king thereupon ordered the Brahmana to be punished according to law. At this the illustrious deity flamed up in wrath. And beholding this, the king wondered much and bent his head low on the ground. And after some time the king bowing low bestowed the daughter of his upon the god Agni, disguised as a Brahmana. And the god Vibhabasu (Agni) accepting that fair-browed daughter of king Nila, became gracious unto that monarch. And Agni, the illustrious gratifier of all desires also asked the monarch to beg a boon of him. And the king begged that his troops might never be struck with panic while engaged in battle. And from that time, O king, those monarchs who from ignorance of this, desire to subjugate king Nila's city, are consumed by Hutasana (Agni). And from that time, O perpetuator of the Kuru race, the girls of the city of Mahishmati became rather unacceptable to others (as wives). And Agni by his boon granted them sexual liberty, so that the women of that town always roam about at will, each unbound to a particular husband. And, O bull of the Bharata race, from that time the monarchs (of other countries) forsake this city for fear of Agni. And the virtuous Sahadeva, beholding his troops afflicted with fear and surrounded by flames of fire, himself stood there immovable as a mountain. And purifying himself and touching water, the hero (Sahadeva) then addressed Agni, the god that sanctifieth everything, in these words,--

"'I bow unto thee, O thou whose track is always marked with smoke. These my exertions are all for thee. O thou sanctifier of all, thou art the mouth of the gods and thou art Sacrifice personified. Thou art called Pavaka because thou sanctifiest everything, and thou art Havyavahana, because thou carriest the clarified butter that is poured on thee. The Veda have sprung for ministering unto thee, and, therefore, thou art called Jataveda. Chief of the gods as thou art, thou art called Chitrabhanu, Anala, Vibhavasu, Hutasana, Jvalana, Sikhi, Vaiswanara, Pingesa, Plavanga, Bhuritejah. Thou art he from whom Kumara (Kartikeya) had his origin; thou art holy; thou art called Rudragarva and Hiranyakrit. Let thee, O Agni, grant me energy, let Vayu grant me life, let Earth grant me nourishment and strength, and let Water grant me prosperity. O Agni, thou who art the first cause of the waters, thou who art of great purity, thou for ministering unto whom the Vedas have sprung, thou who art the foremost of the deities, thou who art their mouth, O purify me by thy truth. Rishis and Brahmanas, Deities and Asuras pour clarified butter every day, according to the ordinance into thee during sacrifices. Let the rays of truth emanating from thee, while thou exhibitest thyself in those sacrifices, purify me. Smoke-bannered as thou art and possessed of flames, thou great purifier from all sins born of Vayu and ever present as thou art in all creatures, O purify me by the rays of thy truth. Having cleansed myself thus cheerfully, O exalted one, do I pray unto thee. O Agni, grant me now contentment and prosperity, and knowledge and gladness.'"

Vaisampayana continued.--"He that will pour clarified butter into Agni reciting these mantras, will ever be blessed with prosperity, and having his soul under complete control will also be cleansed from all his sins.

"Sahadeva, addressing Agni again, said,--'O carrier of the sacrificial libations, it behoveth thee not to obstruct a sacrifice!' Having said this, that tiger among men--the son of Madri--spreading some kusa grass on earth sat down in expectation of the (approaching) fire and in front of those terrified and anxious troops of his. And Agni, too, like the ocean that never transgresseth its continents, did not pass over his head. On the other hand approaching Sahadeva quietly and addressing that prince of the Kuru race, Agni that god of men gave him every assurance and said,--'O thou of the Kuru race, rise up from this posture. O rise up, I was only trying thee. I know all thy purpose, as also those of the son of Dharma (Yudhisthira). But, O best of the Bharata race, as long as there is a descendant of king Nila's line, so long should this town be protected by me. I will, however O son of Pandu, gratify the desires of thy heart.' And at these words of Agni, O bull of the Bharata race, the son of Madri rose up with a cheerful heart, and joining his hands and bending his head worshipped that god of fire, sanctifier of all beings. And at last, after Agni had disappeared, king Nila came there, and at the command of that deity, worshipped with due rites Sahadeva, that tiger among men--that master of battle. And Sahadeva accepted that worship and made him pay tribute. And having brought king Nila under his sway thus, the victorious son of Madri then went further towards the south. The long-armed hero then brought the king of Tripura of immeasurable energy under his sway. And next turning his forces against the Paurava kingdom, he vanquished and reduced to subjection the monarch thereof. And the prince, after this, with great efforts brought Akriti, the king of Saurashtra and preceptor of the Kausikas under his sway. The virtuous prince, while staying in the kingdom of Saurashtra sent an ambassador unto king Rukmin of Bhishmaka within the territories of Bhojakata, who, rich in possessions and intelligence, was the friend of Indra himself. And the monarch along with his son, remembering their relationship with Krishna, cheerfully accepted, O king, the sway of the son of Pandu. And the master of battle then, having exacted jewels and wealth from king Rukmin, marched further to the south. And, endued with great energy and great strength, the hero then reduced to subjection, Surparaka and Talakata, and the Dandakas also. The Kuru warrior then vanquished and brought under his subjection numberless kings of the Mlechchha tribe living on the sea coast, and the Nishadas and the cannibals and even the Karnapravarnas, and those tribes also called the Kalamukhas who were a cross between human beings and Rakshasas, and the whole of the Cole mountains, and also Surabhipatna, and the island called the Copper island, and the mountain called Ramaka. The high-souled warrior, having brought under subjection king Timingila, conquered a wild tribe known by the name of the Kerakas who were men with one leg. The son of Pandu also conquered the town of Sanjayanti and the country of the Pashandas and the Karahatakas by means of his messengers alone, and made all of them pay tributes to him. The hero brought under his subjection and exacted tributes from the Paundrayas and the Dravidas along with the Udrakeralas and the Andhras and the Talavanas, the Kalingas and the Ushtrakarnikas, and also the delightful city of Atavi and that of the Yavanas. And, O king of kings, that slayer of all foes, the virtuous and intelligent son of Madri having arrived at the sea-shore, then despatched with great assurance messengers unto the illustrious Vibhishana, the grandson of Pulastya. And the monarch willingly accepted the sway of the son of Pandu, for that intelligent and exalted king regarded it all as the act of Time. And he sent unto the son of Pandu diverse kinds of jewels and gems, and sandal and also wood, and many celestial ornaments, and much costly apparel, and many valuable pearls. And the intelligent Sahadeva, accepting them all, returned to his own kingdom.

"Thus it was, O king, that slayer of all foes, having vanquished by conciliation and war numerous kings and having also made them pay tribute, came back to his own city. The bull of the Bharata race, having presented the whole of that wealth unto king Yudhisthira the just regarded himself, O Janamejaya, as crowned with success and continued to live happily."

SECTION XXXI

Vaisampayana said,--"I shall now recite to you the deeds and triumphs of Nakula, and how that exalted one conquered the direction that had once been subjugated by Vasudeva. The intelligent Nakula, surrounded by a large host, set out from Khandavaprastha for the west, making this earth tremble with the shouts and the leonine roars of the warriors and the deep rattle of chariot wheels. And the hero first assailed the mountainous country called Rohitaka that was dear unto (the celestial generalissimo) Kartikeya and which was delightful and prosperous and full of kine and every kind of wealth and produce. And the encounter the son of Pandu had with the Mattamyurakas of that country was fierce. And the illustrious Nakula after this, subjugated the whole of the desert country and the region known as Sairishaka full of plenty, as also that other one called Mahetta. And the hero had a fierce encounter with the royal sage Akrosa. And the son of Pandu left that part of the country having subjugated the Dasarnas, the Sivis, the Trigartas, the Amvashtas, the Malavas, the five tribes of the Karnatas, and those twice born classes that were called the Madhyamakeyas and Vattadhanas. And making circuitous journey that bull among men then conquered the (Mlechcha) tribes called the Utsava-sanketas. And the illustrious hero soon brought under subjection the mighty Gramaniya that dwelt on the shore of the sea, and the Sudras and the Abhiras that dwelt on the banks of the Saraswati, and all those tribes that lived upon fisheries, and those also that dwelt on the mountains, and the whole of the country called after the five rivers, and the mountains called Amara, and the country called Uttarayotisha and the city of Divyakutta and the tribe called Dwarapala. And the son of Pandu, by sheer force, reduced to subjection the Ramathas, the Harahunas, and various kings of the west. And while staying there Nakula sent, O Bharata, messengers unto Vasudeva. And Vasudeva with all the Yadavas accepted his sway. And the mighty hero, proceeding thence to Sakala, the city of the Madras, made his uncle Salya accept from affection the sway of the Pandavas. And, O monarch, the illustrious prince deserving the hospitality and entertainment at his uncle's hands, was well entertained by his uncle. And skilled in war, the prince, taking from Salya a large quantity of jewels and gems, left his kingdom. And the son of Pandu then reduced to subjection the fierce Mlechchas residing on the sea coast, as also the wild tribes of the Palhavas, the Kiratas, the Yavanas, and the Sakas. And having subjugated various monarchs, and making all of them pay tributes, Nakula that foremost of the Kurus, full of resources, retraced his way towards his own city. And, O king, so great was the treasure which Nakula brought that ten thousand camels could carry it with difficulty on their backs. And arriving at Indraprastha, the heroic and fortunate son of Madri presented the whole of that wealth unto Yudhishthira.

"Thus, O king, did Nakula subjugate the countries that lay to the west-- the direction that is presided over by the god Varuna, and that had once before been subjugated by Vasudeva himself!"

SECTION XXXII

(Rajasuyika Parva)

Vaisampayana said,--"in consequence of the protection afforded by Yudhisthira the just, and of the truth which he ever cherished in his behaviour, as also of the check under which he kept all foes, the subjects of that virtuous monarch were all engaged in their respective avocations. And by reason of the equitable taxation and the virtuous rule of the monarch, clouds in his kingdom poured as much rain as the people desired, and the cities and the town became highly prosperous. Indeed as a consequence of the monarch's acts every affair of the kingdom, especially cattle breeding, agriculture and trade prospered highly. O king, during those days even robbers and cheats never spoke lies amongst themselves, nor they that were the favourites of the monarch. There were no droughts and floods and plagues and fires and premature deaths in those days of Yudhishthira devoted to virtue. And it was only for doing agreeable services, or for worshipping, or for offering tributes that would not impoverish, that other kings used to approach Yudhisthira (and not for hostility or battle.) The large treasure room of the king became so much filled with hoards of wealth virtuously obtained that it could not be emptied even in a hundred years. And the son of Kunti, ascertaining the state of his treasury and the extent of his possessions, fixed his heart upon the celebration of a sacrifice. His friends and officers, each separately and all together, approaching him said,--'The time hath come, O exalted one, for thy sacrifice. Let arrangements, therefore, be made without loss of time.' While they were thus talking, Hari

(Krishna), that omniscient and ancient one, that soul of the Vedas, that invincible one as described by those that have knowledge, that foremost of all lasting existences in the universe, that origin of all things, as also that in which all things come to be dissolved, that lord of the past, the future, and the present Kesava--the slayer of Kesi, and the bulwark of all Vrishnis and the dispeller of all fear in times of distress and the smiter of all foes, having appointed Vasudeva to the command of the (Yadava) army, and bringing with him for the king Yudhishthira just a large mass of treasure; entered that excellent city of cities. Khandava, himself surrounded by a mighty host and filling the atmosphere with the rattle of his chariot-wheels. And Madhava, that tiger among men enhancing that limitless mass of wealth the Pandavas had by that inexhaustible ocean of gems he had brought, enhanced the sorrows of the enemies of the Pandavas. The capital of the Bharata was gladdened by Krishna's presence just as a dark region is rendered joyful by the sun or a region of still air by a gentle breeze. Approaching him joyfully and receiving him with due respect, Yudhishthira enquired of his welfare. And after Krishna had been seated at ease, that bull among men, the son of Pandu, with Dhaumya and Dwaipayana and the other sacrificial priests and with Bhima and Arjuna and the twins, addressed Krishna thus,--

"'O Krishna it is for thee that the whole earth is under my sway. And, O thou of the Vrishni race, it is through thy grace that vast wealth had been got by me. And, O son of Devaki, O Madhava, I desire to devote that wealth according to the ordinance, unto superior Brahmanas and the carrier of sacrificial libations. And, O thou of the Dasarha race, it behoveth thee, O thou of mighty arms, to grant me permission to celebrate a sacrifice along with thee and my younger brothers. Therefore, O Govinda, O thou of long arms, install thyself at that sacrifice; for, O thou of the Dasarha race, if thou performed the sacrifice, I shall be cleansed of sin. Or, O exalted one, grant permission for myself being installed at the sacrifice along with these my younger brothers, for permitted by thee, O Krishna, I shall be able to enjoy the fruit of an excellent sacrifice.'"

Vaisampayana continued,--"Unto Yudhisthira after he had said this,

Krishna, extolling his virtues, said.--'Thou, O tiger among kings, deservest imperial dignity. Let, therefore, the great sacrifice be performed by thee. And if thou performest that sacrifice and obtainest its fruit we all shall regard ourselves as crowned with success. I am always engaged in seeking good. Perform thou then the sacrifice thou desirest. Employ me also in some office for that purpose, for I should obey all thy commands. Yudhisthira replied--O Krishna, my resolve is already crowned with fruit, and success also is surely mine, when thou, O Harishikesa, hast arrived here agreeably to my wish!'"

Vaisampayana continued,--"Commanded by Krishna, the son of Pandu along with his brothers set himself upon collecting the materials for the performance of the Rajasuya sacrifice. And that chastiser of all foes, the son of Pandu, then commanded Sahadeva that foremost of all warriors and all ministers also, saying,--'Let persons be appointed to collect without loss of time, all those articles which the Brahmanas have directed as necessary for the performance of this sacrifice, and all materials and auspicious necessaries that Dhaumya may order as required for it, each of the kind needed and one after another in due order. Let Indrasena and Visoka and Puru with Arjuna for his charioteer be engaged to collect food if they are to please me. Let these foremost of the Kurus also gather every article of agreeable taste and smell that may delight and attract the hearts of the Brahmanas.'

"Simultaneously with these words of king Yudhisthira the just, Sahadeva that foremost of warriors, having accomplished everything, represented the matter to the king. And Dwaipayana, O king, then appointed as sacrificial priests exalted Brahmanas that were like the Vedas themselves in embodied forms. The son of Satyavati became himself the Brahma of that sacrifice. And that bull of the Dhananjaya race, Susaman, became the chanter of the Vedic (Sama) hymns. Yajnavalkya devoted to Brahma became the Adhyaryu, and Paila--the son of Vasu and Dhaumya became the Hotris. And O bull of the Bharata race, the disciples and the sons of these men, all well-acquainted with the Vedas and the branches of the Vedas, became Hotragis.

And all of them, having uttered benedictions and recited the object of the sacrifice, worshipped, according to the ordinance the large sacrificial compound. Commanded by the Brahmanas, builders and artificers erected numerous edifices there that were spacious and well-perfumed like unto the temples of the gods. After these were finished, that best of kings and that bull among men Yudhishthira commanded his chief adviser Sahadeva, saying,-- 'Despatch thou, without loss of time, messengers endued with speed to invite all to the sacrifice. And Sahadeva, hearing these words of the king, despatched messengers telling them,--"Invite ye all the Brahmanas in the kingdom and all the owners of land (Kshatriyas) and all the Vaisyas and also all the respectable Sudras, and bring them hither!"'"

Vaisampayana continued,--"Endued with speed, these messengers then, thus commanded, invited everybody according to the orders of the Pandava, without losing any time, and brought with them many persons, both friends and strangers. Then, O Bharata, the Brahmanas at the proper time installed Yudhishthira the son of Kunti at the Rajasuya sacrifice. And after the ceremony of installation was over, that foremost of men, the virtuous king Yudhishthira the just like the god Dharma himself in human frame, entered the sacrificial compound, surrounded by thousands of Brahmanas and his brothers and the relatives and friends and counsellors, and by a large number of Kshatriya kings who had come from various countries, and by the officers of State. Numerous Brahmanas, well-skilled in all branches of knowledge and versed in the Vedas and their several branches, began to pour in from various countries. Thousands of craftsmen, at the command of king Yudhishthira the just, erected for those Brahmanas with their attendants separate habitations well-provided with food and clothes and the fruits and flowers of every season. And, O king, duly worshipped by the monarch the Brahmanas continued to reside there passing their time in conversation on diverse topics and beholding the performances of actors and dancers. And the clamour of high-souled Brahmanas, cheerfully eating and talking, was heard there without intermission. 'Give,' and 'Eat' were the words that were heard there incessantly and every day. And, O Bharata, king Yudhishthira the just gave unto each of those Brahmanas thousands of kine and beds and gold coins and damsels.

"Thus commenced on earth the sacrifice of that unrivalled hero, the illustrious son of Pandu, like the sacrifice in heaven of Sakra himself. Then that bull among men, king Yudhishthira despatched Nakula the son of Pandu unto Hastinapura to bring Bhishma and Drona, Dhritarashtra and Vidura and Kripa and those amongst his cousins that were well-disposed towards him."

SECTION XXXIII

Vaisampayana said,--"the ever-victorious Nakula, the son of Pandu, having reached Hastinapura, formally invited Bhishma and Dhritarashtra. The elder of the Kuru race with the preceptor at their head, invited with due ceremonies, came with joyous hearts to that sacrifice, with Brahmanas walking before them. And, O bull of the Bharata race, having heard of king Yudhishthira's sacrifice, hundreds of other Kshatriyas acquainted with the nature of the sacrifice, with joyous hearts came there from various countries, desiring to behold king Yudhishthira the son of Pandu and his sacrificial mansion, and brought with them many costly jewels of various kinds. And Dhritarashtra and Bhishma and Vidura of high intelligence; and all Kaurava brothers with Duryyodhana at their head; and Suvala the king of Gandhara and Sakuni endued with great strength; and Achala, and Vrishaka, and Karna that foremost of all charioteers; and Salya endued with great might and the strong Valhika; and Somadatta, and Bhuri of the Kuru race, and Bhurisravas and Sala; and Aswatthama, Kripa, Drona, and Jayadratha, the ruler of Sindhu; and Yajnasena with his sons, and Salya that lord of earth and that great car warrior king Bhagadatta of Pragjyotisha accompanied by all Mlechcha tribes inhabiting the marshy regions on the sea-shore; and many mountain kings, and king Vrihadvala; and Vasudeva the king of the Paundrayas, and the kings of Vanga and Kalinga; and Akastha and Kuntala and the kings of the Malavas and the Andhrakas; and the Dravidas and the Singhalas and the king of Kashmira, and king Kuntibhoja of great energy and king Gauravahana, and all the other heroic kings of Valhika; and Virata with his two sons, and Mavella endued with great might; and various kings and princes ruling in various countries; and, O Bharata king Sisupala endued with great energy and invincible in battle accompanied by his son--all of them came to the sacrifice of the son of Pandu. And Rama and Aniruddha and Kanaka and Sarana; and Gada, Pradyumna, Shamva, and Charudeshna of great energy; and Ulmuka and Nishatha and the brave Angavaha; and innumerable other Vrishnis--all mighty car-warriors--came there.

"These and many other kings from the middle country came, O monarch, to that great Rajasuya sacrifice of the son of Pandu. And, O king, at the command of king Yudhishthira the just, mansions were assigned to all those monarchs, that were full of various kinds of edibles and adorned with tanks and tall trees. And the son of Dharma worshipped all those illustrious monarchs as they deserved. Worshipped by the king they retired to mansions that were assigned to them. Those mansions were (white and high) like the cliffs of Kailasa, and delightful to behold, and furnished with every kind of furniture. They were enclosed on all sides with well- built and high white-washed walls; their windows were covered with net- works of gold and their interiors were furnished with rows of pearls. Their flights of stairs were easy of ascent and the floors were all laid over with costly carpets. They were all hung over with garlands of flowers and perfumed with excellent aloes. White as snow or the moon, they looked extremely handsome even from the distance of a yojana. Their doors and entrances were set uniformly and were wide enough to admit a crowd of persons. Adorned with various costly articles and built with various metals, they looked like peaks of the Himavat. Having rested a while in those mansions the monarchs beheld king Yudhishthira the just surrounded by numerous Sadasyas (sacrificial priests) and ever performing sacrifices distinguished by large gifts to Brahmanas. That sacrificial mansion wherein were present the kings and Brahmanas and great Rishis looked, O king, as handsome as heaven itself crowded with the gods!"

Thus ends the thirty-fourth section in the Rajasuyika Parva of the Sabha Parva.

Vaisampayana said,--"then, O king, Yudhishthira, having approached and worshipped his grandfather and his preceptor, addressed Bhishma and Drona and Kripa and the son of Drona and Duryyodhana and Vivingsati, and said,-- 'Help me ye all in the matter of this sacrifice. This large treasure that is here is yours. Consult ye with one another and guide me as ye desire.'

"The eldest of the sons of Pandu, who had been installed at the sacrifice, having said this unto all, appointed every one of them to suitable offices. He appointed Dussasana to superintend the department of food and other enjoyable articles. Aswatthama was asked to attend on the Brahmanas. Sanjaya was appointed to offer return-worship unto the kings. Bhishma and Drona, both endued with great intelligence, were appointed to see what was done and what was left undone. And the king appointed Kripa to look after the diamonds and gold and the pearls and gems, as also after the distribution of gifts to Brahmanas. And so other tigers among men were appointed to similar offices. Valhika and Dhritarashtra and Somadatta and Jayadratha, brought thither by Nakula, went about, enjoying themselves as lords of the sacrifice. Vidura otherwise called Kshatta, conversant with every rule of morality, became the disburser. Duryyodhana became the receiver of the tributes that were brought by the kings. Krishna who was himself the centre of all worlds and round whom moved every creature, desirous of acquiring excellent fruits, was engaged at his own will in washing the feet of the Brahmanas.

"And desirous of beholding that sacrificial mansion, as also king Yudhishthira the just, none came there with tribute less than a thousand (in number, weight or measure). Everyone honoured the king Yudhishthira the just with large presents of jewels. And each of the kings made a present of his wealth, flattering himself with the proud belief that the jewels he gave would enable the Kuru king Yudhisthira to complete his sacrifice. And, O monarch, the sacrificial compound of the illustrious son of Kunti looked extremely handsome--with the multitude of palaces built so as to last for ever and crowded with guards and warriors. These were so high that their tops touched the cars of the gods that came to behold that sacrifice; as also with the cars themselves of the celestials, and with the dwelling of the Brahmanas and the mansions made there for the kings resembling the cars of the celestials and adorned with gems and filled with every kind of wealth, and lastly with crowds of the kings that came there all endued with beauty and wealth. Yudhisthira, as though vying with Varuna himself in wealth, commenced the sacrifice (of Rajasuya) distinguished by six fires and large gifts to Brahmanas. The King gratified everybody with presents of great value and indeed with every kind of object that one could desire. With abundance of rice and of every kind of food, as also with a mass of jewels brought as tribute, that vast concourse consisted of persons every one of whom was fed to the full. The gods also were gratified at the sacrifice by the Ida, clarified butter, Homa and libations poured by the great Rishis versed in mantras and pronunciation. Like the gods, the Brahmanas also were gratified with the sacrificial gifts and food and great wealth. And all the other orders of men also were gratified at that sacrifice and filled with joy."

SECTION XXXV

(Arghyaharana Parva)

Vaisampayana said,--"On the last day of the sacrifice when the king was to be sprinkled over with the sacred water, the great Brahmana Rishis ever deserving of respectful treatment, along with the invited kings, entered together the inner enclosure of the sacrificial compound. And those illustrious Rishis with Narada as their foremost, seated at their ease with those royal sages within that enclosure, looked like the gods seated in the mansion of Brahma in the company of the celestial Rishis. Endued with immeasurable energy those Rishis, having obtained leisure, started various topics of conversation. 'This is so,' 'This is not so,' 'This is even so.' 'This cannot be otherwise,'--thus did many of them engage in discussions with one another. Some amongst the disputants, by well-chosen arguments made the weaker position appear the stronger and the stronger the weaker. Some disputants endued with great intelligence fell upon the position urged by others like hawks darting at meat thrown up into the air, while some amongst them versed in the interpretations of religious treatises and others of rigid vows, and well-acquainted with every commentary and gloss engaged themselves in pleasant converse. And, O king, that platform crowded with gods, Brahmanas and great Rishis looked extremely handsome like the wide expanse of the firmament studded with stars. O monarch, there was then no Sudra near that platform of Yudhisthira's mansion, nor anybody that was without vows.

"And Narada, beholding the fortunate Yudhisthira's prosperity that was born of that sacrifice, became highly gratified. Beholding that vast concourse all the Kshatriyas, the Muni Narada, O king of men, became thoughtful. And, O bull amongst men, the Rishi began to recollect the words he had heard of old in the mansion of Brahma regarding the incarnation on earth of portions of every deity. And knowing, O son of the Kuru race, that that was a concourse (of incarnate) gods, Narada thought in his mind of Hari with eyes like lotus-petals. He knew that that creator himself of every object one, that exalted of all gods--Narayana--who had formerly commanded the celestials, saying,--'Be ye born on earth and slay one another and come back to heaven'--that slayer of all the enemies of the gods, that subjugator of all hostile towns, in order to fulfil his own promise, had been born in the Kshatriya order. And Narada knew that the exalted and holy Narayana, also called Sambhu the lord of the universe, having commanded all the celestials thus, had taken his birth in the race of Yadus and that foremost of all perpetuator of races, having sprung from the line of the Andhaka-Vrishnis on earth was graced with great good fortune and was shining like the moon herself among stars. Narada knew that Hari the grinder of foes, whose strength of arm was ever praised by all the celestials with Indra among them, was then living in the world in human form. Oh, the Self-Create will himself take away (from the earth) this vast concourse of Kshatriyas endued with so much strength. Such was the vision of Narada the omniscient who knew Hari or Narayana to be that Supreme Lord whom everybody worshipped with sacrifice. And Narada, gifted with great intelligence and the foremost of all persons and conversant with morality, thinking of all this, sat at that sacrifice of the wise king Yudhisthira the just with feelings of awe.

"Then Bhishma, O king, addressing king Yudhisthira the just, said, 'O Bharata, let Arghya (an article of respect) be offered unto the kings as each of them deserveth. Listen, O Yudhishthira, the preceptor, the sacrificial priest, the relative, the Snataka, the friend, and the king, it hath been said are the six that deserve Arghya. The wise have said that when any of these dwell with one for full one year he deserveth to be worshipped with Arghya. These kings have been staying with us for some time. Therefore, O king, let Arghyas be procured to be offered unto each of them. And let an Arghya be presented first of all unto him among those present who is the foremost.'

"Hearing these words of Bhishma, Yudhishthira said--'O Grandsire, O thou of the Kuru race, whom thou deemest the foremost amongst these and unto whom the Arghya should be presented by us, O tell me.'"

Vaisampayana continued,--"Then, O Bharata, Bhishma the son of Santanu, judged it by his intelligence that on earth Krishna was the foremost of all. And he said--'As is the sun among all luminous objects, so is the one (meaning Krishna) (who shines like the sun) among us all, in consequence of his energy, strength and prowess. And this our sacrificial mansion is illuminated and gladdened by him as a sunless region by the sun, or a region of still air by a gust of breeze. Thus commanded by Bhishma, Sahadeva endued with great prowess duly presented the first Arghya of excellent ingredients unto Krishna of the Vrishni race. Krishna also accepted it according to the forms of the ordinance. But Sisupala could not bear to see that worship offered unto Vasudeva. And this mighty king of Chedi, reproving in the midst of that assembly both Bhishma and. Yudhishthira, censured Vasudeva thereafter.'

SECTION XXXVI

"Sisupala said--'O thou of the Kuru race, this one of the Vrishni race doth not deserve royal worship as if he were a king, in the midst of all these illustrious monarchs. O son of Pandu, this conduct of thine in thus willingly worshipping him with eyes like lotus-petals is not worthy of the illustrious Pandavas. Ye sons of Pandu. Ye are children. Ye know not what morality is, for that is very subtle. Bhishma, this son also of Ganga is of little knowledge and hath transgressed the rules of morality (by giving ye such counsel). And, O Bhishma, if one like thee, possessed of virtue and morality acteth from motives of interest, he is deserving of censure among the honest and the wise. How doth he of the Dasarha race, who is not even a king, accept worship before these kings and how is it that he hath been worshipped by ye? O bull of the Kuru race, if thou regardest Krishna as the oldest in age, here is Vasudeva, and how can his son be said so in his presence? Or, if thou regardest Vasudeva as your well-wisher and supporter, here is Drupada; how then can Madhava deserve the (first) worship? Or, O son of Kuru, regardest thou Krishna as preceptor? When Drona is here, how hast thou worshipped him of the Vrishni race? Or, O son of Kuru, regardest thou Krishna as the Ritwija? When old Dwaipayana is here, how hath Krishna been worshipped by thee? Again when old Bhishma, the son of Santanu, that foremost of men who is not to die save at his own wish is here, why, O king, hath Krishna been worshipped by thee? When the brave Aswatthaman, versed in every branch of knowledge is here, why, O king, hath Krishna, O thou of the Kuru race, been worshipped by thee? When that King of kings, Duryyodhana, that foremost of men, is here, as also Kripa the preceptor of the Bharata princes, why hath Krishna been worshipped by thee? How, O son of Pandu, passing over Druma, the preceptor of the Kimpurusas, hast thou worshipped Krishna? When the invincible Bhishmaka and king Pandya possessed of every auspicious mark, and that foremost of kings--Rukmi and Ekalavya and Salya, the king of the Madras, are here, how, O son of Pandu, hast thou offered the first worship unto Krishna? Here also is Karna ever boasting of his strength amongst all kings, and (really) endued with great might, the favourite disciple of the Brahmana Jamadagnya, the hero who vanquished in battle all monarchs by his own strength alone. How, O Bharata, hast thou, passing him over, offered the first worship unto Krishna? The slayer of Madhu is neither a sacrificial priest nor a preceptor, nor a king. That thou hast notwithstanding all these worshipped him, O chief of the Kurus, could only have been from motives of gain. If, O Bharata, it was your wish to offer the first worship unto the slayer of Madhu, why were these monarchs brought here to be insulted thus? We have not paid tributes to the illustrious son of Kunti from fear, from desire of gain, or from having been won over by conciliation. On the other hand, we have paid him tribute simply because he hath been desirous of the imperial dignity from motives of virtue. And yet he it is that thus insulteth us. O king, from what else, save motives of insult, could it have been that thou hast worshipped Krishna, who possesseth not the insignia of royalty, with the Arghya in the midst of the assembled monarchs? Indeed, the reputation for virtue that the son of Dharma hath acquired, hath been acquired by him without cause, for who would offer such undue worship unto one that hath fallen off from virtue. This wretch born in the race of the Vrishnis unrighteously slew of old the illustrious king Jarasandha. Righteousness hath today been abandoned by Yudhishthira and meanness only hath been displayed by him in consequence of his having offered the Arghya to Krishna. If the helpless sons of Kunti were affrighted and disposed to meanness, thou, O Madhava, ought to have enlightened them as to thy claims to the first worship? Why also, O Janarddana, didst thou accept the worship of which thou art unworthy, although it was offered unto thee by those mean-minded princes? Thou thinkest much of the worship unworthily offered unto thee, like a dog that lappeth in solitude a quantity of clarified butter that it hath obtained. O Janarddana, this is really no insult offered unto the monarchs; on the other hand it is thou whom the Kurus have insulted. Indeed, O slayer of Madhu, as a wife is to one that is without virile power, as a fine show is to one that is blind, so is this royal worship to thee who art no king. What Yudhishthira is, hath been seen; what Bhishma is, hath been seen; and what this Vasudeva is hath been seen. Indeed, all these have been seen as they are!'

"Having spoken these words, Sisupala rose from his excellent seat, and accompanied by the kings, went out of that assembly."

SECTION XXXVII

Vaisampayana said,--"Then the king Yudhishthira hastily ran after Sisupala and spoke unto him sweetly and in a conciliating tone the following words,-- 'O lord of earth, what thou hast said is scarcely proper for thee. O king, it is highly sinful and needlessly cruel. Insult not Bhishma, O king, by saying that he doth not know what virtue is. Behold, these many kings, older than thou art, all approve of the worship offered unto Krishna. It behoveth thee to bear it patiently like them. O ruler of Chedi, Bhishma knoweth Krishna truly. Thou knowest him not so well as this one of the Kuru race.'

"Bhishma also, after this, said,--'He that approveth not the worship offered unto Krishna, the oldest one in the universe, deserveth neither soft words nor conciliation. The chief of warriors of the Kshatriya race who having overcome a Kshatriya in battle and brought him under his power, setteth him free, becometh the guru (preceptor or master) of the vanquished one. I do not behold in this assembly of kings even one ruler of men who hath not been vanquished in battle by the energy of this son of the Satwata race. This one (meaning Krishna) here, of undefiled glory, deserveth to be worshipped not by ourselves alone, but being of mighty arms, he deserveth to be worshipped by the three worlds also. Innumerable warriors among Kshatriyas have been vanquished in battle by Krishna. The whole universe without limit is established in him of the Vrishni race. Therefore do we worship Krishna amongst the best and the oldest, and not others. It behoveth thee not to say so. Let thy understanding be never so. I have, O king, waited upon many persons that are old in knowledge. I have heard from all those wise men, while talking; of the numerous much- regarded attributes of the accomplished Sauri. I have also heard many times all the acts recited by people that Krishna of great intelligence hath performed since his birth. And, O king of Chedi, we do not from caprice, or keeping in view our relationship or the benefits he may confer on us, worship Janarddana who is worshipped by the good on earth and who is the source of the happiness of every creature. We have offered unto him the first worship because of his fame, his heroism, his success. There is none here of even tender years whom we have not taken into consideration. Passing over many persons that are foremost for their virtues, we have regarded Hari as deserving of the first worship. Amongst the Brahmanas one that is superior in knowledge, amongst the Kshatriyas one that is superior in strength, amongst the Vaisyas one that is superior in possessions and wealth, and amongst the Sudras one that is superior in years, deserveth to be worshipped. In the matter of the worship offered unto Govinda, there are two reasons, viz., knowledge of the Vedas and their branches, and also excess of strength. Who else is there in the world of men save Kesava that is so distinguished? Indeed, liberality, cleverness, knowledge of the Vedas, bravery, modesty, achievements, excellent intelligence, humility, beauty, firmness, contentment and prosperity--all dwell for ever in Achyuta. Therefore, ye kings, it behoveth ye to approve of the worship that hath been offered unto Krishna who is of great accomplishments, who as the preceptor, the father, the guru, is worthy of the Arghya and deserving of (everybody's) worship. Hrishikesa is the sacrificial priest, the guru, worthy of being solicited to accept one's daughter in marriage, the Snataka, the king, the friend: therefore hath Achyuta been worshipped by us. Krishna is the origin of the universe and that in which the universe is to dissolve. Indeed, this universe of mobile and immobile creatures hath sprung into existence from Krishna only. He is the unmanifest primal cause (Avyakta Prakriti), the creator, the eternal, and beyond the ken of all creatures. Therefore doth he of unfading glory deserve highest worship. The intellect, the seat of sensibility, the five elements, air, heat, water, ether, earth, and the four species of beings (oviparous, viviparous, born of filthy damp and vegetal) are all established in Krishna. The sun, the moon, the constellations, the planets, all the principal directions, the intermediate directions, are all established in Krishna. As the Agnihotra is the foremost among all Vedic sacrifices, as the Gayatri is the foremost among metres, as the king is the foremost among men, as the ocean is the foremost among all rivers, as the moon is the foremost among all constellations, as the sun is the foremost among all luminous bodies, as the Meru is the foremost among all mountains, as Garuda is the foremost among all birds, so as long as the upward, downward, and sideway course of the universe lasteth, Kesava is the foremost in all the worlds including the regions of the celestials. This Sisupala is a mere boy and hence he knoweth not Krishna, and ever and everywhere speaketh of Krishna thus. This ruler of Chedi will never see virtue in that light in which one that is desirous of acquiring high merit will see it. Who is there among the old and the young or among these illustrious lords of earth that doth not regard Krishna as deserving of worship or that doth not worship Krishna? If Sisupala regardeth this worship as undeserved, it behoveth him to do what is proper in this matter.'"

SECTION XXXVIII

Vaisampayana said,--"The mighty Bhishma ceased, having said this. Sahadeva then answered (Sisupala) in words of grave import, saying,--'If amongst ye there be any king that cannot bear to see Kesava of dark hue, the slayer of Kesi, the possessor of immeasurable energy, worshipped by me, this my foot is placed on the heads of all mighty ones (like him). When I say this, let that one give me an adequate reply. And let those kings that possess intelligence approve the worship of Krishna who is the preceptor, the father, the guru, and deserveth the Arghya and the worship (already offered unto him).'

"When Sahadeva thus showed his foot, no one among those intelligent and wise and proud and mighty monarchs said anything. And a shower of flowers fell on Sahadeva's head, and an incorporeal voice said--'Excellent, excellent.' Then Narada clad in black deer-skin, speaking of both the future and the past, that dispeller of all doubts, fully acquainted with all the worlds, said in the midst of innumerable creatures, these words of the clearest import,--'Those men that will not worship the lotus-eyed Krishna should be regarded as dead though moving, and should never be talked to on any occasion.'"

Vaisampayana continued,--"Then that god among men, Sahadeva cognisant of the distinction between a Brahmana and a Kshatriya, having worshipped those that deserved worship, completed that ceremony. But upon Krishna having received the first worship, Sunitha (Sisupala) that mower of foes-- with eyes red as copper from anger, addressed those rulers of men and said,- -'When I am here to head ye all, what are ye thinking of now? Arrayed let us stand in battle against the assembled Vrishnis and the Pandavas?' And the bull of the Chedis, having thus stirred the kings up, began to consult with them how to obstruct the completion of the sacrifice. All the invited monarchs who had come to the sacrifice, with Sunitha as their chief, looked angry and their faces became pale. They all said, 'We must so act that the final sacrificial rite performed by Yudhishthira and the worship of Krishna may not be regarded as having been acquiesced in by us.' And impelled by a belief in their power and great assurance, the kings, deprived of reason through anger, began to say this. And being moved by self-confidence and smarting under the insult offered unto them, the monarchs repeatedly exclaimed thus. Though their friends sought to appease them, their faces glowed with anger like those of roaring lions driven away from their preys. Krishna then understood that the vast sea of monarchs with its countless waves of troops was preparing for a terrific rush."

SECTION XXXIX

(Sisupala-badha Parva)

Vaisampayana said,--"Beholding that vast assembly of kings agitated with wrath, even like the terrific sea agitated by the winds that blow at the time of the universal dissolution, Yudhishthira addressing the aged Bhishma, that chief of intelligent men and the grandsire of the Kurus, even like Puruhita (Indra) that slayer of foes, of abundant energy addressing Vrihaspati, said,-- 'This vast ocean of kings, hath been agitated by wrath. Tell me, O Grandsire, what I should do in view of this. O Grandsire, now what I should do that my sacrifice may not be obstructed and my subjects may not be injured.'

"When king Yudhishthira the just, conversant with morality, said this, Bhishma the grandsire of the Kurus, spoke these words in reply,--'Fear not, O tiger of the Kurus. Can the dog slay the lion? I have before this found out a way that is both beneficial and comfortable to practise. As dogs in a pack approaching the lion that is asleep bark together, so are all these lords of earth. Indeed, O child, like dogs before the lion, these (monarchs) are barking in rage before the sleeping lion of the Vrishni race. Achyuta now is like a lion that is asleep. Until he waketh up, this chief of the Chedis--this lion among men--maketh these monarchs look like lions. O child, O thou foremost of all monarchs, this Sisupala possessed of little intelligence is desirous of taking along with him all these kings, through the agency of him who is the soul of the universe, to the regions of Yama. Assuredly, O Bharata Vishnu hath been desirous of taking back unto himself the energy that existeth in this Sisupala. O Chief of all intelligent men, O son of Kunti, the intelligence of this wicked- minded king of the Chedis, as also of all these monarchs, hath become perverse. Indeed, the intelligence of all those whom this tiger among men desireth to take unto himself, becometh perverse even like that of this king of the Chedis. O Yudhishthira, Madhava is the progenitor as also the destroyer of all created beings of the four species, (oviparous, etc.,) existing in the three worlds.'"

Vaisampayana continued--"Then the ruler of Chedis, having heard these words of Bhishma, addressed the latter, O Bharata, in words that were stern and rough.

SECTION XL

"Sisupala said,--'Old and infamous wretch of thy race, art thou not ashamed of affrighting all these monarchs with these numerous false terrors! Thou art the foremost of the Kurus, and living as thou dost in the third state (celibacy) it is but fit for thee that thou shouldst give such counsel that is so wide of morality. Like a boat tied to another boat or the blind following the blind, are the Kurus who have thee for their guide. Thou hast once more simply pained our hearts by reciting particularly the deeds of this one (Krishna), such as the slaying of Putana and others. Arrogant and ignorant as thou art, and desirous of praising Kesava, why doth not this tongue of thine split up into a hundred parts? How dost thou, superior as thou art in knowledge, desire to praise that cow-boy in respect of whom even men of little intelligence may address invectives? If Krishna in his infancy slew a vulture, what is there remarkable in that, or in that other feat of his, O Bhishma, viz., in his slaughter of Aswa and Vrishava, both of whom were unskilled in battle? If this one threw drown by a kick an inanimate piece of wood, viz., a car, what is there, O Bhishma, wonderful in that? O Bhishma, what is there remarkable in this one's having supported for a week the Govardhan mount which is like an anthill? "While sporting on the top of a mountain this one ate a large quantity of food,"--hearing these words of thine many have wondered exceedingly. But, O thou who art conversant with the rules of morality, is not this still more wrongful that that great person, viz., Kansa, whose food this one ate, hath been slain by him? Thou infamous one of the Kuru race, thou art ignorant of the rules of morality. Hast thou not ever heard, from wise men speaking unto thee, what I would now tell thee? The virtuous and the wise always instruct the honest that weapons must never be made to descend upon women and kine and Brahmanas and upon those whose food hath been taken, as also upon those whose shelter hath been enjoyed. It seemeth, O Bhishma, that all these teachings hath been thrown away by thee. O infamous one of the Kuru race, desiring to praise Kesava, thou describest him before me as great and superior in knowledge and in age, as if I knew nothing. If at thy word, O Bhishma, one that hath slain women (meaning Putana) and kine be worshipped, then what is to become of this great lesson? How can one who is such, deserve praise, O Bhishma? "This one is the foremost of all wise men,"--"This one is the lord of the universe"-- hearing these words of thine, Janarddana believeth that these are all true. But surely, they are all false. The verses that a chanter sings, even if he sings them often, produce no impression on him. And every creature acts according to his disposition, even like the bird Bhulinga (that picks the particles of flesh from between the lion's teeth, though preaching against rashness). Assuredly thy disposition is very mean. There is not the least doubt about it. And so also, it seemeth, that the sons of Pandu who regard Krishna as deserving of worship and who have thee for their guide, are possessed of a sinful disposition. Possessing a knowledge of virtue, thou hast fallen off from the path of the wise. Therefore thou art sinful. Who, O Bhishma, knowing himself to be virtuous and superior in knowledge, will so act as thou hast done from motives of virtue? If thou knowest the ways of the morality, if thy mind is guided by wisdom, blessed be thou. Why then, O

Bhishma, was that virtuous girl Amva, who had set her heart upon another, carried off by thee, so proud of wisdom and virtue? Thy brother Vichitravirya conformably to the ways of the honest and the virtuous, knowing that girl's condition, did not marry her though brought by thee. Boasting as thou dost of virtue, in thy very sight, upon the widow of thy brother were sons begotten by another according to the ways of the honest. Where is thy virtue, O Bhishma? This thy celibacy, which thou leadest either from ignorance or from impotence, is fruitless. O thou who art conversant with virtue, I do not behold thy well-being. Thou who expoundest morality in this way dost not seem to have ever waited upon the old. Worship, gift, study,--sacrifices distinguished by large gifts to the Brahmanas,--these all equal not in merit even one- sixteenth part of that which is obtainable by the possession of a son. The merit, O Bhishma, that is acquired by numberless vows and fasts assuredly becomes fruitless in the case of one that is childless. Thou art childless and old and the expounder of false morality. Like the swan in the story, thou shalt now die at the hands of thy relatives. Other men possessed of knowledge have said this of old. I will presently recite it fully in thy hearing.

"'There lived of yore an old swan on the sea-coast. Ever speaking of morality, but otherwise in his conduct, he used to instruct the feathery tribe. "Practise ye virtue and forego sin,"--these were the words that other truthful birds, O Bhishma, constantly heard him utter. And the other oviparous creatures ranging the sea, it hath been heard by us, O Bhishma use for virtue's sake to bring him food. And, O Bhishma, all those other birds, keeping their eggs, with him, ranged and dived in the waters of the sea. And the sinful old swan, attentive to his own pursuits, used to eat up the eggs of all those birds that foolishly trusted in him. After a while when the eggs were decreasing in number, a bird of great wisdom had his suspicions roused and he even witnessed (the affair) one day. And having witnessed the sinful act of the old swan, that bird in great sorrow spoke unto all the other birds. Then, O thou best of the Kurus, all those birds witnessing with their own eyes the act of the old swan, approached that wretch of false conduct and slew him.

"'Thy behaviour, O Bhishma, is even like that of the old swan. These lords of earth might slay thee in anger like those creatures of the feathery tribe slaying the old swan. Persons conversant with the Puranas recite a proverb, O Bhishma, as regards this occurrence, I shall, O Bharata, repeat it to thee fully. It is even this: O thou that supportest thyself on thy wings, though thy heart is affected (by the passions), thou preachest yet (of virtue); but this thy sinful act of eating up the eggs transgresseth thy speech!'

SECTION XLI

"Sisupala said,--'That mighty king Jarasandha who desired not to fight with Krishna, saying "He is a slave," was worthy of my greatest esteem. Who will regard as praiseworthy the act which was done by Kesava, as also by Bhima and Arjuna, in the matter of Jarasandha's death? Entering by an improper gate, disguised as a Brahmana, thus Krishna observed the strength of king Jarasandha. And when that monarch offered at first unto this wretch water to wash his feet, it was then that he denied his Brahmanahood from seeming motives of virtue. And when Jarasandha, O thou of the Kuru race, asked Krishna and Bhima and Dhananjaya to eat, it was this Krishna that refused that monarch's request. If this one is the lord of the universe, as this fool representeth him to be, why doth he not regard himself as a Brahmana? This, however, surpriseth me greatly that though thou leadest the Pandavas away from the path of the wise, they yet regard thee as honest. Or, perhaps, this is scarcely a matter of surprise in respect of those that have thee, O Bharata, womanish in disposition and bent down with age, for their counsellor in everything.'"

Vaisampayana continued,--"Hearing these words of Sisupala, harsh both in import and sound, that foremost of mighty men, Bhimasena endued with energy became angry. And his eyes, naturally large and expanding and like unto lotus leaves became still more extended and red as copper under the influence of that rage. And the assembled monarchs beheld on his forehead three lines of wrinkles like the Ganga of treble currents on the treble- peaked mountain. When Bhimasena began to grind his teeth in rage, the monarchs beheld his face resembling that of Death himself, at the end of the Yuga, prepared to swallow every creature. And as the hero endued with great energy of mind was about to leap up impetuously, the mighty-armed Bhishma caught him like Mahadeva seizing Mahasena (the celestial generalissimo). And, O Bharata, Bhima's wrath was soon appeased by Bhishma, the grand-sire of the Kurus, with various kinds of counsel. And Bhima, that chastiser of foes, could not disobey Bhishma's words, like the ocean that never transgresseth (even when swollen with the waters of the rainy season) its continents. But, O king, even though Bhima was angry, the brave Sisupala depending on his own manhood, did not tremble in fear. And though Bhima was leaping up impetuously every moment, Sisupala bestowed not a single thought on him, like a lion that recks not a little animal in rage. The powerful king of Chedi, beholding Bhima of terrible prowess in such rage, laughingly said,--'Release him, O Bhishma! Let all the monarchs behold him scorched by my prowess like an insect in fire.' Hearing these words of the ruler of the Chedis, Bhishma, that foremost of the Kurus and chief of all intelligent men, spoke unto Bhima these words.

SECTION XLII

"Bhishma said,--'This Sisupala was born in the line of the king of Chedi with three eyes and four hands. As soon as he was born, he screamed and brayed like an ass. On that account, his father and mother along with their relatives, were struck with fear. And beholding these extraordinary omens, his parents resolved to abandon him. But an incorporeal voice, about this time, said unto the king and his wife with their ministers and priest, all with hearts paralysed by anxiety, those words,--"This thy son, O king, that hath been born will become both fortunate and superior in strength. Therefore thou hast no fear from him. Indeed cherish the child without anxiety. He will not die (in childhood). His time is not yet come. He that will slay him with weapons hath also been born." Hearing these words, the mother, rendered anxious by affection for her son, addressed the invisible Being and said,--"I bow with joined hands unto him that hath uttered these words respecting my son; whether he be an exalted divinity or any other being, let him tell me another word. I desire to hear who will be the slayer of this my son." The invisible Being then said,--"He upon whose lap this child being placed the superfluous arms of his will fall down upon the ground like a pair of five-headed snakes, and at the sight of whom his third eye on the forehead will disappear, will be his slayer?" Hearing of the child's three eyes and four arms as also of the words of the invisible Being, all the kings of the earth went to Chedi to behold him. The king of Chedi worshipping, as each deserved, the monarchs that came, gave his child upon their laps one after another. And though the child was placed upon the laps of a thousand kings, one after another, yet that which the incorporeal voice had said came not to pass. And having heard of all this at Dwaravati, the mighty Yadava heroes Sankarshana and Janarddana also went to the capital of the Chedis, to see their father's sister--that daughter of the Yadavas (the queen of Chedi). And saluting everybody according to his rank and the king and queen also, and enquiring after every body's welfare, both Rama and Kesava took their seats. And after those heroes had been worshipped, the queen with great pleasure herself placed the child on the lap of Damodara. As soon as the child was placed on his lap, those superfluous arms of his fell down and the eye on his forehead also disappeared. And beholding this, the queen in alarm and anxiety begged of Krishna a boon. And she said,--"O mighty-armed Krishna, I am afflicted with fear; grant me a boon. Thou art the assurer of all afflicted ones and that the dispeller of everybody's fear." Thus addressed by her, Krishna, that son of the Yadu race, said--"Fear not, O respected one. Thou art acquainted with morality. Thou needest have no fear from me. What boon shall I give thee? What shall I do, O aunt? Whether able or not, I shall do thy bidding."--Thus spoken to by Krishna, the queen said, "O thou of great strength, thou wilt have to pardon the offences of Sisupala for my sake. O tiger of the Yadu race. Know O lord, even this is the boon that I ask." Krishna then said, "O aunt, even when he will deserve to be slain, I will pardon an hundred offences of his. Grieve thou not.'"

"Bhishma continued,--'Even thus, O Bhima, is this wretch of a king--Sisupala of wicked heart, who, proud of the boon granted by Govinda, summons thee to battle!'

SECTION XLIII

"Bhishma said,--'The will under which the ruler of Chedi summoneth thee to fight though thou art of strength that knoweth no deterioration, is scarcely his own intention. Assuredly, this is the purpose of Krishna himself, the lord of the universe. O Bhima, what king is there on earth that would dare abuse me thus, as this wretch of his race, already possessed by Death, hath done to-day? This mighty-armed one is, without doubt, a portion of Hari's energy. And surely, the Lord desireth to take back unto himself that energy of his own.' In consequence of this, O tiger of the Kuru race, this tiger-like king of Chedi, so wicked of heart, roareth in such a way caring little for us all."

Vaisampayana continued,--"Hearing these words of Bhishma, the king of Chedi could bear no more. He then replied in rage unto Bhishma in these words.--

"'Let our foes, O Bhishma, be endued with that prowess which this Kesava hath, whom thou like a professional chanter of hymns praisest, rising repeatedly from thy seat. If thy mind, O Bhishma, delighteth so in praising others, then praise thou these kings, leaving off Krishna. Praise thou this excellent of kings, Darada, the ruler of Valhika, who rent this earth as soon as he was born. Praise thou, O Bhishma, this Karna, the ruler of the territories of Anga and Vanga, who is equal in strength unto him of a thousand eyes, who draweth a large bow, who endued with mighty arms owneth celestial ear-rings of heavenly make with which he was born and this coat of mail possessing the splendour of the rising sun, who vanquished in a wrestling encounter the invincible Jarasandha equal unto Vasava himself, and who tore and mangled that monarch. O Bhishma, praise Drona and Aswatthaman, who both father and son, are mighty warriors, worthy of praise, and the best of Brahmanas, and either of whom, O Bhishma, if enraged could annihilate this earth with its mobile and immobile creatures, as I believe. I do not behold, O Bhishma, the king that is equal in battle unto

Drona or Aswatthaman. Why wishest thou not to praise them? Passing over Duryyodhana, that mighty-armed king of kings, who is unequalled in whole earth girt with her seas and king Jayadratha accomplished in weapons and endued with great prowess, and Druma the preceptor of the Kimpurushas and celebrated over the world for prowess, and Saradwata's son, old Kripa, the preceptor of the Bharata princes and endued with great energy, why dost thou praise Kesava? Passing over that foremost of bowmen--that excellent of kings, Rukmin of great energy, why praisest thou Kesava? Passing over Bhishmaka of abundant energy, and king Dantavakra, and Bhagadatta known for his innumerable sacrificial stakes, and Jayatsena the king of the Magadha, and Virata and Drupada, and Sakuni and Vrihadvala, and Vinda and Anuvinda of Avant Pandya, Sweta Uttama Sankhya of great prosperity, the proud Vrishasena, the powerful Ekalavya, and the great charioteer Kalinga of abundant energy, why dost thou praise Kesava? And, O Bhishma, if thy mind is always inclined to sing the praises of others, why dost thou not praise Salya and other rulers of the earth? O king, what can be done by me when (it seemeth) thou hast not heard anything before from virtuous old men giving lessons in morality? Hast thou never heard, O Bhishma, that reproach and glorification, both of self and others, are not practices of those that are respectable? There is no one that approveth thy conduct, O Bhishma, in unceasingly praising with devotion, from ignorance alone, Kesava so unworthy of praise. How dost thou, from thy wish alone, establish the whole universe in the servitor and cowherd of Bhoja (Kansa)? Perhaps, O Bharata, this thy inclination is not conformable to thy true nature, like to what may be in the bird Bhulinga, as hath already been said by me. There is a bird called Bhulinga living on the other side of the Himavat. O Bhishma, that bird ever uttereth words of adverse import. "Never do anything rash,"--this is what she always sayeth, but never understandeth that she herself always acteth very rashly. Possessed of little intelligence that bird picketh from the lion's mouth the pieces of flesh sticking between the teeth, and at a time when the lion is employed in eating. Assuredly, O Bhishma, that bird liveth at the pleasure of the lion. O sinful wretch, thou always speakest like that bird. And assuredly, O Bhishma, thou art alive at the pleasure only of these kings. Employed in acts contrary to the opinions of all, there is none else like thee!'"

Vaisampayana continued,--"Hearing these harsh words of the ruler of Chedi, Bhishma, O king, said in the hearing of the king of Chedi,--'Truly am I alive at the pleasure of these rulers of earth. But I do regard these kings as not equal to even a straw.' As soon as these words were spoken by Bhishma, the kings became inflamed with wrath. And the down of some amongst them stood erect and some began to reprove Bhishma. And hearing those words of Bhishma, some amongst them, that were wielders of large bows exclaimed, 'This wretched Bhishma, though old, is exceedingly boastful. He deserveth not our pardon. Therefore, ye kings, incensed with rage as this Bhishma is, it is well that this wretch were slain like an animal, or, mustering together, let us burn him in a fire of grass or straw.' Hearing these words of the monarchs, Bhishma the grand-sire of the Kurus, endued with great intelligence, addressing those lords of earth, said,--'I do not see the end of our speeches, for words may be answered with words. Therefore, ye lords of earth, listen ye all unto what I say. Whether I be slain like an animal or burnt in a fire of grass and straw, thus do I distinctly place my foot on the heads of ye all. Here is Govinda, that knoweth no deterioration. Him have we worshipped. Let him who wisheth for speedy death, summon to battle Madhava of dark hue and the wielder of the discus and the mace; and falling enter into and mingle with the body of this god!'"

SECTION XLIV

Vaisampayana said,--"Hearing these words of Bhishma, the ruler of Chedi endued with exceeding prowess, desirous of combating with Vasudeva addressed him and said,--'O Janarddana, I challenge thee. Come, fight with me until I slay thee today with all the Pandavas. For, O Krishna, the sons of Pandu also, who disregarding the claims of all these kings, have worshipped thee who art no king, deserve to be slain by me along with thee. Even this is my opinion, O Krishna, that they who from childishness have worshipped thee, as if thou deservest it, although thou art unworthy of worship, being only a slave and a wretch and no king, deserve to be slain by me.' Having said this, that tiger among kings stood there roaring in anger. And after

Sisupala had ceased, Krishna addressing all the kings in the presence of the Pandavas, spoke these words in a soft voice.--'Ye kings, this wicked-minded one, who is the son of a daughter of the Satwata race, is a great enemy of us of the Satwata race; and though we never seek to injure him, he ever seeketh our evil. This wretch of cruel deeds, ye kings, hearing that we had gone to the city of Pragjyotisha, came and burnt Dwaraka, although he is the son of my father's sister. While king Bhoja was sporting on the Raivataka hill, this one fell upon the attendants of that king and slew and led away many of them in chains to his own city. Sinful in all his purpose, this wretch, in order to obstruct the sacrifice of my father, stole the sacrificial horse of the horse-sacrifice that had been let loose under the guard of armed men. Prompted by sinful motives, this one ravished the reluctant wife of the innocent Vabhru (Akrura) on her way from Dwaraka to the country of the Sauviras. This injurer of his maternal uncle, disguising himself in the attire of the king of Karusha, ravished also the innocent Bhadra, the princess of Visala, the intended bride of king Karusha. I have patiently borne all these sorrows for the sake of my father's sister. It is, however, very fortunate that all this hath occurred today in the presence of all the kings. Behold ye all today the hostility this one beareth towards me. And know ye also all that he hath done me at my back. For the excess of that pride in which he hath indulged in the presence of all these monarchs, he deserveth to be slain by me. I am ill able to pardon today the injuries that he hath done me. Desirous of speedy death, this fool had desired Rukmini. But the fool obtained her not, like a Sudra failing to obtain the audition of the Vedas.'

Vaisampayana continued,--"Hearing these words of Vasudeva, all the assembled monarchs began to reprove the ruler of Chedi. But the powerful Sisupala, having heard these words, laughed aloud and spoke thus,--'O Krishna, art thou not ashamed in saying in this assembly, especially before all these kings that Rukmini (thy wife) had been coveted by me? O slayer of Madhu, who else is there than thee, who regarding himself a man would say in the midst of respectable men that his wife had been intended for some body else? O Krishna, pardon me if thou pleasest, or pardon me not. But angry or friendly, what canst thou do unto me?'

"And while Sisupala was speaking thus, the exalted slayer of Madhu thought in his mind of the discus that humbleth the pride of the Asuras. And as soon as the discus came into his hands, skilled in speech the illustrious one loudly uttered these words,--'Listen ye lords of earth, why this one had hitherto been pardoned by me. As asked by his mother, a hundred offences (of his) were to be pardoned by me. Even this was the boon she had asked, and even this I granted her. That number, ye kings, hath become full. I shall now slay him in your presence, ye monarchs.' Having said this, the chief of the Yadus, that slayer of all foes, in anger, instantly cut off the head of the ruler of Chedi by means of his discus. And the mighty-armed one fell down like a cliff struck with thunder. And, O monarch, the assembled kings then beheld a fierce energy, like unto the sun in the sky, issue out of the body of the king of Chedi, and O king, that energy then adored Krishna, possessed of eyes like lotus leaves and worshipped by all the worlds, and entered his body. And all the kings beholding the energy which entered that mighty-armed chief of men regarded it as wonderful. And when Krishna had slain the king of Chedi, the sky, though cloudless, poured showers of rain, and blasting thunders were hurled, and the earth itself began to tremble. There were some among the kings who spoke not a word during those unspeakable moments but merely sat gazing at Janarddana. And some there were that rubbed in rage their palms with their forefingers. And there were others who deprived of reason by rage bit their lips with their teeth. And some amongst the kings applauded him of the Vrishni race in private. And some there were that became excited with anger; while others became mediators. The great Rishis with pleased hearts praised Kesava and went away. And all the high-souled Brahmanas and the mighty kings that were there, beholding Krishna's prowess, became glad at heart and praised him.

"Yudhishthira then commanded his brothers to perform without delay the funeral rites of king Sisupala, the brave son of Damaghosha, with proper respect. The sons of Pandu obeyed the behest of their brother. And Yudhishthira then, with all the kings, installed the son of king Sisupala in the sovereignty of the Chedis.

"Then that sacrifice, O monarch, of the king of the Kurus possessed of great energy, blessed with every kind of prosperity, became exceedingly handsome and pleasing unto all young men. And commenced auspiciously, and all impediments removed, and furnished with abundance of wealth and corn, as also with plenty of rice and every kind of food, it was properly watched by Kesava. And Yudhishthira in due time completed the great sacrifice. And the mighty-armed Janarddana, the exalted Sauri, with his bow called Saranga and his discus and mace, guarded that sacrifice till its completion. And all the Kshatriya monarchs, having approached the virtuous Yudhishthira who had bathed after the conclusion of the sacrifice, said these words: 'By good fortune thou hast come out successful. O virtuous one, thou hast obtained the imperial dignity. O thou of the Ajamida race, by thee hath been spread the fame of thy whole race. And, O king of kings, by this act of thine, thou hast also acquired great religious merit. We have been worshipped by thee to the full extent of our desires. We now tell thee that we are desirous of returning to our own kingdoms. It behoveth thee to grant us permission.'

"Hearing these words of the monarchs, king Yudhishthira the just, worshipping each as he deserved, commanded his brothers, saying, 'These monarchs had all come to us at their own pleasure. These chastisers of foes are now desirous of returning to their own kingdoms, bidding me farewell. Blest be ye, follow ye these excellent kings to the confines of our own dominions.' Hearing these words of their brother, the virtuous Pandava princes followed the kings, one after another as each deserved. The powerful Dhrishtadyumna followed without loss of time king Virata: and Dhananjaya followed the illustrious and mighty charioteer Yajnasena; and the mighty Bhimasena followed Bhishma and Dhritarashtra: and Sahadeva, that master of battle, followed the brave Drona and his son; and Nakula, O king, followed Suvala with his son; and the sons of Draupadi with the son of Subhadra followed those mighty warriors--the kings of the mountainous countries. And other bulls among Kshatriyas followed other Kshatriyas. And the Brahmanas by thousands also went away, duly worshipped.

"After all the Kings and the Brahmanas had gone away, the powerful Vasudeva addressing Yudhishthira said,--'O son of the Kuru race, with thy leave, I also desire to go to Dwaraka. By great good fortune, thou hast accomplished the foremost of sacrifices--Rajasuya!' Thus addressed by Janarddana, Yudhishthira replied, 'Owing to thy grace, O Govinda, I have accomplished the great sacrifice. And it is owing to thy grace that the whole Kshatriya world having accepted my sway, had come hither with valuable tribute. O hero, without thee, my heart never feeleth any delight. How can I, therefore, O hero, give thee, O sinless one, leave to go? But thou must have to go to the city of Dwaraka.' The virtuous Hari of worldwide fame, thus addressed by Yudhishthira, cheerfully went with his cousin to Pritha and said,--'O aunt, thy sons have now obtained the imperial dignity. They have obtained vast wealth and been also crowned with success. Be pleased with all this. Commanded by thee, O aunt, I desire to go to Dwaraka.' After this, Kesava bade farewell to Draupadi and Subhadra. Coming out then of the inner apartments accompanied by Yudhishthira, he performed his ablutions and went through the daily rites of worship, and then made the Brahmanas utter benedictions. Then the mighty armed Daruka came there with a car of excellent design and body resembling the clouds. And beholding that Garuda-bannered car arrived thither, the high-souled one, with eyes like lotus leaves, walked round it respectfully and ascending on it set out for Dwaravati. And king Yudhishthira the just, blessed with prosperity, accompanied by his brothers, followed on foot the mighty Vasudeva. Then Hari with eyes like lotus leaves, stopping that best of cars for a moment, addressing Yudhishthira the son of Kunti, said,--'O king of kings, cherishest thou thy subjects with ceaseless vigilance and patience. And as the clouds are unto all creatures, as the large tree of spreading bough is unto birds, as he of a thousand eyes is unto the immortals, be thou the refuge and support of thy relatives.' And Krishna and Yudhishthira having thus talked unto each other took each other's leave and returned to their respective homes. And, O king, after the chief of the Satwata race had gone to Dwaravati, king Duryodhana alone, with king Suvala's son, Sakuni,--these bulls among men,--continued to live in that celestial assembly house."

SECTION XLV

(Dyuta Parva)

Vaisampayana said,--"when that foremost of sacrifices, the Rajasuya so difficult of accomplishment, was completed, Vyasa surrounded by his disciples presented himself before Yudhishthira. And Yudhishthira, upon beholding him quickly rose from his seat, surrounded by his brothers, and worshipped the Rishi who was his grand-father, with water to wash his feet and the offer of a seat. The illustrious one having taken his seat on a costly carpet inlaid with gold, addressed king Yudhishthira the just and said.--'Take thy seat'. And after the king had taken his seat surrounded by his brothers, the illustrious Vyasa, truthful in speech said,--'O son of Kunti, thou growest from good fortune. Thou hast obtained imperial sway so difficult of acquisition. And O perpetuator of the Kuru race, all the Kauravas have prospered in consequence of thee. O Emperor, I have been duly worshipped. I desire now to go with thy leave!' King Yudhishthira the just, thus addressed by the Rishi of dark hue, saluted (him) his grandfather and touching his feet said,--'O chief of men, a doubt difficult of being dispelled, hath risen within me. O bull among regenerate ones, save thee there is none to remove it. The illustrious Rishi Narada said that (as a consequence of the Rajasuya sacrifice) three kinds of portents, viz., celestial, atmospherical and terrestrial ones happen. O grandsire, have those portents been ended by the fall of the king of the Chedis?'"

Vaisampayana continued,--"Hearing these words of the king, the exalted son of Parasara, the island-born Vyasa of dark hue, spoke these words,--'For thirteen years, O king, those portents will bear mighty consequences ending in destruction, O king of kings, of all the Kshatriyas. In course of time, O bull of the Bharata race, making thee the sole cause, the assembled Kshatriyas of the world will be destroyed, O Bharata, for the sins of Duryodhana and through the might of Bhima and Arjuna. In thy dream, O king of kings thou wilt behold towards the end of this might the blue throated Bhava, the slayer of Tripura, ever absorbed in meditation, having the bull for his mark, drinking off the human skull, and fierce and terrible, that lord of all creatures, that god of gods, the husband of Uma, otherwise called Hara and Sarva, and Vrisha, armed with the trident and the bow called Pinaka, and attired in tiger skin. And thou wilt behold Siva, tall and white as the Kailasa cliff and seated on his bull, gazing unceasingly towards the direction (south) presided over by the king of the Pitris. Even this will be the dream thou wilt dream today, O king of kings. Do not grieve for dreaming such a dream. None can rise superior to the influence of Time. Blest be thou! I will now proceed towards the Kailasa mountain. Rule thou the earth with vigilance and steadiness, patiently bearing every privation!'"

Vaisampayana continued,--"Having said this, the illustrious and island-born Vyasa of dark hue, accompanied by his disciples ever following the dictates of the Vedas, proceeded towards Kailasa. And after the grand- father had thus gone away, the king afflicted with anxiety and grief, began to think continuously upon what the Rishi hath said. And he said to himself, 'Indeed what the Rishi hath said must come to pass. We will succeed in warding off the fates by exertion alone?' Then Yudhishthira endued with great energy addressing all his brothers, said, 'Ye tigers among men, ye have heard what the island-born Rishi hath told me. Having heard the words of the Rishi, I have arrived at this firm resolution viz., that I should die, as I am ordained to be the cause of the destruction of all Kshatriyas. Ye my dear ones, if Time hath intended so what need is there for me to live?' Hearing these words of the king, Arjuna replied, 'O king, yield not thyself to this terrible depression that is destructive of reason. Mustering fortitude, O great king, do what would be beneficial.' Yudhishthira then, firm in truth, thinking all the while of Dwaipayana's words answered his brothers thus,--'Blest be ye. Listen to my vow from this day. For thirteen years, what ever purpose have I to live for, I shall not speak a hard word to my brothers or to any of the kings of the earth. Living under the command of my relatives, I shall practise virtue, exemplifying my vow. If I live in this way, making no distinction between my own children and others, there will be no disagreement (between me and others). It is disagreement that is the cause of war in the world. Keeping war at a distance, and ever doing what is agreeable to others, evil reputation will not be mine in the world, ye bulls among men.' Hearing these words of their eldest brother, the Pandavas, always engaged in doing what was agreeable to him, approved of them. And Yudhishthira the just, having pledged so, along with his brothers in the midst of that assembly, gratified his priests as also the gods with due ceremonies. And, O bull of the Bharata race, after all the monarchs had gone away, Yudhishthira along with his brothers, having performed the usual auspicious rites, accompanied by his ministers entered his own palace. And, O ruler of men, king Duryodhana and Sakuni, the son of Suvala, continued to dwell in that delightful assembly house."

SECTION XLVI

Vaisampayana said,--"That bull among men, Duryodhana, continued to dwell in that assembly house (of the Pandavas). And with Sakuni, the Kuru prince slowly examined the whole of that mansion, and the Kuru prince beheld in it many celestial designs, which he had never seen before in the city called after the elephant (Hastinapore). And one day king Duryodhana in going round that mansion came upon a crystal surface. And the king, from ignorance, mistaking it for a pool of water, drew up his clothes. And afterwards finding out his mistake the king wandered about the mansion in great sorrow. And sometime after, the king, mistaking a lake of crystal water adorned with lotuses of crystal petals for land, fell into it with all his clothes on. Beholding Duryodhana fallen into the lake, the mighty Bhima laughed aloud as also the menials of the palace. And the servants, at the command of the king, soon brought him dry and handsome clothes. Beholding the plight of Duryodhana, the mighty Bhima and Arjuna and both the twins--all laughed aloud. Being unused to putting up with insults, Duryodhana could not bear that laugh of theirs. Concealing his emotions he even did not cast his looks on them. And beholding the monarch once more draw up his clothes to cross a piece of dry land which he had mistaken for water, they all laughed again. And the king sometime after mistook a closed door made of crystal as open. And as he was about to pass through it his head struck against it, and he stood with his brain reeling. And mistaking as closed another door made of crystal that was really open, the king in attempting to open it with stretched hands, tumbled down. And coming upon another door that was really open, the king thinking it as closed, went away from it. And, O monarch, king Duryodhana beholding that vast wealth in the Rajasuya sacrifice and having become the victim of those numerous errors within the assembly house at last returned, with the leave of the Pandavas, to Hastinapore."

"And the heart of king Duryodhana, afflicted at sight of the prosperity of the Pandavas, became inclined to sin, as he proceeded towards his city reflecting on all he had seen and suffered. And beholding the Pandavas happy and all the kings of the earth paying homage to them, as also everybody, young and old, engaged in doing good unto them, and reflecting also on the splendour and prosperity of the illustrious sons of Pandu, Duryodhana, the son of Dhritarashtra, became pale. In proceeding (to his city) with an efflicted heart, the prince thought of nothing else but that assembly house and that unrivalled prosperity of the wise Yudhishthira. And Duryodhana, the son of Dhritarashtra, was so taken up with his thoughts then that he spoke not a word to Suvala's son even though the latter addressed him repeatedly. And Sakuni, beholding him absent-minded, said,--'O Duryodhana, why art thou proceeding thus'?

"Duryodhana replied,--'O uncle, beholding this whole earth owning the sway of Yudhishthira in consequence of the might of the illustrious Arjuna's weapons and beholding also that sacrifice of the son of Pritha like unto the sacrifice of Sakra himself of great glory among the celestials, I, being filled with jealousy and burning day and night, am being dried up like a shallow tank in the summer season. Behold, when Sisupala was slain by the chief of the Satwatas, there was no man to take the side of Sisupala. Consumed by the fire of the Pandava, they all forgave that offence; otherwise who is there that could forgive it? That highly improper act of grave consequence done by Vasudeva succeeded in consequence of the power of the illustrious son of Pandu. And so many monarchs also brought with them various kinds of wealth for king Yudhishthira, the son of Kunti, like tribute-paying Vaisyas!

Beholding Yudhishthira's prosperity of such splendour, my heart burneth, efflicted with jealously, although it behoveth me not to be jealous.'

"Having reflected in this way, Duryodhana, as if burnt by fire, addressed the king of Gandhara again and said,--'I shall throw myself upon a flaming fire or swallow poison or drown myself in water. I cannot live. What man is there in the world possessed of vigour who can bear to see his foes in the enjoyment of prosperity and himself in destitution? Therefore I who bear to see that accession of prosperity and fortune (in my foes) am neither a woman nor one that is not a woman, neither also a man nor one that is not a man. Beholding their sovereignty over the world and vast affluence, as also that sacrifice, who is there like me that would not smart under all that? Alone I am incapable of acquiring such royal prosperity; nor do I behold allies that could help me in the matter. It is for this that I am thinking of self-destruction. Beholding that great and serene prosperity of the son of Kunti, I regard Fate as supreme and exertions fruitless. O son of Suvala, formerly I strove to compass his destruction. But baffling all my efforts he hath grown in prosperity even like the lotus from within a pool of water. It is for this that I regard Fate as supreme and exertions fruitless. Behold, the sons of Dhritarashtra are decaying and the sons of Pritha are growing day by day. Beholding that prosperity of the Pandavas, and that assembly house of theirs, and those menials laughing at me, my heart burneth as if it were on fire. Therefore, O uncle, know me now as deeply grieved and filled with jealousy, and speak of it to Dhritarashtra.'

SECTION XLVII

"Sakuni said.--'O Duryodhana, thou shouldst not be jealous of Yudhishthira. The sons of Pandu are enjoying what they deserve in consequence of their own good fortune. O slayer of foes, O great king, thou couldst not destroy them by repeatedly devising numberless plans, many of which thou hadst even put to practice. Those tigers among men out of sheer luck escaped all those machinations. They have obtained Draupadi for wife and Drupada with his sons as also Vasudeva of great prowess as allies, capable of helping them in subjugating the whole world. And O king, having inherited the paternal share of the kingdom without being deprived of it they have grown in consequence of their own energy. What is there to make thee sorry for this? Having gratified Hustasana, Dhananjaya hath obtained the bow Gandiva and the couple of inexhaustible quivers and many celestial weapons. With that unique bow and by the strength of his own arms also he hath brought all the kings of the world under his sway. What is there to make thee sorry for this? Having saved the Asura Maya from a conflagration, Arjuna, that slayer of foes, using both his hands with equal skill, caused him to build that assembly house. And it is for this also that commanded by Maya, those grim Rakshasas called Kinkaras supported that assembly house. What is there in this to make thee sorry? Thou hast said, O king, that thou art without allies. This, O Bharata, is not true. These thy brothers are obedient to thee. Drona of great prowess and wielding the large bow along with his son, Radha's son Karna, the great warrior Gautama (Kripa), myself with my brothers and king Saumadatti--these are thy allies. Uniting thyself with these, conquer thou the whole of the earth.'

"Duryodhana said,--'O king, with thee, as also with these great warriors, I shall subjugate the Pandavas, if it pleases thee. If I can now subjugate them, the world will be mine and all the monarchs, and that assembly house so full of wealth.'

"Sakuni replied,--'Dhananjaya and Vasudeva, Bhimasena and Yudhishthira, Nakula and Sahadeva and Drupada with his sons,--these cannot be vanquished in battle by even the celestials, for they are all great warriors wielding the largest bows, accomplished in weapons, and delighting in battle. But, O king, I know the means by which Yudhishthira himself may be vanquished. Listen to me and adopt it.'

"Duryodhana said,--'without danger to our friends and other illustrious men, O uncle, tell me if there is any way by which I may vanquish him.'

"Sakuni said,--'The son of Kunti is very fond of dice-play although he doth not know how to play. That king if asked to play, is ill able to refuse. I am skillful at dice. There is none equal to me in this respect on earth, no, not even in the three worlds, O son of Kuru. Therefore, ask him to play at dice. Skilled at dice, I will win his kingdom, and that splendid prosperity of his for thee, O bull among men. But, O Duryodhana, represent all this unto the king (Dhritarashtra). Commanded by thy father I will win without doubt the whole of Yudhishthira's possessions.'

"Duryodhana said 'O son of Suvala, thou thyself represent properly all this to Dhritarashtra, the chief of the Kurus. I shall not be able to do so.'"

SECTION XLVIII

Vaisampayana said--"O king, impressed with the great Rajasuya sacrifice of king Yudhishthira, Sakuni, the son of Suvala, having learnt before the intentions of Duryodhana, while accompanying him in the way from the assembly house, and desirous of saying what was agreeable to him, approached Dhritarashtra endued with great wisdom, and finding the monarch deprived of his eye seated (in his throne), told him these words,-- 'Know, O great king, O bull of the Bharata race, that Duryodhana, having lost colour, hath become pale and emaciated and depressed and a prey to anxiety. Why dost thou not, after due enquiry, ascertain the grief that is in the heart of thy eldest son, the grief that is caused by the foe?'

"Dhritarashtra said,--'Duryodhana, what is the reason of thy great affliction, O son of the Kuru race? If it is fit for me to hear it, then tell me the reason. This Sakuni here says that thou hast lost colour, become pale and emaciated, and a prey to anxiety. I do not know what can be the reason of the sorrow. This vast wealth of mine is at thy control. Thy brothers and all our relations never do anything that is disagreeable to thee. Thou wearest the best apparel and eatest the best food that is prepared with meat. The best of horse carries thee. What it is, therefore, that hath made thee pale and emaciated? Costly beds, beautiful damsels, mansions decked with excellent furniture, and sport of the delightful kind, without doubt these all wait but at thy command, as in the case of the gods themselves. Therefore, O proud one, why dost thou grieve, O son, as if thou wert destitute.'

"Duryodhana said,--'I eat and dress myself like a wretch and pass my time all the while a prey to fierce jealousy. He indeed is a man, who incapable of bearing the pride of the foe, liveth having vanquished that foe with the desire of liberating his own subjects from the tyranny of the foe. Contentment, as also pride, O Bharata, are destructive of prosperity; and those other two qualities also, viz., compassion and fear. One who acteth under the influence of these, never obtaineth anything high. Having beheld Yudhishthira's prosperity, whatever I enjoy brings me no gratification. The prosperity of Kunti's son that is possessed of such splendour maketh me pale. Knowing the affluence of the foe and my own destitution, even though that affluence is not before me, I yet see it before me. Therefore, have I lost colour and become melancholy, pale and emaciated. Yudhishthira supporteth eighty-eight thousand Snataka Brahmanas leading domestic lives, giving unto each of them thirty slave-girls. Beside this, thousand other Brahmanas daily eat at his palace the best of food on golden plates. The king of Kambhoja sent unto him (as tribute) innumerable skins, black, darkish, and red, of the deer Kadali, as also numberless blankets of excellent textures. And hundreds and thousands and thousands of she- elephants and thirty thousand she-camels wander within the palace, for the kings of the earth brought them all as tribute to the capital of the Pandavas. And, O lord of earth, the kings also brought unto this foremost of sacrifices heaps upon heaps of jewels and gems for the son of Kunti. Never before did I see or hear of such enormous wealth as was brought unto the sacrifice of the intelligent sons of Pandu. And, O king, beholding that enormous collection of wealth belonging to the foe, I can not enjoy peace of mind. Hundreds of Brahmanas supported by the grants that Yudhishthira hath given them and possessing wealth of kine, waited at the palace gate with three thousands of millions of tribute but were prevented by the keepers from entering the mansion. Bringing with them clarified butter in handsome Kamandalus made of gold, they did not obtain admission into the palace, and Ocean himself brought unto him in vessels of white copper the nectar that is generated within his waters and which is much superior to that which flowers and annual plants produce for Sakra. And Vasudeva (at the conclusion of the sacrifice) having brought an excellent conch bathed the Sun of Pritha with sea water brought in thousand jars of gold, all well adorned with numerous gems. Beholding all this I became feverish with jealousy. Those jars had been taken to the Eastern and the Southern oceans. And they had also been taken on the shoulders of men to the Western ocean, O bull among men. And, O father, although none but birds only can go to the Northern region Arjuna, having gone thither, exacted as tribute a vast quantity of wealth. There is another wonderful incident also which I will relate to thee. O listen to me. When a hundred thousand Brahmanas were fed, it had been arranged that to notify this act every day conches would be blown in a chorus. But, O Bharata, I continually heard conches blown there almost repeatedly. And hearing those notes my hair stood on end. And, O great king, that palatial compound, filled with innumerable monarchs that came there as spectators, looked exceedingly handsome like the cloudless firmament with stars. And, O king of men, the monarchs came into that sacrifice of the wise son of Pandu bringing with them every kind of wealth. And the kings that came there became like Vaisyas the distributors of food unto the Brahmanas that were fed. And O king, the prosperity that I beheld of Yudhishthira was such that neither the chief himself of the celestials, nor Yama or Varuna, nor the lord of the Guhyakas owneth the same. And beholding that great prosperity of the son of Pandu, my heart burneth and I cannot enjoy peace.'

"Hearing these words of Duryodhana, Sakuni replied,--'Hear how thou mayest obtain this unrivalled prosperity that thou beholdest in the son of Pandu, O thou that hast truth for thy prowess. O Bharata, I am an adept at dice, superior to all in the world. I can ascertain the success or otherwise of every throw, and when to stake and when not. I have special knowledge of the game. The Son of Kunti also is fond of dice playing though he possesseth little skill in it. Summoned to play or battle, he is sure to come forward, and I will defeat him repeatedly at every throw by practising deception. I promise to win all that wealth of his, and thou, O Duryodhana, shalt then enjoy the same.'"

Vaisampayana continued,--"King Duryodhana, thus addressed by Sakuni, without allowing a moment to elapse, said unto Dhritarashtra,--'This, Sakuni, an adept at dice, is ready to win at dice, O king, the wealth of the sons of Pandu. It behoveth thee to grant him permission to do so.'

"Dhritarashtra replied,--'I always follow the counsels of Kshatta, my minister possessed of great wisdom. Having consulted with him, I will inform thee what my judgment is in respect of this affair. Endued with great foresight, he will, keeping morality before his eyes, tell us what is good and what is proper for both parties, and what should be done in this matter.'

"Duryodhana said,--'If thou consultest with Kshatta he will make thee desist. And if thou desist, O king, I will certainly kill myself. And when I am dead, O king, thou wilt become happy with Vidura. Thou wilt then enjoy the whole earth; what need hast thou with me?'"

Vaisampayana continued,--"Dhritarashtra, hearing these words of affliction uttered by Duryodhana from mixed feeling, himself ready to what Duryodhana had dictated, commanded his servant, saying,--'Let artificers be employed to erect without delay a delightful and handsome and spacious palace with an hundred doors and a thousand columns. And having brought carpenters and joiners, set ye jewels and precious stones all over the walls. And making it handsome and easy of access, report to me when everything is complete.' And, O monarch, king Dhritarashtra having made this resolution for the pacification of Duryodhana, sent messengers unto Vidura for summoning him. For without taking counsel with Vidura never did the monarch form any resolution. But as regards the matter at hand, the king although he knew the evils of gambling, was yet attracted towards it. The intelligent Vidura, however, as soon as he heard of it, knew that the arrival of Kali was at hand. And seeing that the way to destruction was about to open, he quickly came to Dhritarashtra. And Vidura approaching his illustrious eldest brother and bowing down unto his feet, said these words:

"'O exalted king, I do not approve of this resolution that thou hast formed. It behave thee, O king, to act in such a way that no dispute may arise between thy children on account of this gambling match.'

"Dhritarashtra replied,--'O Kshatta, if the gods be merciful unto us, assuredly no dispute will ever arise amongst my sons. Therefore, auspicious or otherwise, beneficial or otherwise, let this friendly challenge at dice proceed. Even this without doubt is what fate hath ordained for us. And, O son of the Bharata race, when I am near, and Drona and Bhishma and thou too, nothing evil that even Fate might have ordained is likely to happen. Therefore, go thou on a car yoking thereto horses endued with the speed of the wind, so that thou mayest reach Khandavaprastha even today and bring thou Yudhishthira with thee. And, O Vidura, I tell that even this is my resolution. Tell me nothing. I regard Fate as supreme which bringeth all this.' Hearing these words of Dhritarashtra and concluding that his race was doomed, Vidura in great sorrow went unto Bhishma with great wisdom."

SECTION XLIX

Janamejaya said,--"O thou foremost of all conversant with the Vedas, how did that game at dice take place, fraught with such evil to the cousins and through which my grand-sires, the son of Pandu, were plunged into such sorrow? What kings also were present in that assembly, and who amongst them approved of the gambling match and who amongst them forbade it? O sinless one, O chief of regenerate ones, I desire thee to recite in detail all about this, which, indeed, was the cause of the destruction of the world."

Santi said,--"Thus addressed by the king, the disciple of Vyasa, endued with great energy and conversant with the entire Vedas, narrated everything that had happened."

Vaisampayana said,--"O best of the Bharatas, O great king, if thou desirest to hear, then listen to me as I narrate to thee everything again in detail.

"Ascertaining the opinion of Vidura, Dhritarashtra the son of Amvika, calling Duryodhana told him again in private--'O son of Gandhari, have nothing to do with dice. Vidura doth not speak well of it. Possessed of great wisdom, he will never give me advice that is not for my good. I also regard what Vidura sayeth as exceedingly beneficial for me. Do that, O son, for I regard it all as for thy good also. Indeed, Vidura knoweth with all its mysteries the science (of political morality) that the illustrious and learned and wise Vrihaspati, the celestial Rishi who is the spiritual guide of Vasava-- had unfolded unto the wise chief of the immortals. And O son, I always accept what Vidura adviseth. O king, as the wise Uddhava is ever regarded amongst the Vrishnis, so is Vidura possessed of great intelligence esteemed as the foremost of the Kurus. Therefore, O son, have nothing to do with dice. It is evident that dice soweth dissensions. And dissensions are the ruin of the kingdom. Therefore, O son, abandon this idea of gambling. O son, thou hast obtained from us what, it hath been ordained, a father and a mother should give unto their son, viz., ancestral rank and possessions. Thou art educated and clever in every branch of knowledge, and hast been brought up with affection in thy paternal dwelling. Born the eldest among all thy brothers, living within thy own kingdom, why regardest thou thyself as unhappy? O thou of mighty arms, thou obtainest food and attire of the very best kind and which is not obtainable by ordinary men. Why dost thou grieve yet. O son, O mighty- armed one, ruling thy large ancestral kingdom swelling with people and wealth, thou shinest as splendidly as the chief of the celestials in heaven. Thou art possessed of wisdom. It behoveth thee to tell me what can be the root of this grief that hath made thee so melancholy.'

"Duryodhana replied,--'I am a sinful wretch, O king, because I eat and dress beholding (the prosperity of the foes). It hath been said that man is a wretch who is not filled with jealousy at the sight of his enemy's prosperity. O exalted one, this kind of prosperity of mine doth not gratify me. Beholding that blazing prosperity of the son of Kunti, I am very much pained. I tell thee strong must be my vitality, in as much as I am living even at the sight of the whole earth owning the sway of Yudhishthira. The Nipas, the Chitrakas, the Kukkuras, the Karaskaras, and the Lauha-janghas are living in the palace of

Yudhishthira like bondsmen. The Himavat, the ocean, the regions on the sea-shore, and the numberless other regions that yield jewels and gems, have all acknowledged superiority of the mansion of Yudhishthira in respect of wealth it containeth. And, O Monarch, regarding me as the eldest and entitled to respect, Yudhishthira having received me respectfully, appointed me in receiving the jewels and gems (that were brought as tribute). O Bharata, the limit and the like of the excellent and invaluable jewels that were brought there have not been seen. And O king, my hands were fatigued in receiving that wealth. And when I was tired, they that brought those valuable articles from distant regions used to wait till I was able to resume my labour. Bringing jewels from the lake Vindu, the Asura architect Maya constructed (for the Pandavas) a lake-like surface made of crystal. Beholding the (artificial) lotuses with which it was filled, I mistook it, O king for water. And seeing me draw up my clothes (while about to cross it), Vrikodara (Bhima) laughed at me, regarding me as wanting in jewels and having lost my head at the sight of the affluence of my enemy. If I had the ability, I would, O king, without the loss of a moment, slay Vrikodara for that. But, O monarch, if we endeavour to slay Bhima now, without doubt, ours will be the fate of Sisupala. O Bharata, that insult by the foe burneth me. Once again, O king, beholding a similar lake that is really full of water but which I mistook for a crystal surface, I fell into it. At that, Bhima with Arjuna once more laughed derisively, and Draupadi also accompanied by other females joined in the laughter. That paineth my heart exceedingly. My apparel having been wet, the menials at the command of the king gave me other clothes. That also is my great sorrow. And O king, hear now of another mistake that I speak of. In attempting to pass through what is exactly of the shape of a door but through which there was really no passage, I struck my forehead against stone and injured myself. The twins Nakula and Sahadeva beholding from a distance that I was so hit at the head came and supported me in their arms, expressing great concern for me. And Sahadeva repeatedly told me, as if with a smile,--"This O king, is the door. Go this way!" And Bhimasena, laughing aloud, addressed me and said,--"O son of Dhritarashtra, this is the door." And, O king I had not even heard of the names of those gems that I saw in that mansion. And it is for these reasons that my heart so acheth.'

SECTION L

"Duryodhana said,--'Listen now, O Bharata, about all the most costly articles I saw, belonging unto the sons of Pandu, and brought one after another by the kings of the earth. Beholding that wealth of the foe, I lost my reason and scarcely knew myself. And, O Bharata, listen as I describe that wealth consisting of both manufactures and the produce of the land. The king of Kamboja gave innumerable skins of the best kind, and blankets made of wool, of the soft fur of rodents and other burroughers, and of the hair of cats,--all inlaid with threads of gold. And he also gave three hundred horses of the Titteti and the Kalmasha species possessing noses like parrots. And he also gave three hundred camels and an equal number of she-asses, all fattened with the olives and the Pilusha. And innumerable Brahmanas engaged in rearing cattle and occupied in low offices for the gratification of the illustrious king Yudhishthira the just waited at the gate with three hundred millions of tribute but they were denied admission into the palace. And hundred upon hundreds of Brahmanas possessing wealth of kine and living upon the lands that Yudhishthira had given them, came there with their handsome golden Kamandalus filled with clarified butter. And though they had brought such tribute, they were refused admission into the palace. And the Sudra kings that dwelt in the regions on the seacoast, brought with them, O king, hundred thousands of serving girls of the Karpasika country, all of beautiful features and slender waist and luxuriant hair and decked in golden ornaments; and also many skins of the Ranku deer worthy even of Brahmanas as tribute unto king Yudhishthira. And the tribes Vairamas, Paradas, Tungas, with the Kitavas who lived upon crops that depended on water from the sky or of the river and also they who were born in regions on the sea-shore, in woodlands, or countries on the other side of the ocean waited at the gate, being refused permission to enter, with goats and kine and asses and camels and vegetable, honey and blankets and jewels and gems of various kinds. And that great warrior king Bhagadatta, the brave ruler of Pragjyotisha and the mighty sovereign of the mlechchas, at the head of a large number of Yavanas waited at the gate unable to enter, with a considerable tribute comprising of horses of the best breed and possessing the speed of the wind. And king Bhagadatta (beholding the concourse) had to go away from the gate, making over a number of swords with handles made of the purest ivory and well-adorned with diamonds and every kind of gems. And many tribes coming from different regions, of whom some possess two eyes, some three and some had eyes on their foreheads, and those also called Aushmikas, and Nishadas, and Romakas, some cannibals and many possessing only one leg, I say, O king, standing at the gate, being refused permission to enter. And these diverse rulers brought as tribute ten thousand asses of diverse hues and black necks and huge bodies and great speed and much docility and celebrated all over the world. And these asses were all of goodly size and delightful colour. And they were all bred on the coast of Vankhu. And there were many kings that gave unto Yudhishthira much gold and silver. And having given much tribute they obtained admission into the palace of Yudhishthira. The people that came there possessing only one leg gave unto Yudhishthira many wild horses, some of which were as red as the cochineal, and some white, and some possessing the hues of the rainbow and some looking like evening clouds, and some that were of variegated colour. And they were all endued with the speed of the mind. And they also gave unto the king enough gold of superior quality. I also saw numberless Chins and Sakas and Uddras and many barbarous tribes living in the woods, and many Vrishnis and Harahunas, and dusky tribes of the Himavat, and many Nipas and people residing in regions on the sea-coast, waiting at the gate being refused permission to enter. And the people of Valhika gave unto him as tribute ten thousand asses, of goodly size and black necks and daily running two hundred miles, And those asses were of many shapes. And they were well-trained and celebrated all over the world. And possessed of symmetrical proportion and excellent colour, their skins were pleasant to the touch. And the Valhikas also presented numerous blankets of woollen texture manufactured in Chin and numerous skins of the Ranku deer, and clothes manufactured from jute, and others woven with the threads spun by insects. And they also gave thousands of other clothes not made of cotton, possessing the colour of the lotus. And these were all of smooth texture. And they also gave soft sheep-skins by thousands. And they also gave many sharp and long swords and scimitars, and hatchets and fine-edged battle-axes manufactured in the western countries. And having presented perfumes and jewels and gems of various kinds by thousands as tribute, they waited at the gate, being refused admission into the palace. And the Sakas and Tukhatas and Tukharas and Kankas and Romakas and men with horns bringing with them as tribute numerous large elephants and ten thousand horses, and hundreds and hundreds of millions of gold waited at the gate, being refused permission to enter. And the kings of the eastern countries having presented numerous valuable articles including many costly carpets and vehicles and beds, and armours of diverse hues decked with jewels and gold and ivory, and weapons of various kinds, and cars of various shapes and handsome make and adorned with gold, with well-trained horses trimmed with tiger skins, and rich and variegated blankets for caprisoning elephants, and various kinds of jewels and gems, arrows long and short and various other kinds of weapons, obtained permission to enter the sacrificial palace of the illustrious Pandava!'

SECTION LI

"Duryodhana said,--'O sinless one, listen to me as I describe that large mass of wealth consisting of various kinds of tribute presented unto Yudhishthira by the kings of the earth. They that dwell by the side of the river Sailoda flowing between the mountains of Mer and Mandara and enjoy the delicious shade of topes of the Kichaka bamboo, viz., the Khashas, Ekasanas, the Arhas, the Pradaras, the Dirghavenus, the Paradas, the Kulindas, the Tanganas, and the other Tanganas, brought as tribute heaps of gold measured in dronas (jars) and raised from underneath the earth by ants and therefore called after these creatures. The mountain tribes endued with great strength having brought as tribute numerous Chamaras (long brushes) soft and black and others white as moon-beam and sweet honey extracted from the flowers growing on the Himavat as also from the Mishali champaka and garlands of flowers brought from the region of the northern Kurus, and diverse kinds of plants from the north even from Kailasa, waited with their heads bent down at the gate of king Yudhishthira, being refused permission to enter. I also beheld there numberless chiefs of the Kiratas armed with cruel weapons and ever engaged in cruel deeds, eating of fruits and roots and attired in skins and living on the northern slopes of the Himavat and on the mountain from behind which the sun rises and in the region of Karusha on the sea-coast and on both sides of the Lohitya mountains. And, O king, having brought with them as tribute loads upon loads of sandal and aloe as also black aloe, and heaps upon heaps of valuable skins and gold and perfumes, and ten thousand serving-girls of their own race, and many beautiful animals and birds of remote countries, and much gold of great splendour procured from mountains, the Kiratas waited at the gate, being refused permission to enter. The Kairatas, the Daradas, the Darvas, the Suras, the Vaiamakas, the Audumvaras, the Durvibhagas, the Kumaras, the Paradas along with the Vahlikas, the Kashmiras, the Ghorakas, the Hansakayanas, the Sivis, the Trigartas, the Yauddheyas, the ruler of Madras and the Kaikeyas, the Amvashtas, the Kaukuras, the Tarkshyas, the Vastrapas along with the Palhavas, the Vashatayas, the Mauleyas along with the Kshudrakas, and the Malavas, the Paundrayas, the Kukkuras, the Sakas, the Angas, the Vangas, the Punras, the Sanavatyas, and the Gayas--these good and well-born Kshatriyas distributed into regular clans and trained to the use of arms, brought tribute unto king Yudhishthira by hundreds and thousands. And the Vangas, the Kalingas, the Magadhas, the Tamraliptas, the Supundrakas, the Dauvalikas, the Sagarakas, the Patrornas, the Saisavas, and innumerable Karnapravaranas, who presented themselves at the gate, were told by the gate-keepers at the command of the king, that if they could wait and bring good tribute they could obtain admission. Then the kings of those nations each gave a thousand elephants furnished with tusks like unto the shafts of ploughs and decked with girdles made of gold, and covered with fine blankets and therefore, resembling the lotus in hue. And they were all darkish as rocks and always musty, and procured from the sides of the Kamyaka lake, and covered with defensive armour. And they were also exceedingly patient and of the best breed. And having made these presents, those kings were permitted to enter. O king, these and many others, coming from various regions, and numberless other illustrious kings, brought jewels and gems unto this sacrifice. And Chitraratha, also the king of Gandharvas, the friend of Indra, gave four hundred horses gifted with the speed of the wind. And the Gandharva Tumvuru gladly gave a hundred horses of the colour of mango leaf and decked in gold. And, O thou of the Kuru race, the celebrated king of the Mlechcha tribe, called the Sukaras, gave many hundreds of excellent elephants. And Virata, the king of Matsya, gave as tribute two thousand elephants decked in gold. And king Vasudana from the kingdom of Pansu presented unto the son of Pandu six and twenty elephants and two thousand horses, O king, all decked in gold and endued with speed and strength and in full vigour of youth, and diverse other kinds of wealth. And Yajnasena presented unto the sons of Pandu for the sacrifice, fourteen thousand serving-girls and ten thousand serving-men with their wives, many hundreds of excellent elephants, six and twenty cars with elephants yoked unto them, and also his whole kingdom. And Vasudeva of the Vrishni race, in order to enhance the dignity of Arjuna, gave fourteen thousands of excellent elephants. Indeed, Krishna is the soul of Arjuna and Arjuna is the soul of Krishna, and whatever Arjuna may say Krishna is certain to accomplish. And Krishna is capable of abandoning heaven itself for the sake of Arjuna, and Arjuna also is capable of sacrificing his life for the sake of Krishna. And the Kings of Chola and Pandya, though they brought numberless jars of gold filled with fragrant sandal juice from the hills of Malaya, and loads of sandal and aloe wood from the Dardduras hills, and many gems of great brilliancy and fine cloths inlaid with gold, did not obtain permission (to enter). And the king of the Singhalas gave those best of sea-born gems called the lapis lazuli, and heaps of pearls also, and hundreds of coverlets for elephants. And numberless dark-coloured men with the ends of their eyes red as copper, attired in clothes decked with gems, waited at the gate with those presents. And numberless Brahmanas and Kshatriyas who had been vanquished, and Vaisyas and serving Sudras, from love of Yudhishthira, brought tribute unto the son of Pandu. And even all the Mlechchas, from love and respect, came unto Yudhishthira. And all orders of men, good, indifferent and low, belonging to numberless races, coming from diverse lands made Yudhishthira's habitation the epitome of the world.'

"'And beholding the kings of the earth to present unto the foes such excellent and valuable presents, I wished for death out of grief. And O king, I will now tell thee of the servants of the Pandavas, people for whom Yudhishthira supplieth food, both cooked and uncooked. There are a hundred thousand billions of mounted elephants and cavalry and a hundred millions of cars and countless foot soldiers. At one place raw provisions are being measured out; at another they are being cooked; and at another place the foods are being distributed. And the notes of festivity are being heard everywhere. And amongst men of all orders I beheld not a single one in the mansion of Yudhishthira that had not food and drink and ornaments. And eighty-eight thousands of Snataka Brahmanas leading domestic lives, all supported by Yudhishthira, with thirty serving-girls given unto each, gratified by the king, always pray with complacent hearts for the destruction of his foes. And ten thousands of other ascetics with vital seed drawn up, daily eat of golden plates in Yudhishthira's palace. And, O king, Yajnaseni, without having eaten herself, daily seeth whether everybody, including even the deformed and the dwarfs, hath eaten or not. And, O Bharata, only two do not pay tribute unto the son of Kunti, viz., the Panchalas in consequence of their relationship by marriage, and the Andhakas and Vrishnis in consequence of their friendship.'

SECTION LII

"Duryodhana said,--'Those kings that are revered over all the world, who are devoted to truth and who are pledged to the observance of rigid vows, who are possessed of great learning and eloquence, who are fully conversant with the Vedas and their branches as also with sacrifices, who have piety and modesty, whose souls are devoted to virtue, who possess fame, and who have enjoyed the grand rites of coronation, all wait upon and worship Yudhishthira. And, O king, I beheld there many thousands of wild kine with as many vessels of white copper for milking them, brought thither by the kings of the earth as sacrificial presents to be given away by Yudhishthira unto the Brahmana. And, O Bharata, for bathing Yudhishthira at the conclusion of the sacrifice, many kings with the greatest alacrity, themselves brought there in a state of purity many excellent jars (containing water). And king Vahlika brought there a car decked with pure gold. And king Sudakshina himself yoked thereto four white horses of Kamboja breed, and Sunitha of great might fitted the lower pole and the ruler of Chedi with his own hands took up and fitted the flag-staff. And the king of the Southern country stood ready with the coat of mail; the ruler of Magadha, with garlands of flowers and the head-gear; the great warrior Vasudana with a sixty years old elephant, the king of Matsya, with the side-fittings of the car, all encased in gold; king Ekalavya, with the shoes; the king of Avanti, with diverse kinds of water for the final bath; king Chekitana, with the quiver; the king of Kasi, with the bow; and Salya, with a sword whose hilt and straps were adorned with gold. Then Dhaumya and Vyasa, of great ascetic merit, with Narada and Asita's son Devala, standing before performed the ceremony of sprinkling the sacred water over the king. And the great Rishis with cheerful hearts sat where the sprinkling ceremony was performed. And other illustrious Rishis conversant with the Vedas, with Jamadagni's son among them, approached Yudhishthira, the giver of large sacrificial presents, uttering mantras all the while, like the seven Rishis, approaching the great Indra in heaven. And Satyaki of unbaffled prowess held the umbrella (over the king's head). And Dhananjaya and Bhima were engaged in tanning the king; while the twins held a couple of chamaras in their hands. And the Ocean himself brought in a sling that big conch of Varuna which the celestial artificer Viswakarman had constructed with a thousand Nishkas of gold, and which Prajapati had in a former Kalpa, presented unto Indra. It was with that conch that Krishna bathed Yudhishthira after the conclusion of the sacrifice, and beholding it, I swooned away. People go to the Eastern or the Western seas and also to the Southern one. But, O father, none except birds can ever go to the Northern sea. But the Pandavas have spread their dominion even there, for I heard hundreds of conches that had been brought thence blown (in the sacrificial mansion) indicative of auspicious rejoicing. And while those conches blew simultaneously, my hair stood on end. And those among the kings, who were weak in strength fell down. And Dhrishtadyumna and Satyaki and the sons of Pandu and Kesava,--those eight, endued with strength and prowess and handsome in person, beholding the kings deprived of consciousness and myself in that plight, laughed outright. Then Vibhatsu (Arjuna) with a cheerful heart gave, O Bharata, unto the principal Brahmanas five hundred bullocks with horns plated with gold. And king Yudhishthira, the son of Kunti, having completed the Rajasuya sacrifice, obtained like the exalted Harishchandra such prosperity that neither Rantideva nor Nabhaga, nor Jauvanaswa, nor Manu, nor king Prithu the son of Vena, nor Bhagiratha, Yayati, nor Nahusha, had obtained its like. And beholding, O exalted one, such prosperity, in the son of Pritha which is even like that which Harishchandra had, I do not see the least good in continuing to live, O Bharata! O ruler of men, a yoke that is tied (to the bullock's shoulders) by a blind man becomes loosened. Even such is the case with us. The younger ones are growing while the elder ones are decaying. And beholding all this, O chief of the Kurus, I cannot enjoy peace even with the aid of reflection. And it is for this, O king, that I am plunged into grief and becoming pale and emaciated.'

SECTION LIII

"Dhritrashtra said,--'Thou art my eldest son and born also of my eldest wife. Therefore, O son, be not jealous of the Pandavas. He that is jealous is always unhappy and suffereth the pangs of death. O bull of the Bharata race, Yudhishthira knoweth not deception, possesseth wealth equal unto thine, hath thy friends for his, and is not jealous of thee. Why shouldst thou, therefore, be jealous of him? O king, in respect of friends and allies thou art equal unto Yudhishthira. Why shouldst thou, therefore, covet, from folly, the property of thy brother? Be not so. Cease to be jealous. Do not grieve. O bull of the Bharata race, if thou covetest the dignity attaching to the performance of a sacrifice, let the priests arrange for thee the great sacrifice, called the Saptatantu. The kings of the earth will then, cheerfully and with great respect, bring for thee also much wealth and gems and ornaments. O child, coveting other's possessions is exceedingly mean. He, on the other hand, enjoyeth happiness, who is content with his own being engaged in the practices of his own order. Never striving to obtain the wealth of others, persevering in one's own affairs, and protecting what hath been earned,--

these are the indications of true greatness. He that is unmoved in calamity, skilled in his own business, ever exerting vigilance and humble, always beholdeth prosperity. The sons of Pandu are as thy arms. Do not lop off those arms of thine. Plunge not into internal dissensions for the sake of that wealth of thy brothers. O king, be not jealous of the sons of Pandu. Thy wealth is equal unto that of thy brothers in his entirety. There is great sin in quarrelling with friends. They that are thy grandsires are theirs also. Give away in charity on occasions of sacrifices, gratify every dear object of thy desire, disport in the company of women freely, and enjoy thou peace.'

SECTION LIV

"Duryodhana said,--'He that is devoid of intellect but hath merely heard of many things, can scarcely understand the real import of the scriptures, like the spoon that hath no perception of the taste of the soup it toucheth. Thou knowest everything, but yet confoundest me. Like a boat fastened to another, thou and I are tied to each other. Art thou unmindful of thy own interests? Or, dost thou entertain hostile feeling towards me? These thy sons and allies are doomed to destruction, inasmuch as they have thee for their ruler, for thou describest as attainable in the future what is to be done at the present moment. He often trippeth whose guide acts under the instructions of others. How then can his followers expect to come across a right path? O king, thou art of mature wisdom; thou hast the opportunity to listen to the words of old, and thy senses also are under thy control. It behoveth thee not to confound us who are ready to seek our own interests. Vrihaspati hath said that the usage of kings are different from those of common people. Therefore kings should always attend to their own interests with vigilance. The attainment of success is the sole criterion that should guide the conduct of a Kshatriya. Whether, therefore, the means is virtuous or sinful, what scruples can there be in the duties of one's own order? He that is desirous of snatching the blazing prosperity of his foe, should, O bull of the Bharata race, bring every direction under his subjection like the charioteer taming the steeds with his whip. Those used to handling weapons say that, a weapon is not simply an instrument that cuts but is a means, whether covert or overt, that can defeat a foe. Who is to be reckoned a foe and who a friend, doth not depend on one's figure or dimensions. He that paineth another is, O king, to be regarded a foe by him that is pained. Discontent is the root of prosperity. Therefore, O king, I desire to be discontented. He that striveth after the acquisition of prosperity is, O king, a truly politic person. Nobody should be attached to wealth and affluence, for the wealth that hath been earned and hoarded may be plundered. The usages of kings are even such. It was during a period of peace that Sakra cut off the head of Namuchi after having given a pledge to the contrary, and it was because he approved of this eternal usage towards the enemy that he did so. Like a snake that swalloweth up frogs and other creatures living in holes, the earth swalloweth up a king that is peaceful and a Brahmana that stirreth not out of home. O king, none can by nature be any person's foe. He is one's foe, and not anybody else, who hath common pursuits with one. He that from folly neglecteth a growing foe, hath his vitals cut off as by a disease that he cherished without treatment. A foe, however insignificant, if suffered to grow in prowess, swalloweth one like the white ants at the root of a tree eating off the tree itself. O Bharata, O Ajamida, let not the prosperity of the foe be acceptable to thee. This policy (of neglecting the foe) should always be borne on their heads by the wise even like a load. He that always wisheth for the increase of his wealth, ever groweth in the midst of his relatives even like the body naturally growing from the moment of birth. Prowess conferreth speedy growth. Coveting as I do the prosperity of the Pandavas, I have not yet made it my own. At present I am a prey to doubts in respect of my ability. I am determined to resolve those doubts of mine. I will either obtain that prosperity of theirs, or lie down having perished in battle. O king when the state of my mind is such, what do I care now for life, for the Pandavas are daily growing while our possessions know no increase?'

SECTION LV

"Sakuni said,--'O thou foremost of victorious persons, I will snatch (for thee) this prosperity of Yudhishthira, the son of Pandu, at the sight of which thou grievest so. Therefore, O king, let Yudhishthira the son of Kunti be summoned. By throwing dice a skilful man, himself uninjured, may vanquish one that hath no skill. Know, O Bharata, that betting is my bow, the dice are my arrows, the marks on them my bow-string, and the dice-board my car.'

"Duryodhana said,--'This Sukuni skilled at dice, is ready, O king, to snatch the prosperity of the son of Pandu by means of dice. It behoveth thee to give him permission.'

"Dhritarashtra said,--'I am obedient to the counsels of my brother, the illustrious Vidura. Consulting with him, I shall tell what should be done in this matter.'

"Duryodhana said,--'Vidura is always engaged in doing good to the sons of Pandu. O Kaurava, his feelings towards us are otherwise. He will, therefore, without doubt, withdraw thy heart from the proposed act. No man should set himself to any task depending upon the counsels of another, for, O son of Kuru's race, the minds of two persons seldom agree in any particular act. The fool that liveth shunning all causes of fear wasteth himself like an insect in the rainy season. Neither sickness nor Yama waiteth till one is in prosperity. So long, therefore, as there is life and health, one should (without waiting for prosperity) accomplish his purpose.'

"Dhritarashtra said,--'O son, hostility with those that are strong, is what never recommendeth itself to me. Hostility bringeth about a change of feelings, and that itself is a weapon though not made of steel. Thou regardest, O Prince, as a great blessing what will bring in its train the terrible consequences of war. What is really fraught with mischief. If once it beginneth, it will create sharp swords and pointed arrows.'

"Duryodhana replied,--'Men of the most ancient times invented the use of dice. There is no destruction in it, nor is there any striking with weapons. Let the words of Sakuni, therefore, be acceptable to thee, and let thy command be issued for the speedy construction of the assembly house. The door of heaven, leading us to such happiness, will be opened to us by gambling. Indeed, they that betake to gambling (with such aid) deserve such good fortune. The Pandavas then will become thy equals (instead of, as now, superiors); therefore, gamble thou with the Pandavas.'

"Dhritarashtra said.--'The words uttered by thee do not recommend themselves to me. Do what may be agreeable to thee, O ruler of men. But thou shall have to repent for acting according to these words; for, words that are fraught with such immorality can never bring prosperity in the future. Even this was foreseen by the learned Vidura ever treading the path of truth and wisdom. Even the great calamity, destructive of the lives of the Kshatriyas, cometh as destined by fate.'"

Vaisampayana continued--"Having said this, the weak-minded Dhritarashtra regarded fate as supreme and unavoidable. And the king deprived of reason by Fate, and obedient to the counsels of his son, commanded his men in loud voice, saying--'Carefully construct, without loss of time, an assembly house of the most beautiful description, to be called the crystal- arched palace with a thousand columns, decked with gold and lapis lazuli, furnished with a hundred gates, and full two miles in length and in breadth the same.' Hearing those words of his, thousands of artificers endued with intelligence and skill soon erected the palace with the greatest alacrity, and having erected it brought thither every kind of article. And soon after they cheerfully represented unto the king that the palace had been finished, and that it as delightful and handsome and furnished with every kind of gems and covered with many-coloured carpets inlaid with gold. Then king Dhritarashtra, possessed of learning, summoning Vidura the chief of his ministers, said:--'Repairing, (to Khandavaprastha), bring prince Yudhishthira here without loss of time. Let him come hither with his brothers, and behold this handsome assembly house of mine, furnished with countless jewels and gems, and costly beds and carpets, and let a friendly match at dice commence here.'"

SECTION LVI

Vaisampayana said,--"King Dhritarashtra, ascertaining the inclinations of his son and knowing that Fate is inevitable, did what I have said. Vidura, however, that foremost of intelligent men, approved not his brother's words and spoke thus, 'I approve not, O king, of this command of thine. Do not act so. I fear, this will bring about the destruction of our race. When thy sons lose their unity, dissension will certainly ensue amongst them. This I apprehend, O king, from this match at dice.'

"Dhritarashtra said,--'If Fate be not hostile, this quarrel will not certainly grieve me. The whole universe moveth at the will of its Creator, under the controlling influence of Fate. It is not free. Therefore, O Vidura, going unto king Yudhishthira at my command, bring thou soon that invincible son of Kunti.'"

SECTION LVII

Vaisampayana said,--"Vidura then, thus commanded against his will by king Dhritarashtra, set out, with the help of horses of high mettle and endued with great speed and strength, and quiet and patient, for the abode of the wise sons of Pandu. Possessed of great intelligence, Vidura proceeded by the way leading to the capital of the Pandavas. And having arrived at the city of king Yudhishthira, he entered it and proceeded towards the palace, worshipped by numberless Brahmanas. And coming to the palace which was even like unto the mansion of Kuvera himself, the virtuous Vidura approached Yudhishthira, the son of Dharma. Then the illustrious Ajamida devoted to truth and having no enemy on earth, reverentially saluted Vidura, and asked him about Dhritarashtra and his sons. And Yudhishthira said, 'O Kshatta, thy mind seemeth to be cheerless. Dost thou come here in happiness and peace? The sons of Dhritarashtra, I hope, are obedient to their old father. The people also, I hope, are obedient to Dhritarashtra's rule.'

"Vidura said,--'The illustrious king, with his sons, is well and happy, and surrounded by his relatives he reigneth even like Indra himself. The king is happy with his sons who are all obedient to him and hath no grief. The illustrious monarch is bent on his own aggrandisement. The king of the Kurus hath commanded me to enquire after thy peace and prosperity, and to ask thee to repair to Hastinapore with thy brothers and to say, after beholding king Dhritarashtra's newly erected palace, whether that one is equal to thy own. Repairing thither, O son of Pritha, with thy brothers, enjoy ye in that mansion and sit to a friendly match at dice. We shall be glad if thou goest, as the Kurus have already arrived there. And thou wilt see there those gamblers and cheats that the illustrious king Dhritarashtra hath already brought thither. It is for this, O king, that I have come hither. Let the king's command be approved by thee.'

"Yudhishthira said,--'O Kshatta, if we sit to a match at dice, we may quarrel. What man is there, who knowing all this, will consent to gamble? What dost thou think fit for us? We all are obedient to thy counsels.'

"Vidura said,--'I know that gambling is the root of misery, and I strove to dissuade the king from it. The king, however, hath sent me to thee. Having known all this, O learned one, do what is beneficial.'

"Yudhishthira said,--'Besides the sons of Dhritarashtra what other dishonest gamblers are there ready for play? Tell us, O Vidura, who they are and with whom we shall have to play, staking hundreds upon hundreds of our possessions.'

"Vidura said,--'O monarch, Sakuni, the king of Gandhara, an adept at dice, having great skill of hand and desperate in stakes, Vivingati, king Chitrasena, Satyavrata, Purumitra and Jaya, these, O king, are there.'

"Yudhishthira said,--'It would seem then that some of the most desperate and terrible gamblers always depending upon deceit are there. This whole universe, however, is at the will of its Maker, under the control of fate. It is not free. O learned one, I do not desire, at the command of king Dhritarashtra to engage myself in gambling. The father always wisheth to benefit his son. Thou art our master, O Vidura. Tell me what is proper for us. Unwilling as I am to gamble, I will not do so, if the wicked Sakuni doth not summon me to it in the Sabha? If, however, he challengeth me, I will never refuse. For that, as settled, is my eternal vow.'"

Vaisampayana continued,--"King Yudhishthira the just having said this unto Vidura, commanded that preparations for his journey might be made without loss of time. And the next day, the king accompanied by his relatives and attendants and taking with him also the women of the household with Draupadi in their midst, set out for the capital of the Kurus. 'Like some brilliant body falling before the eyes, Fate depriveth us of reason, and man, tied as it were with a cord, submitteth to the sway of Providence,' saying this, king Yudhishthira, that chastiser of the foe, set out with Kshatta, without deliberating upon that summons from Dhritarashtra. And that slayer of hostile heroes, the son of Pandu and Pritha, riding upon the car that had been given him by the king of Valhika, and attired also in royal robes, set out with his brothers. And the king, blazing as it were with royal splendour, with Brahmanas walking before him, set out from his city, summoned by Dhritarashtra and impelled by what hath been ordained by Kala (Time). And arriving at Hastinapore he went to the palace of Dhritarashtra. And going there, the son of Pandu approached the king. And the exalted one then approached Bhishma and Drona and Karna, and Kripa, and the son of Drona, and embraced and was embraced by them all. And the mighty-armed one, endued with great prowess, then approached Somadatta, and then Duryodhana and Salya, and the son of Suvala, and those other kings also that had arrived there before him. The king then went to the brave Dusshasana and then to all his (other) brothers and then to Jayadratha and next to all the Kurus one after another. And the mighty- armed one, then surrounded by all his brothers, entered the apartment of the wise king Dhritarashtra. And then Yudhishthira beheld the reverend Gandhari, ever obedient to her lord, and surrounded by her daughters-in- law like Rohini by the stars. And saluting Gandhari and blessed by her in return, the king then beheld his old uncle, that illustrious monarch whose wisdom was his eye. King Dhritarashtra then, O monarch, smelt his head as also the heads of those four other princes of the Kuru race, viz., the sons of Pandu with Bhimasena as their eldest. And, O king, beholding the handsome Pandava those tigers among men, all the Kurus became exceedingly glad. And commanded by the king, the Pandavas then retired to the chambers allotted to them and which were all furnished with jewels and gems. And when they had retired into the chambers, the women of Dhritarashtra's household with Dussala taking the lead visited them. And the daughters-in- law of Dhritarashtra beholding the blazing and splendid beauty and prosperity of Yajnaseni, became cheerless and filled with jealousy. And those tigers among men, having conversed with the ladies went through their daily physical exercises and then performed the religious rites of the day. And having finished their daily devotions, they decked their persons with sandal paste of the most fragrant kind. And desiring to secure good luck and prosperity they caused (by gifts) the Brahmanas to utter benedictions. And then eating food that was of the best taste they retired to their chambers for the night. And those bulls among the Kurus then were put to sleep with music by handsome females. And obtaining from them what came in due succession, those subjugators of hostile towns passed with cheerful hearts that delightful night in pleasure and sport. And waked by the bards with sweet music, they rose from their beds, and having passed the night thus in happiness, they rose at dawn and having gone through the usual rites, they entered into the assembly house and were saluted by those that were ready there for gambling."

SECTION LVIII

Vaisampayana said,--"The sons of Pritha with Yudhishthira at their head, having entered that assembly house, approached all the kings that were present there. And worshipping all those that deserved to be worshipped, and saluting others as each deserved according to age, they seated themselves on seats that were clean and furnished with costly carpets. After they had taken their seats, as also all the kings, Sakuni the son of Suvala addressed Yudhishthira and said, 'O king, the assembly is full. All had been waiting for thee. Let, therefore, the dice be cast and the rules of play be fixed, O Yudhishthira.'

"Yudhishthira replied, 'Deceitful gambling is sinful. There is no Kshatriya prowess in it. There is certainly no morality in it. Why, then, O king, dost thou praise gambling so? The wise applaud not the pride that gamesters feel in deceitful play. O Sakuni, vanquish us, not like a wretch, by deceitful means.'

"Sakuni said,--'That high-souled player who knoweth the secrets of winning and losing, who is skilled in baffling the deceitful arts of his confrere, who is united in all the diverse operations of which gambling consisteth, truly knoweth the play, and he suffereth all in course of it. O son of Pritha, it is the staking at dice, which may be lost or won that may injure us. And it is for that reason that gambling is regarded as a fault. Let us, therefore, O king, begin the play. Fear not. Let the stakes be fixed. Delay not!'

"Yudhishthira said,--'That best of Munis, Devala, the son of Asita, who always instructeth us about all those acts that may lead to heaven, hell, or the other regions, hath said, that it is sinful to play deceitfully with a gamester. To obtain victory in battle without cunning or stratagem is the best sport. Gambling, however, as a sport, is not so. Those that are respectable never use the language of the Mlechchas, nor do they adopt deceitfulness in their behaviour. War carried on without crookedness and cunning, this is the act of men that are honest. Do not, O Sakuni, playing desperately, win of us that wealth with which according to our abilities, we strive to learn how to benefit the Brahmanas. Even enemies should not be vanquished by desperate stakes in deceitful play. I do not desire either happiness or wealth by means of cunning. The conduct of one that is a gamester, even if it be without deceitfulness, should not be applauded.'

"Sakuni said,--'O Yudhishthira, it is from a desire of winning, which is not a very honest motive, that one high-born person approacheth another (in a contest of race superiority). So also it is from a desire of defeating, which is not a very honest motive, that one learned person approacheth another (in a contest of learning). Such motives, however, are scarcely regarded as really dishonest. So also, O Yudhishthira, a person skilled at dice approacheth one that is not so skilled from a desire of vanquishing him. One also who is conversant with the truths of science approacheth another that is not from desire of victory, which is scarcely an honest motive. But (as I have already said) such a motive is not really dishonest. And, O Yudhishthira, so also one that is skilled in weapons approacheth one that is not so skilled; the strong approacheth the weak. This is the practice in every contest. The motive is victory, O Yudhishthira. If, therefore, thou, in approaching me, regardest me to be actuated by motives that are dishonest, if thou art under any fear, desist then from play.'

"Yudhishthira said,--'Summoned, I do not withdraw. This is my established vow. And, O king, Fate is all powerful. We all are under the control of Destiny. With whom in this assembly am I to play? Who is there that can stake equally with me? Let the play begin.'

"Duryodhana said,--'O monarch, I shall supply jewels and gems and every kind of wealth. And it is for me that this Sakuni, my uncle, will play.'

"Yudhishthira said,--'Gambling for one's sake by the agency of another seemeth to me to be contrary to rule. Thou also, O learned one, will admit this. If, however, thou art still bent on it, let the play begin.'"

SECTION LIX

Vaisampayana said,--"When the play commenced, all those kings with Dhritarashtra at their head took their seats in that assembly. And, O Bharata, Bhishma and Drona and Kripa and the high-souled Vidura with cheerless hearts sat behind. And those kings with leonine necks and endued with great energy took their seats separately and in pairs upon many elevated seats of beautiful make and colour. And, O king, that mansion looked resplendent with those assembled kings like heaven itself with a conclave of the celestials of great good fortune. And they were all conversant with the Vedas and brave and of resplendent countenances. And, O great king, the friendly match at dice then commenced.

"Yudhishthira said,--'O king, this excellent wealth of pearls of great value, procured from the ocean by churning it (of old), so beautiful and decked with pure gold, this, O king, is my stake. What is thy counter stake, O great king,--the wealth with which thou wishest to play with me?'

"Duryodhana said,--'I have many jewels and much wealth. But I am not vain of them. Win thou this stake.'"

Vaisampayana continued,--"Then Sakuni, well-skilled at dice, took up the dice and (casting them) said unto Yudhishthira, 'Lo, I have won!'

SECTION LX

"Yudhishthira said,--'Thou hast won this stake of me by unfair means. But be not so proud, O Sakuni. Let us play staking thousands upon thousands. I have many beautiful jars each full of a thousand Nishkas in my treasury, inexhaustible gold, and much silver and other minerals. This, O king, is the wealth with which I will stake with thee!'"

Vaisampayana continued,--"Thus addressed, Sakuni said unto the chief of the perpetuators of the Kuru race, the eldest of the sons of Pandu, king Yudhishthira, of glory incapable of sustaining any diminution. 'Lo, I have won!'

"Yudhishthira said,--'This my sacred and victorious and royal car which gladdeneth the heart and hath carried us hither, which is equal unto a thousand cars, which is of symmetrical proportions and covered with tiger-skin, and furnished with excellent wheels and flag-staffs which is handsome, and decked with strings of little bells, whose clatter is even like the roar of the clouds or of the ocean, and which is drawn by eight noble steeds known all over the kingdom and which are white as the moon- beam and from whose hoofs no terrestrial creature can escape--this, O king, is my wealth with which I will stake with thee!'"

Vaisampayana continued,--"Hearing these words, Sakuni ready with the dice, and adopting unfair means, said unto Yudhishthira, 'Lo, I have won!'

"Yudhishthira said,--'I have a hundred thousand serving-girls, all young, and decked with golden bracelets on their wrists and upper arms, and with nishkas round their necks and other ornaments, adorned with costly garlands and attired in rich robes, daubed with the sandal paste, wearing jewels and gold, and well-skilled in the four and sixty elegant arts, especially versed in dancing and singing, and who wait upon and serve at my command the celestials, the Snataka Brahmanas, and kings. With this wealth, O king, I will stake with thee!'"

Vaisampayana continued,--"Hearing these words, Sakuni ready with the dice, adopting unfair means, said unto Yudhishthira. 'Lo, I have won!'

"Yudhishthira said,--'I have thousands of serving-men, skilled in waiting upon guests, always attired in silken robes, endued with wisdom and intelligence, their senses under control though young, and decked with ear-rings, and who serve all guests night and day with plates and dishes in hand. With this wealth, O king, I will stake with thee!'"

Vaisampayana continued,--"Hearing these words, Sakuni, ready with the dice, adopting unfair means said unto Yudhishthira, 'Lo, I have won!'

"Yudhishthira said,--'I have, O son of Suvala, one thousand musty elephants with golden girdles, decked with ornaments, with the mark of the lotus on their temples and necks and other parts, adorned with golden garlands, with fine white tusks long and thick as plough-shafts, worthy of carrying kings on their backs, capable of bearing every kind of noise on the field of battle, with huge bodies, capable of battering down the walls of hostile towns, of the colour of new-formed clouds, and each possessing eight she-elephants. With this wealth, O king, I will stake with thee.'"

Vaisampayana continued,--"Unto Yudhishthira who had said so, Sakuni, the son of Suvala, laughingly said, 'Lo, I have won it!'

"Yudhishthira said,--'I have as many cars as elephants, all furnished with golden poles and flag-staffs and well-trained horses and warriors that fight wonderfully and each of whom receiveth a thousand coins as his monthly pay whether he fighteth or not. With this wealth, O king, I will stake with thee!'"

Vaisampayana continued,--"When these words had been spoken, the wretch Sakuni, pledged to enmity, said unto Yudhishthira, 'Lo, I have won it.'

"Yudhishthira said.--'The steeds of the Tittiri, Kalmasha, and Gandharva breeds, decked with ornaments, which Chitraratha having been vanquished in battle and subdued cheerfully gave unto Arjuna, the wielder of the Gandiva. With this wealth, O king, I will stake with thee.'"

Vaisampayana continued, "Hearing this, Sakuni, ready at dice, adopting unfair means, said unto Yudhishthira: 'Lo, I have won!'

"Yudhishthira said,--'I have ten thousand cars and vehicles unto which are yoked draught animals of the foremost breed. And I have also sixty thousand warriors picked from each order by thousands, who are all brave and endued with prowess like heroes, who drink milk and eat good rice, and all of whom have broad chests. With this wealth, O king, I will stake with thee.'"

Vaisampayana continued,--"Hearing this, Sakuni ready at dice, adopting unfair means said unto Yudhishthira, 'Lo, I have won!'

"Yudhishthira said,--'I have four hundred Nidis (jewels of great value) encased in sheets of copper and iron. Each one of them is equal to five draunikas of the costliest and purest leaf gold of the Jatarupa kind. With this wealth, O king, I will stake with thee.'"

Vaisampayana continued,--"Hearing this, Sakuni ready at dice, adopting foul means, said unto Yudhishthira, 'Lo, I have won it!'"

SECTION LXI

Vaisampayana said,--"During the course of this gambling, certain to bring about utter ruin (on Yudhishthira), Vidura, that dispeller of all doubts, (addressing Dhritarashtra) said, 'O great king, O thou of the Bharata race, attend to what I say, although my words may not be agreeable to thee, like medicine to one that is ill and about to breathe his last. When this Duryodhana of sinful mind had, immediately after his birth, cried discordantly like a jackal, it was well known that he had been ordained to bring about the destruction of the Bharata race. Know, O king, that he will be the cause of death of ye all. A jackal is living in thy house, O king, in the form of Duryodhana. Thou knowest it not in consequence of thy folly. Listen now to the words of the Poet (Sukra) which I will quote. They that collect honey (in mountains), having received what they seek, do not notice that they are about to fall. Ascending dangerous heights, abstracted in the pursuit of what they seek, they fall down and meet with destruction. This Duryodhana also, maddened with the play at dice, like the collector of honey, abstracted in what he seeketh, marketh not the consequences. Making enemies of these great warriors, he beholdeth not the fall that is before him. It is known to thee, O thou of great wisdom, that amongst the Bhojas, they abandoned, for the good of the citizens a son that was unworthy of their race. The Andhakas, the Yadavas, and the Bhojas uniting together, abandoned Kansa. And afterwards, when at the command of the whole tribe, the same Kansa had been slain by Krishna that slayer of foes, all the men of the tribe became exceedingly happy for a hundred years. So at thy command, let Arjuna slay this Suyodhana. And in consequence of the slaying of this wretch, let the Kurus be glad and pass their days in happiness. In exchange of a crow, O great king, buy these peacocks--the Pandavas; and in exchange of a jackal, buy these tigers. For the sake of a family a member may be sacrificed; for the sake of a village a family may be sacrificed, for the sake of a province a village may be sacrificed and for the sake of one's own soul the whole earth may be sacrificed. Even this was what the omniscient Kavya himself, acquainted with the thoughts of every creature, and a source of terror unto all foes, said unto the great Asuras to induce them to abandon Jambha at the moment of his birth. It is said that a certain king, having caused a number of wild birds that vomited gold to take up their quarters in his own house, afterwards killed them from temptation. O slayer of foes, blinded by temptation and the desire of enjoyment, for the sake of gold, the king destroyed at the same time both his present and future gains. Therefore, O king, prosecute not the Pandavas from desire of profit, even like the king in story. For then, blinded by folly thou wilt have to repent afterwards, even like the person that killed the birds. Like a flower-seller that plucketh (many flowers) in the garden from trees that he cherisheth with affection from day to day, continue, O Bharata, to pluck flowers day by day from the Pandavas. Do not scorch them to their roots like a fire- producing breeze that reduceth everything to black charcoal. Go not, O king, unto the region of Yama, with thy sons and troops, for who is there that is capable of fighting with the sons of Pritha, together? Not to speak of others, is the chief of the celestials at the head of the celestials themselves, capable of doing so?'

SECTION LXII

"Vidura said,--'Gambling is the root of dissensions. It bringeth about disunion. Its consequences are frightful. Yet having recourse to this, Dhritarashtra's son Duryodhana createth for himself fierce enmity. The descendants of Pratipa and Santanu, with their fierce troops and their allies the Vahlikas, will, for the sins of Duryodhana meet with destruction. Duryodhana, in consequence of this intoxication, forcibly driveth away luck and prosperity from his kingdom, even like an infuriate bull breaking his own horns himself. That brave and learned person who disregarding his own foresight, followeth, O king, (the bent of) another man's heart, sinketh in terrible affliction even like one that goeth into the sea in a boat guided by a child. Duryodhana is gambling with the son of Pandu, and thou art in raptures that he is winning. And it is such success that begeteth war, which endeth in the destruction of men. This fascination (of gambling) that thou has well-devised only leadeth to dire results. Thus hast thou simply brought on by these counsels great affliction to thy heart. And this thy quarrel with Yudhishthira, who is so closely related to thee, even if thou hadst not foreseen it, is still approved by thee. Listen, ye sons of Santanu, ye descendants of Pratipa, who are now in this assembly of the Kauravas, to these words of wisdom. Enter ye not into the terrible fire that hath blazed forth following the wretch. When Ajatasatru, the son of Pandu, intoxicated with dice, giveth way to his wrath, and Vrikodara and Arjuna and the twins (do the same), who, in that hour of confusion, will prove your refuge? O great king, thou art thyself a mine of wealth. Thou canst earn (by other means) as much wealth as thou seekest to earn by gambling. What dost thou gain by winning from the Pandavas their vast wealth? Win the Pandavas themselves, who will be to thee more than all the wealth they have. We all know the skill of Suvala in play. This hill-king knoweth many nefarious methods in gambling. Let Sakuni return whence he came. War not, O Bharata, with the sons of Pandu!'

SECTION LXIII

"Duryodhana said,--'O Kshatta, thou art always boasting of the fame of our enemies, deprecating the sons of Dhritarashtra. We know, O Vidura, of whom thou art really fond. Thou always disregardest us as children. That man standeth contest, who wisheth for success unto those that are near to him and defeat unto those that are not his favourites. His praise and blame are applied accordingly. Thy tongue and mind betray thy heart. But the hostility thou showeth in speech is even greater than what is in thy heart. Thou hast been cherished by us like a serpent on our lap. Like a cat thou wishest evil unto him that cherisheth thee. The wise have said that there is no sin graver than that of injuring one's master. How is it, O Kshatta, that thou dost not fear this sin? Having vanquished our enemies we have obtained great advantages. Use not harsh words in respect of us. Thou art always willing to make peace with the foes. And it is for this reason that thou hatest us always. A man becometh a foe by speaking words that are unpardonable. Then again in praising the enemy, the secrets of one's own party should not be divulged. (Thou however, transgressest this rule). Therefore, O thou parasite, why dost thou obstruct us so? Thou sayest whatever thou wishest. Insult us not. We know thy mind. Go and learn sitting at the feet of the old. Keen up the reputation that thou hast won. Meddle not with the affairs of other men. Do not imagine that thou art our chief. Tell us not harsh words always, O Vidura. We do not ask thee what is for our good. Cease, irritate not those that have already borne too much at thy hands. There is only one Controller, no second. He controlleth even the child that is in the mother's womb. I am controlled by Him. Like water that always floweth in a downward course, I am acting precisely in the way in which He is directing me. He that breaketh his head against a stone-wall, and he that feedeth a serpent, are guided in those acts of theirs by their own intellect. (Therefore, in this matter I am guided by my own intelligence). He becometh a foe who seeketh to control others by force. When advice, however, is offered in a friendly spirit, the learned bear with it. He again that hath set fire to such a highly inflammable object as camphor, beholdeth not its ashes, if he runneth immediately to extinguish it. One should not give shelter to another who is the friend of his foes, or to another who is ever jealous of his protector or to another who is evil-minded. Therefore, O Vidura, go whither-so-ever thou pleasest. A wife that is unchaste, however well-treated, forsaketh her husband yet.'

"Vidura addressing Dhritarashtra, said, 'O monarch, tell us (impartially) like a witness what thou thinkest of the conduct of those who abandon their serving-men thus for giving instruction to them. The hearts of kings are, indeed, very fickle. Granting protection at first, they strike with clubs at last. O prince (Duryodhana), thou regardest thyself as mature in intellect, and, O thou of bad heart, thou regardest me as a child. But consider that he is a child who having first accepted one for a friend, subsequently findeth fault with him. An evil-hearted man can never be brought to the path of rectitude, like an unchaste wife in the house of a well-born person. Assuredly, instruction is not agreeable to this bull of the Bharata race like a husband of sixty years to a damsel that is young. After this, O king, if thou wishest to hear words that are agreeable to thee, in respect of all acts good or bad, ask thou women and idiots and cripples or persons of that description. A sinful man speaking words that are agreeable may be had in this world. But a speaker of words that are disagreeable though sound as regimen, or a hearer of the same, is very rare. He indeed, is a king's true ally who disregarding what is agreeable or disagreeable to his master beareth himself virtuously and uttereth what may be disagreeable but necessary as regimen. O great king, drink thou that which the honest drink and the dishonest shun, even humility, which is like a medicine that is bitter, pungent, burning, unintoxicating, disagreeable, and revolting. And drinking it, O king, regain thou thy sobriety. I always wish Dhritarashtra and his sons affluence and fame. Happen what may unto thee, here I bow to thee (and take my leave). Let the Brahmanas wish me well. O son of Kuru, this is the lesson I carefully inculcate, that the wise should never enrage such as adders as have venom in their very glances!'

SECTION LXIV

"Sakuni said,--'Thou hast, O Yudhishthira, lost much wealth of the Pandavas. If thou hast still anything that thou hast not yet lost to us, O son of Kunti, tell us what it is!'

"Yudhishthira said,--'O son of Suvala, I know that I have untold wealth. But why is it, O Sakuni, that thou askest me of my wealth? Let tens of thousands and millions and millions and tens of millions and hundreds of millions and tens of billions and hundreds of billions and trillions and tens of trillions and hundreds of trillions and tens of quadrillions and hundreds of quadrillions and even more wealth be staked by thee. I have as much. With that wealth, O king, I will play with thee.'"

Vaisampayana said,--"Hearing this, Sakuni, ready with the dice, adopting unfair means, said unto Yudhishthira, 'Lo, I have won!'

"Yudhishthira said,--'I have, O son of Suvala, immeasurable kine and horses and milch cows with calves and goats and sheep in the country extending from the Parnasa to the eastern bank of the Sindu. With this wealth, O king, I will play with thee.'"

Vaisampayana said,--"Hearing this Sakuni, ready with the dice, adopting unfair means, said unto Yudhishthira, 'Lo, I have won!'

"Yudhishthira said,--'I have my city, the country, land, the wealth of all dwelling therein except of the Brahmanas, and all those persons themselves except Brahmanas still remaining to me. With this wealth, O king, I will play with thee.'"

Vaisampayana said,--"Hearing this, Sakuni, ready with the dice, adopting foul means, said unto Yudhishthira, 'Lo! I have won.'

"Yudhishthira said,--'These princes here, O king, who look resplendent in their ornaments and their ear-rings and Nishkas and all the royal ornaments on their persons are now my wealth. With this wealth, O king, I play with thee.'"

Vaisampayana said,--"Hearing this, Sakuni, ready with his dice, adopting foul means, said unto Yudhishthira, 'Lo! I have won them.'

"Yudhishthira said,--'This Nakula here, of mighty arms and leonine neck, of red eyes and endued with youth, is now my one stake. Know that he is my wealth.'

"Sakuni said,--'O king Yudhishthira, prince Nakula is dear to thee. He is already under our subjection. With whom (as stake) wilt thou now play?'"

Vaisampayana said,--"Saying this, Sakuni cast those dice, and said unto Yudhishthira, 'Lo! He hath been won by us.'

"Yudhishthira said,--'This Sahadeva administereth justice. He hath also acquired a reputation for learning in this world. However undeserving he may be to be staked in play, with him as stake I will play, with such a dear object as it, indeed, he were not so!'"

Vaisampayana said,--"Hearing this, Sakuni, ready with the dice, adopting foul means, said unto Yudhishthira, 'Lo! I have won.'

"Sakuni continued,--'O king, the sons of Madri, dear unto thee, have both been won by me. It would seem, however, that Bhimasena and Dhananjaya are regarded very much by thee.'

"Yudhishthira said,--'Wretch! thou actest sinfully in thus seeking to create disunion amongst us who are all of one heart, disregarding morality.'

"Sakuni said,--'One that is intoxicated falleth into a pit (hell) and stayeth there deprived of the power of motion. Thou art, O king, senior to us in age, and possessed of the highest accomplishments. O bull of the Bharata race, I (beg my pardon and) bow to thee. Thou knowest, O Yudhishthira, that gamesters, while excited with play, utter such ravings that they never indulge in the like of them in their waking moments nor even in dream.'

"Yudhishthira said,--'He that taketh us like a boat to the other shore of the sea of battle, he that is ever victorious over foes, the prince who is endued with great activity, he who is the one hero in this world, (is here). With that Falguna as stake, however, undeserving of being made so, I will now play with thee.'"

Vaisampayana said,--"Hearing this, Sakuni, ready with the dice, adopting foul means, said unto Yudhishthira, 'Lo! I have won.'

"Sakuni continued,--'This foremost of all wielders of the bow, this son of Pandu capable of using both his hands with equal activity hath now been won by me. O play now with the wealth that is still left unto thee, even with Bhima thy dear brother, as thy stake, O son of Pandu.'

"Yudhishthira said,--'O king, however undeserving he may be of being made a stake, I will now play with thee by staking Bhimasena, that prince who is our leader, who is the foremost in fight,--even like the wielder of the thunder-bolt--the one enemy of the Danavas,--the high-souled one with leonine neck and arched eye-brows and eyes looking askance, who is incapable of putting up with an insult, who hath no equal in might in the world, who is the foremost of all wielders of the mace, and who grindeth all foes,'"

Vaisampayana said,--"Hearing this, Sakuni, ready with the dice adopting foul means, said unto Yudhishthira. 'Lo! I have won.'

"Sakuni continued,--'Thou hast, O son of Kunti, lost much wealth, horses and elephants and thy brothers as well. Say, if thou hast anything which thou hast not lost.'

"Yudhishthira, said--'I alone, the eldest of all my brothers and dear unto them, am still unwon. Won by thee, I will do what he that is won will have to do.'"

Vaisampayana said,--"Hearing this Sakuni, ready with the dice, adopting foul means, said unto Yudhishthira, 'Lo! I have won.'

"Sakuni continued,--'Thou hast permitted thyself to be won. This is very sinful. There is wealth still left to thee, O king. Therefore, thy having lost thyself is certainly sinful.'"

Vaisampayana continued,--"Having said this, Sakuni, well-skilled at dice, spoke unto all the brave kings present there of his having won, one after another, all the Pandavas. The son of Suvala then, addressing Yudhishthira said,--'O king, there is still one stake dear to thee that is still unwon. Stake thou Krishna, the princess of Panchala. By her, win thyself back.'

"Yudhishthira said,--'With Draupadi as stake, who is neither short nor tall, neither spare nor corpulent, and who is possessed of blue curly locks, I will now play with thee. Possessed of eyes like the leaves of the autumn lotus, and fragrant also as the autumn lotus, equal in beauty unto her (Lakshmi) who delighteth in autumn lotuses, and unto Sree herself in symmetry and every grace she is such a woman as a man may desire for wife in respect of softness of heart, and wealth of beauty and of virtues. Possessed of every accomplishment and compassionate and sweet-speeched, she is such a woman as a man may desire for wife in respect of her fitness for the acquisition of virtue and pleasure and wealth. Retiring to bed last and waking up first, she looketh after all down to the cowherds and the shepherds. Her face too, when covered with sweat, looketh as the lotus or the jasmine. Of slender waist like that of the wasp, of long flowing locks, of red lips, and body without down, is the princess of Panchala. O king, making the slender-waisted Draupadi, who is even such as my stake, I will play with thee, O son of Suvala.'"

Vaisampayana continued,--"When the intelligent king Yudhishthira the just has spoken thus,--'Fie!' 'Fie!' were the words that were uttered by all the aged persons that were in the assembly. And the whole conclave was agitated, and the kings who were present there all gave way to grief. And Bhishma and Drona and Kripa were covered with perspiration. And Vidura holding his head between his hands sat like one that had lost his reason. He sat with face downwards giving way to his reflections and sighing like a snake. But Dhritarashtra glad at heart, asked repeatedly, 'Hath the stake been won?' 'Hath the stake been won?' and could not conceal his emotions. Karna with Dussassana and others laughed aloud, while tears began to flow from the eyes of all other present in the assembly. And the son of Suvala, proud of success and flurried with excitement and repeating. Thou hast one stake, dear to thee, etc. said,--'Lo! I have won' and took up the dice that had been cast.

"Duryodhana said,--'Come, Kshatta, bring hither Draupadi the dear and loved wife of the Pandavas. Let her sweep the chambers, force her thereto, and let the unfortunate one stay where our serving-women are.'

"Vidura said,--'Dost thou not know, O wretch, that by uttering such harsh words thou art tying thyself with cords? Dost thou not understand that thou art hanging on the edge of a precipice? Dost thou not know that being a deer thou provokest so many tigers to rage? Snakes of deadly venom, provoked to ire, are on thy head! Wretch, do not further provoke them lest thou goest to the region of Yama. In my judgement, slavery does not attach to Krishna, in as much as she was staked by the King after he had lost himself and ceased to be his own master. Like the bamboo that beareth fruit only when it is about to die, the son of Dhritarashtra winneth this treasure at play. Intoxicated, he perceiveth not in these his last moments that dice bring about enmity and frightful terrors. No man should utter harsh speeches and pierce the hearts of the others. No man should subjugate his enemies by dice and such other foul means. No one should utter such words as are disapproved by the Vedas and lead to hell and annoy others. Some one uttereth from his lips words that are harsh. Stung by them another burneth day and night. These words pierce the very heart of another. The learned, therefore, should never utter them, pointing them at others. A goat had once swallowed a hook, and when it was pierced with it, the hunter placing the head of the animal on the ground tore its throat frightfully in drawing it out. Therefore, O Duryodhana, swallow not the wealth of the Pandavas. Make them not thy enemies. The sons of Pritha never use words such as these. It is only low men that are like dogs who use harsh words towards all classes of people, viz., those that have retired to the woods, those leading domestic lives, those employed in ascetic devotions and those that are of great learning. Alas! the son of Dhritarashtra knoweth not that dishonesty is one of the frightful doors of hell. Alas! many of the Kurus with Dussasana amongst them have followed him in the path of dishonesty in the matter of this play at dice. Even gourds may sink and stones may float, and boats also may always sink in water, still this foolish king, the son of Dhritarashtra, listeneth not to my words that are even as regimen unto him. Without doubt, he will be the cause of the destruction of the Kurus. When the words of wisdom spoken by friends and which are even as fit regimen are not listened to, but on the other hand temptation is on the increase, a frightful and universal destruction is sure to overtake all the Kurus.'"

SECTION LXVI

Vaisampayana said,--"Intoxicated with pride, the son of Dhritarashtra spake,--'Fie on Kshatta! and casting his eyes upon the Pratikamin in attendance, commanded him, in the midst of all those reverend seniors, saying,--'Go Pratikamin, and bring thou Draupadi hither. Thou hast no fear from the sons of Pandu. It is Vidura alone that raveth in fear. Besides, he never wisheth our prosperity!'"

Vaisampayana continued,--"Thus commanded, the Pratikamin, who was of the Suta caste, hearing the words of the king, proceeded with haste, and entering the abode of the Pandavas, like a dog in a lion's den, approached the queen of the sons of Pandu. And he said,--'Yudhishthira having been intoxicated with dice, Duryodhana, O Draupadi, hath won thee. Come now, therefore, to the abode of Dhritarashtra. I will take thee, O Yajnaseni, and put thee in some menial work.'

"Draupadi said,--'Why, O Pratikamin, dost thou say so? What prince is there who playeth staking his wife? The king was certainly intoxicated with dice. Else, could he not find any other object to stake?'

"The Pratikamin said,--'When he had nothing else to stake, it was then that Ajatasatru, the son of Pandu, staked thee. The king had first staked his brothers, then himself, and then thee, O princess.'

"Draupadi said,--'O son of the Suta race, go, and ask that gambler present in the assembly, whom he hath lost first, himself, or me. Ascertaining this, come hither, and then take me with thee, O son of the Suta race.'"

Vaisampayana continued,--"The messenger coming back to the assembly told all present the words of Draupadi. And he spoke unto Yudhishthira sitting in the midst of the kings, these words,--'Draupadi hath asked thee, Whose lord wert thou at the time thou lost me in play? Didst thou lose thyself first or me?' Yudhishthira, however sat there like one demented and deprived of reason and gave no answer good or ill to the Suta.

"Duryodhana then said,--'Let the princess of Panchala come hither and put her question. Let every one hear in this assembly the words that pass between her and Yudhishthira.'"

Vaisampayana continued,--"The messenger, obedient to the command of Duryodhana, going once again to the palace, himself much distressed, said unto Draupadi,--'O princess, they that are in the assembly are summoning thee. It seemeth that the end of the Kauravas is at hand. When Duryodhana, O princess, is for taking thee before the assembly, this weak-brained king will no longer be able to protect his prosperity.'

"Draupadi said,--'The great ordainer of the world hath, indeed, ordained so. Happiness and misery pay their court to both the wise and unwise. Morality, however, it hath been said, is the one highest object in the world. If cherished, that will certainly dispense blessings to us. Let not that morality now abandon the Kauravas. Going back to those that are present in that assembly, repeat these my words consonant with morality. I am ready to do what those elderly and virtuous persons conversant with morality will definitely tell me.'"

Vaisampayana continued,--"The Suta, hearing these words of Yajnaseni, came back to the assembly and repeated the words of Draupadi. But all sat with faces downwards, uttering not a word, knowing the eagerness and resolution of Dhritarashtra's son.

"Yudhishthira, however, O bull of the Bharata race, hearing of Duryodhana's intentions, sent a trusted messenger unto Draupadi, directing that although she was attired in one piece of cloth with her navel itself exposed, in consequence of her season having come, she should come before her father-in-law weeping bitterly. And that intelligent messenger, O king, having gone to Draupadi's abode with speed, informed her of the intentions of Yudhishthira. The illustrious Pandavas, meanwhile, distressed and sorrowful, and bound by promise, could not settle what they should do. And casting his eyes upon them, king Duryodhana, glad at heart, addressed the Suta and said,--'O Pratikamin, bring her hither. Let the Kauravas answer her question before her face.' The Suta, then, obedient to his commands, but terrified at the (possible) wrath of the daughter of Drupada, disregarding his reputation for intelligence, once again said to those that were in the assembly,--'what shall I say unto Krishna?'

"Duryodhana, hearing this, said,--'O Dussasana, this son of my Suta, of little intelligence, feareth Vrikodara. Therefore, go thou thyself and forcibly bring hither the daughter of Yajnasena. Our enemies at present are dependent on our will. What can they do thee?' Hearing the command of his brother, prince Dussasana rose with blood-red eyes, and entering the abode of those great warriors, spake these words unto the princess, 'Come, come, O Krishna, princess of Panchala, thou hast been won by us. And O thou of eyes large as lotus leaves, come now and accept the Kurus for thy lords. Thou hast been won virtuously, come to the assembly.' At these words, Draupadi, rising up in great affliction, rubbed her pale face with her hands, and distressed she ran to the place where the ladies of Dhritarashtra's household were. At this, Dussasana roaring in anger, ran after her and seized the queen by her locks, so long and blue and wavy. Alas! those locks that had been sprinkled with water sanctified with mantras in the great Rajasuya sacrifice, were now forcibly seized by the son of Dhritarashtra disregarding the prowess of the Pandavas. And Dussasana dragging Krishna of long long locks unto the presence of the assembly--as if she were helpless though having powerful protectors--and pulling at her, made her tremble like the banana plant in a storm. And dragged by him, with body bent, she faintly cried--'Wretch! it ill behoveth thee to take me before the assembly. My season hath come, and I am now clad in one piece of attire.' But Dussasana dragging Draupadi forcibly by her black locks while she was praying piteously unto Krishna and Vishnu who were Narayana and Nara (on earth), said unto her--'Whether thy season hath come or not, whether thou art attired in one piece of cloth or entirely naked, when thou hast been won at dice and made our slave, thou art to live amongst our serving-women as thou pleasest.'"

Vaisampayana continued,--"With hair dishevelled and half her attire loosened, all the while dragged by Dussasana, the modest Krishna consumed with anger, faintly said--'In this assembly are persons conversant with all the branches of learning devoted to the performance of sacrifices and other rites, and all equal unto Indra, persons some of whom are really my superiors and others who deserve to be respected as such. I can not stay before them in this state. O wretch! O thou of cruel deeds, drag me not so. Uncover me not so. The princes (my lords) will not pardon thee, even if thou hast the gods themselves with Indra as thy allies. The illustrious son of Dharma is now bound by the obligations of morality. Morality, however, is subtle. Those only that are possessed of great clearness of vision can ascertain it. In speech even I am unwilling to admit an atom of fault in my lord forgetting his virtues. Thou draggest me who am in my season before these Kuru heroes. This is truly an unworthy act. But no one here rebuketh thee. Assuredly, all these are of the same mind with thee. O fie! Truly hath the virtue of the Bharata gone! Truly also hath the usage of those acquainted with the Kshatriya practice disappeared! Else these Kurus in this assembly would never have looked silently on this act that transgresseth the limits of their practices. Oh! both Drona and Bhishma have lost their energy, and so also hath the high-souled Kshatta, and so also this king. Else, why do these foremost of the Kuru elders look silently on this great crime?'"

Vaisampayana continued,--"Thus did Krishna of slender waist cry in distress in that assembly. And casting a glance upon her enraged lords-- the Pandavas--who were filled with terrible wrath, she inflamed them further with that glance of hers. And they were not so distressed at having been robbed of their kingdom, of their wealth, of their costliest gems, as with that glance of Krishna moved by modesty and anger. And Dussasana, beholding Krishna looking at her helpless lords, dragging her still more forcibly, and addressed her, 'Slave, Slave' and laughed aloud. And at those words Karna became very glad and approved of them by laughing aloud. And Sakuni, the son of Suvala, the Gandhara king, similarly applauded Dussasana. And amongst all those that were in the assembly except these three and Duryodhana, every one was filled with sorrow at beholding Krishna thus dragged in sight of that assembly. And beholding it all, Bhishma said, 'O blessed one, morality is subtle. I therefore am unable to duly decide this point that thou hast put, beholding that on the one hand one that hath no wealth cannot stake the wealth belonging to others, while on the other hand wives are always under the orders and at the disposal of their lords. Yudhishthira can abandon the whole world full of wealth, but he will never sacrifice morality. The son of Pandu hath said--"I am won." Therefore, I am unable to decide this matter. Sakuni hath not his equal among men at dice-play. The son of Kunti still voluntarily staked with him. The illustrious Yudhishthira doth not himself regard that Sakuni hath played with him deceitfully. Therefore, I can not decide this point.'

"Draupadi said,--'The king was summoned to this assembly and though possessing no skill at dice, he was made to play with skilful, wicked, deceitful and desperate gamblers. How can he said then to have staked voluntarily? The chief of the Pandavas was deprived of his senses by wretches of deceitful conduct and unholy instincts, acting together, and then vanquished. He could not understand their tricks, but he hath now done so. Here, in this assembly, there are Kurus who are the lords of both their sons and their daughters-in-law! Let all of them, reflecting well upon my words, duly decide the point that I have put.'"

Vaisampayana continued,--"Unto Krishna who was thus weeping and crying piteously, looking at times upon her helpless lord, Dussasana spake many disagreeable and harsh words. And beholding her who was then in her season thus dragged, and her upper garments loosened, beholding her in that condition which she little deserved, Vrikodara afflicted beyond endurance, his eyes fixed upon Yudhishthira, gave way to wrath.

"Bhima said,--'O Yudhishthira, gamblers have in their houses many women of loose character. They do not yet stake those women having kindness for them even. Whatever wealth and other excellent articles the king of Kasi gave, whatever, gems, animals, wealth, coats of mail and weapons that other kings of the earth gave, our kingdom, thyself and ourselves, have all been won by the foes. At all this my wrath was not excited for thou art our lord. This, however, I regard as a highly improper act--this act of staking Draupadi. This innocent girl deserveth not this treatment. Having obtained the Pandavas as her lords, it is for thee alone that she is being thus persecuted by the low, despicable, cruel, and mean-minded Kauravas. It is for her sake, O king, that my anger falleth on thee. I shall burn those hands of thine. Sahadeva, bring some fire.'

"Arjuna hearing this, said,--'Thou hast never, O Bhimasena, before this uttered such words as these. Assuredly thy high morality hath been destroyed by these cruel foes. Thou shouldst not fulfil the wishes of the enemy. Practise thou the highest morality. Whom doth it behave to transgress his virtuous eldest brother? The king was summoned by the foe, and remembering the usage of the Kshatriyas, he played at dice against his will. That is certainly conducive to our great fame.'

"Bhima said,--'If I had not known, O Dhananjaya, that the king had acted according to Kshatriya usage, then I would have, taking his hands together by sheer force, burnt them in a blazing fire.'"

Vaisampayana continued,--"Beholding the Pandavas thus distressed and the princess of Panchala also thus afflicted, Vikarna the son of Dhritarashtra said--'Ye kings, answer ye the question that hath been asked by Yajnaseni. If we do not judge a matter referred to us, all of us will assuredly have to go to hell without delay. How is that Bhishma and Dhritarashtra, both of whom are the oldest of the Kurus, as also the high-souled Vidura, do not say anything! The son of Bharadwaja who is the preceptor of us, as also Kripa, is here. Why do not these best of regenerate ones answer the question? Let also those other kings assembled here from all directions answer according to their judgment this question, leaving aside all motives of gain and anger. Ye kings, answer ye the question that hath been asked by this blessed daughter of king Drupada, and declare after reflection on which side each of ye is.' Thus did Vikarna repeatedly appeal to those that were in that assembly. But those kings answered him not one word, good or ill. And Vikarna having repeatedly appealed to all the kings began to rub his hands and sigh like a snake. And at last the prince said--'Ye kings of the earth, ye Kauravas, whether ye answer this question or not, I will say what I regard as just and proper. Ye foremost of men, it hath been said that hunting, drinking, gambling, and too much enjoyment of women, are the four vices of kings. The man, that is addicted to these, liveth forsaking virtue. And people do not regard the acts done by a person who is thus improperly engaged, as of any authority. This son of Pandu, while deeply engaged in one of these vicious acts, urged thereto by deceitful gamblers, made Draupadi a stake. The innocent Draupadi is, besides, the common wife of all the sons of Pandu. And the king, having first lost himself offered her as a stake. And Suvala himself desirous of a stake, indeed prevailed upon the king to stake this Krishna. Reflecting upon all these circumstances, I regard Draupadi as not won.'

"Hearing these words, a loud uproar rose from among those present in that assembly. And they all applauded Vikarna and censured the son of Suvala. And at that sound, the son of Radha, deprived of his senses by anger, waving his well-shaped arms, said these words,--'O Vikarna, many opposite and inconsistent conditions are noticeable in this assembly. Like fire produced from a faggot, consuming the faggot itself, this thy ire will consume thee. These personages here, though urged by Krishna, have not uttered a word. They all regard the daughter of Drupada to have been properly won. Thou alone, O son of Dhritarashtra in consequence of thy immature years, art bursting with wrath, for though but a boy thou speakest in the assembly as if thou wert old. O younger brother of Duryodhana, thou dost not know what morality truly is, for thou sayest like a fool that this Krishna who hath been (justly) won as not won at all. O son of Dhritarashtra, how dost thou regard Krishna as not won, when the eldest of the Pandavas before this assembly staked all his possessions? O bull of the Bharata race, Draupadi is included in all the possessions (of Yudhishthira). Therefore, why regardest thou Krishna who hath been justly won as not won? Draupadi had been mentioned (by Suvala) and approved of as a stake by the Pandavas. For what reason then dost thou yet regard her as not won? Or, if thou thinkest that bringing her hither attired in a single piece of cloth, is an action of impropriety, listen to certain excellent reasons I will give. O son of the Kuru race, the gods have ordained only one husband for one woman. This Draupadi, however, hath many husbands. Therefore, certain it is that she is an unchaste woman. To bring her, therefore, into this assembly attired though she be in one piece of cloth-- even to uncover her is not at all an act that may cause surprise. Whatever wealth the Pandavas had--she herself and these Pandavas themselves,--have all been justly won by the son of Suvala. O Dussasana, this Vikarna speaking words of (apparent) wisdom is but a boy. Take off the robes of the Pandavas as also the attire of Draupadi.' Hearing these words the Pandavas, O Bharata, took of their upper garments and throwing them down sat in that assembly. Then Dussasana, O king, forcibly seizing Draupadi's attire before the eyes of all, began to drag it off her person."

Vaisampayana continued,--"When the attire of Draupadi was being thus dragged, the thought of Hari, (And she herself cried aloud, saying), 'O Govinda, O thou who dwellest in Dwaraka, O Krishna, O thou who art fond of cow-herdesses (of Vrindavana). O Kesava, seest thou not that the Kauravas are humiliating me. O Lord, O husband of Lakshmi, O Lord of Vraja (Vrindavana), O destroyer of all afflictions, O Janarddana, rescue me who am sinking in the Kaurava Ocean. O Krishna, O Krishna, O thou great yogin, thou soul of the universe, Thou creator of all things, O Govinda, save me who am distressed,--who am losing my senses in the midst of the Kurus.' Thus did that afflicted lady resplendent still in her beauty, O king covering her face cried aloud, thinking of Krishna, of Hari, of the lord of the three worlds. Hearing the words of Draupadi, Krishna was deeply moved. And leaving his seat, the benevolent one from compassion, arrived there on foot. And while Yajnaseni was crying aloud to Krishna, also called Vishnu and Hari and Nara for protection, the illustrious Dharma, remaining unseen, covered her with excellent clothes of many hues. And, O monarch as the attire of Draupadi was being dragged, after one was taken off, another of the same kind, appeared covering her. And thus did it continue till many clothes were seen. And, O exalted one, owing to the protection of Dharma, hundreds upon hundreds of robes of many hues came off Draupadi's person. And there arose then a deep uproar of many many voices. And the kings present in that assembly beholding that most extraordinary of all sights in the world, began to applaud Draupadi and censure the son of Dhritarashtra. And Bhima then, squeezing his hands, with lips quivering in rage, swore in the midst of all those kings a terrible oath in a loud voice.

"And Bhima said,--'Hear these words of mine, ye Kshatriyas of the world. Words such as these were never before uttered by other men, nor will anybody in the future ever utter them. Ye lords of earth, if having spoken these words I do not accomplish them hereafter, let me not obtain the region of my deceased ancestors. Tearing open in battle, by sheer force, the breast of this wretch, this wicked-minded scoundrel of the Bharata race, if I do not drink his life-blood, let me not obtain the region of my ancestors.'"

Vaisampayana continued,--"Hearing these terrible words of Bhima that made the down of the auditors to stand on end, everybody present there applauded him and censured the son of Dhritarashtra. And when a mass of clothes had been gathered in that assembly, all dragged from the person of Draupadi, Dussasana, tired and ashamed, sat down. And beholding the sons of Kunti in that state, the persons--those gods among men--that were in that assembly all uttered the word 'Fie!' (on the son of Dhritarashtra). And the united voices of all became so loud that they made the down of anybody who heard them stand on end. And all the honest men that were in that assembly began to say,--'Alas! the Kauravas answer not the question that hath been put to them by Draupadi.' And all censuring Dhritarashtra together, made a loud clamour. Then Vidura, that master of the science of morality, waving his hands and silencing every one, spake these words;-- 'Ye that are in this assembly, Draupadi having put her question is weeping helplessly. Ye are not answering her. Virtue and morality are being persecuted by such conduct. An afflicted person approacheth an assembly of good men, like one that is being consumed by fire. They that are in the assembly quench that fire and cool him by means of truth and morality. The afflicted person asketh the assembly about his rights, as sanctioned by morality. They that are in the assembly should, unmoved by interest and anger, answer the question. Ye kings, Vikarna hath answered the question, according to his own knowledge and judgment. Ye should also answer it as ye think proper. Knowing the rules of morality, and having attended an assembly, he that doth not answer a query that is put, incurreth half the demerit that attacheth to a lie. He, on the other hand, who, knowing the rules of morality and having joined an assembly answereth falsely, assuredly incurreth the sin of a lie. The learned quote as an example in this connection the old history of Prahlada and the son of Angirasa.

"'There was of old a chief of the Daityas of the name Prahlada. He had a son named Virochana. And Virochana, for the sake of obtaining a bride, quarrelled with Sudhanwan, the son of Angiras. It hath been heard by us that they mutually wagered their lives, saying--"I am superior,"--"I am superior,"--for the sake of obtaining a bride. And after they had thus quarrelled with each other, they both made Prahlada the arbitrator to decide between them. And they asked him, saying;--"Who amongst us is superior (to the other)? Answer this question. Speak not falsely." Frightened at this quarrel, Prahlada cast his eyes upon Sudhanwan. And Sudhanwan in rage, burning like unto the mace of Yama, told him,--"If thou answerest falsely, or dost not answer at all thy head will then be split into a hundred pieces by the wielder of the thunderbolt with that bolt of his."--Thus addressed by Sudhanwan, the Daitya, trembling like a leaf of the fig tree, went to Kasyapa of great energy, for taking counsel with him. And Prahlada said,--"Thou art, O illustrious and exalted one, fully conversant with the rules of morality that should guide both the gods and the Asuras and the Brahmanas as well. Here, however, is a situation of great difficulty in respect of duty. Tell me, I ask thee, what regions are obtainable by them who upon being asked a question, answer it not, or answer it falsely." Kasyapa thus asked answered.--"He that knoweth, but answereth not a question from temptation, anger or fear, casteth upon himself a thousand nooses of Varuna. And the person who, cited as a witness with respect to any matter of ocular or auricular knowledge, speaketh carelessly, casteth a thousand nooses of Varuna upon his own person. On the completion of one full year, one such noose is loosened. Therefore, he that knoweth, should speak the truth without concealment. If virtue, pierced by sin, repaireth to an assembly (for aid), it is the duty of every body in the assembly to take off the dart, otherwise they themselves would be pierced with it. In an assembly where a truly censurable act is not rebuked, half the demerit of that act attacheth to the head of that assembly, a fourth to the person acting censurably and a fourth unto those others that are there. In that assembly, on the other hand, when he that deserveth censure is rebuked, the head of the assembly becometh freed from all sins, and the other members also incur none. It is only the perpetrator himself of the act that becometh responsible for it. O Prahlada, they who answer falsely those that ask them about morality destroy the meritorious acts of their seven upper and seven lower generations. The grief of one who hath lost all his wealth, of one who hath lost a son, of one who is in debt, of one who is separated from his companions, of a woman who hath lost her husband, of one that hath lost his all in consequence of the king's demand, of a woman who is sterile, of one who hath been devoured by a tiger (during his last struggles in the tiger's claws), of one who is a co-wife, and of one who hath been deprived of his property by false witnesses, have been said by the gods to be uniform in degree. These different sorts of grief are his who speaketh false. A person becometh a witness in consequence of his having seen, heard, and understood a thing. Therefore, a witness should always tell the truth. A truth-telling witness never loseth his religious merits and earthly possessions also." Hearing these words of Kasyapa, Prahlada told his son, "Sudhanwan is superior to thee, as indeed, (his father) Angiras is superior to me. The mother also of Sudhanwan is superior to thy mother.

Therefore, O Virochana, this Sudhanwan is now the lord of the life." At these words of Prahlada, Sudhanwan said, "Since unmoved by affection for thy child, thou hast adhered to virtue, I command, let this son of thine live for a hundred years.'"

"Vidura continued,--'Let all the persons, therefore, present in this assembly hearing these high truths of morality, reflect upon what should be the answer to the question asked by Draupadi.'"

Vaisampayana continued,--"The kings that were there hearing these words of Vidura, answered not a word, yet Karna alone spoke unto Dussasana, telling him. Take away this serving-woman Krishna into the inner apartments. And thereupon Dussasana began to drag before all the spectators the helpless and modest Draupadi, trembling and crying piteously unto the Pandavas her lords.

SECTION LXVIII

"Draupadi said,--'Wait a little, thou worst of men, thou wicked-minded Dussasana. I have an act to perform--a high duty that hath not been performed by me yet. Dragged forcibly by this wretch's strong arms, I was deprived of my senses. I salute these reverend seniors in this assembly of the Kurus. That I could not do this before cannot be my fault.'"

Vaisampayana said,--"Dragged with greater force than before, the afflicted and helpless Draupadi, undeserving of such treatment, falling down upon the ground, thus wept in that assembly of the Kurus,--

"'Alas, only once before, on the occasion of the Swayamvara, I was beheld by the assembled kings in the amphitheatre, and never even once beheld afterwards. I am to-day brought before this assembly. She whom even the winds and the sun had seen never before in her palace is to-day before this assembly and exposed to the gaze of the crowd. Alas, she whom the sons of Pandu could not, while in her palace, suffer to be touched even by the wind, is to-day suffered by the Pandavas to be seized and dragged by this wretch. Alas, these Kauravas also suffer their daughter-in-law, so unworthy of such treatment, to be thus afflicted before them. It seemeth that the times are out of joint. What can be more distressing to me, than that though high-born and chaste, I should yet be compelled to enter this public court? Where is that virtue for which these kings were noted? It hath been heard that the kings of ancient days never brought their wedded wives into the public court. Alas, that eternal usage hath disappeared from among the Kauravas. Else, how is it that the chaste wife of the Pandavas, the sister of Prishata's son, the friend of Vasudeva, is brought before this assembly? Ye Kauravas, I am the wedded wife of king Yudhishthira the just, hailing from the same dynasty to which the King belonged. Tell me now if I am a serving-maid or otherwise. I will cheerfully accept your answer. This mean wretch, this destroyer of the name of the Kurus, is afflicting me hard. Ye Kauravas, I cannot bear it any longer. Ye kings, I desire ye to answer whether ye regard me as won or unwon. I will accept your verdict whatever it be.'

"Hearing these words, Bhishma answered, 'I have already said, O blessed one that the course of morality is subtle. Even the illustrious wise in this world fail to understand it always. What in this world a strong man calls morality is regarded as such by others, however otherwise it may really be; but what a weak man calls morality is scarcely regarded as such even if it be the highest morality. From the importance of the issue involved, from its intricacy and subtlety, I am unable to answer with certitude the question thou hast asked. However, it is certain that as all the Kurus have become the slaves of covetousness and folly, the destruction of this our race will happen on no distant date. O blessed one, the family into which thou hast been admitted as a daughter-in-law, is such that those who are born in it, however much they might be afflicted by calamities, never deviate from the paths of virtue and morality. O Princess of Panchala, this conduct of thine also, viz. that though sunk in distress, thou still easiest thy eyes on virtue and morality, is assuredly worthy of thee. These persons, Drona and others, of mature years and conversant with morality, sit heads downwards like men that are dead, with bodies from which life hath departed. It seemeth to me, however, that Yudhishthira is an authority on this question. It behoveth him to declare whether thou art won or not won.'"

SECTION LXIX

Vaisampayana said,--"The kings present in that assembly, from fear of Duryodhana, uttered not a word, good or ill, although they beheld Draupadi crying piteously in affliction like a female osprey, and repeatedly appealing to them. And the son of Dhritarashtra beholding those kings and sons and grand sons of kings all remaining silent, smiled a little, and addressing the daughter of the king of Panchala, said,--'O Yajnaseni, the question thou hast put dependeth on thy husbands--on Bhima of mighty strength, on Arjuna, on Nakula, on Sahadeva. Let them answer thy question. O Panchali, let them for thy sake declare in the midst of these respectable men that Yudhishthira is not their lord, let them thereby make king Yudhishthira the just a liar. Thou shalt then be freed from the condition of slavery. Let the illustrious son of Dharma, always adhering to virtue, who is even like Indra, himself declare whether he is not thy lord. At his words, accept thou the Pandavas or ourselves without delay. Indeed, all the Kauravas present in this assembly are floating in the ocean of thy distress. Endued with magnanimity, they are unable to answer thy question, looking at thy unfortunate husbands.'"

Vaisampayana continued,--"Hearing these words of the Kuru king, all who were present in the assembly loudly applauded them. And shouting approvingly, they made signs unto one another by motions of their eyes and lips. And amongst some that were there, sounds of distress such as 'O!' and 'Alas!' were heard. And at these words of Duryodhana, so delightful (to his partisans), the Kauravas present in that assembly became exceedingly glad. And the kings, with faces turned sideways, looked upon Yudhishthira conversant with the rules of morality, curious to hear what he would say. And every one present in that assembly became curious to hear what Arjuna, the son of Pandu never defeated in battle, and what Bhimasena, and what the twins also would say. And when that busy hum of many voices became still, Bhimasena, waving his strong and well-formed arms smeared with sandalpaste spake these words,--'If this high-souled king Yudhishthira the just, who is our eldest brother, had not been our lord, we would never have forgiven the Kuru race (for all this). He is the lord of all our religious and ascetic merits, the lord of even our lives. If he regardeth himself as won, we too have all been won. If this were not so, who is there amongst creatures touching the earth with their feet and mortal, that would escape from me with his life after having touched those locks of the princess of Panchala? Behold these mighty, well-formed arms of mine, even like maces of iron. Having once come within them, even he of a hundred sacrifices is incapable of effecting an escape. Bound by the ties of virtue and the reverence that is due to our eldest brother, and repeatedly urged by Arjuna to remain silent, I am not doing anything terrible. If however, I am once commanded by king Yudhishthira the just, I would slay these wretched sons of Dhritarashtra, making slaps do the work of swords, like a lion slaying a number of little animals.'"

Vaisampayana continued,--"Unto Bhima who had spoken these words Bhishma and Drona and Vidura said, 'Forbear, O Bhima. Everything is possible with thee.'

SECTION LXX

"Karna said,--'Of all the persons in the assembly, three, viz., Bhishma, Vidura, and the preceptor of the Kurus (Drona) appear to be independent; for they always speak of their master as wicked, always censure him, and never wish for his prosperity. O excellent one, the slave, the son, and the wife are always dependent. They cannot earn wealth, for whatever they earn belongeth to their master. Thou art the wife of a slave incapable of possessing anything on his own account. Repair now to the inner apartments of king Dhritarashtra and serve the king's relatives. We direct that that is now thy proper business. And, O princess, all the sons of Dhritarashtra and not the sons of Pritha are now thy masters. O handsome one, select thou another husband now,--one who will not make thee a slave by gambling. It is well-known that women, espccially that are slaves, are not censurable if they proceed with freedom in electing husbands. Therefore let it be done by thee. Nakula hath been won, as also Bhimasena, and Yudhishthira also, and Sahadeva, and Arjuna. And, O Yajnaseni, thou art now a slave. Thy husbands that are slaves cannot continue to be thy lords any longer. Alas, doth not the son of Pritha regards life, prowess and manhood as of no use that he offereth this daughter of Drupada, the king of Panchala, in the presence of all this assembly, as a stake at dice?'"

Vaisampayana continued,--"Hearing these words, the wrathful Bhima breathed hard, a very picture of woe. Obedient to the king and bound by the tie of virtue and duty, burning everything with his eyes inflamed by anger, he said,--'O king, I cannot be angry at these words of this son of a Suta, for we have truly entered the state of servitude. But O king, could our enemies have said so unto me, it thou hadst not played staking this princess?'"

Vaisampayana continued,--"Hearing these words of Bhimasena king Duryodhana addressed Yudhishthira who was silent and deprived of his senses, saying,-- 'O king, both Bhima and Arjuna, and the twins also, are under thy sway. Answer thou the question (that hath been asked by Draupadi). Say, whether thou regardest Krishna as unwon.' And having spoken thus unto the son of Kunti, Duryodhana desirous of encouraging the son of Radha and insulting Bhima, quickly uncovered his left thigh that was like unto the stem of a plantain tree or the trunk of an elephant and which was graced with every auspicious sign and endued with the strength of thunder, and showed it to Draupadi in her very sight. And beholding this, Bhimasena expanding his red eyes, said unto Duryodhana in the midst of all those kings and as if piercing them (with his dart-like words),--'Let not Vrikodara attain to the regions, obtained by his ancestors, if he doth not break that thigh of thine in the great conflict.' And sparkles of fire began to be emitted from every organ of sense of Bhima filled with wrath, like those that come out of every crack and orifice in the body of a blazing tree.

"Vidura then, addressing everybody, said,--'Ye kings of Pratipa's race, behold the great danger that ariseth from Bhimasena. Know ye for certain that this great calamity that threatens to overtake the Bharatas hath been sent by Destiny itself. The sons of Dhritarashtra have, indeed, gambled disregarding every proper consideration. They are even now disputing in this assembly about a lady (of the royal household). The prosperity of our kingdom is at an end. Alas, the Kauravas are even now engaged in sinful consultations. Ye Kauravas, take to your heart this high precept that I declare. If virtue is persecuted, the whole assembly becometh polluted. If Yudhishthira had staked her before he was himself won, he would certainly have been regarded as her master. If, however a person staketh anything at a time when he himself is incapable of holding any wealth, to win it is very like obtaining wealth in a dream. Listening to the words of the king of Gandhara, fall ye not off from this undoubted truth.'

"Duryodhana, hearing Vidura thus speak, said,--'I am willing to abide by the words of Bhima, of Arjuna and of the twins. Let them say that Yudhishthira is not their master. Yajnaseni will then be freed from her state of bondage.'

"Arjuna at this, said,--'This illustrious son of Kunti, king Yudhishthira the just, was certainly our master before he began to play. But having lost himself, let all the Kauravas judge whose master he could be after that.'"

Vaisampayana continued,--"Just then, a jackal began to cry loudly in the homa-chamber of king Dhritarashtra's palace. And, O king, unto the jackal that howled so, the asses began to bray responsively. And terrible birds also, from all sides, began to answer with their cries. And Vidura conversant with everything and the daughter of Suvala, both understood the meaning of those terrible sounds. And Bhishma and Drona and the learned Gautama loudly cried,--Swashti! Swashti! [Footnote 1] Then Gandhari and the learned Vidura beholding that frightful omen, represented everything, in great affliction, unto the king. And the king (Dhritarashtra) thereupon said,--

[Footnote 1. A word of benediction, similar to 'Amen.']

"'Thou wicked-minded Duryodhana, thou wretch, destruction hath all ready overtaken thee when thou insultest in language such as this the wife of these bulls among the Kurus, especially their wedded wife Draupadi.' And having spoken those words, the wise Dhritarashtra endued with knowledge, reflecting with the aid of his wisdom and desirous of saving his relatives and friends from destruction, began to console Krishna, the princess of Panchala, and addressing her, the monarch said,--'Ask of me any boon, O princess of Panchala, that thou desirest. Chaste and devoted to virtue, thou art the first of all my daughters-in-law.'

"Draupadi said,--'O bull of the Bharata race, if thou will grant me a boon, I ask the handsome Yudhishthira, obedient to every duty, be freed from slavery. Let not unthinking children call my child Prativindhya endued with great energy of mind as the son of a slave. Having been a prince, so superior to all men, and nurtured by kings it is not proper that he should be called the child of a slave.'

"Dhritarashtra said unto her,--'O auspicious one, let it be as thou sayest. O excellent one, ask thou another boon, for I will give it. My heart inclineth to give thee a second boon. Thou dost not deserve only one boon.'

"Draupadi said,--'I ask, O king, that Bhimasena and Dhananjaya and the twins also, with their cars and bows, freed from bondage, regain their liberty.'

"Dhritarashtra said,--'O blessed daughter, let it be as thou desirest. Ask thou a third boon, for thou hast not been sufficiently honoured with two boons. Virtuous in thy behaviour, thou art the foremost of all my daughters-in-law.'

"Draupadi said,--'O best of kings, O illustrious one, covetousness always bringeth about loss of virtue. I do not deserve a third boon. Therefore I dare not ask any. O king of kings, it hath been said that a Vaisya may ask one boon; a Kshatriya lady, two boons; a Kshatriya male, three, and a Brahmana, a hundred. O king, these my husbands freed from the wretched state of bondage, will be able to achieve prosperity by their own virtuous acts!'

SECTION LXXI

"Karna said,--'We have never heard of such an act (as this one of Draupadi), performed by any of the women noted in this world for their beauty. When the sons of both Pandu and Dhritarashtra were excited with wrath, this Draupadi became unto the sons of Pandu as their salvation. Indeed the princess of Panchala, becoming as a boat unto the sons of Pandu who were sinking in a boatless ocean of distress, hath brought them in safety to the shore.'"

Vaisampayana continued,--"Hearing these words of Karna in the midst of the Kurus,--viz., that the sons of Pandu were saved by their wife,--the angry Bhimasena in great affliction said (unto Arjuna),--'O Dhananjaya, it hath been said by Devala three lights reside in every person, viz., offspring, acts and learning, for from these three hath sprung creation. When life becometh extinct and the body becometh impure and is cast off by relatives, these three become of service to every person. But the light that is in us hath been dimmed by this act of insult to our wife. How, O Arjuna, can a son born from this insulted wife of ours prove serviceable to us?'

"Arjuna replied,--'Superior persons, O Bharata, never prate about the harsh words that may or may not be uttered by inferior men. Persons that have earned respect for themselves, even if they are able to retaliate, remember not the acts of hostility done by their enemies, but, on the other hand, treasure up only their good deeds.'

"Bhima said,--'Shall I, O king, slay, without loss of time all these foes assembled together, even here, or shall I destroy them, O Bharata, by the roots, outside this palace? Or, what need is there of words or of command? I shall slay all these even now, and rule thou the whole earth, O king, without a rival.' And saying this, Bhima with his younger brothers, like a lion in the midst of a herd of inferior animals, repeatedly cast his angry glances around. But Arjuna, however, of white deeds, with appealing looks began to pacify his elder brother. And the mighty-armed hero endued with great prowess began to burn with the fire of his wrath. And, O king, this fire began to issue out of Vrikodara's ears and other senses with smoke and sparks and flames. And his face became terrible to behold in consequence of his furrowed brows like those of Yama himself at the time of the universal destruction. Then Yudhishthira forbade the mighty hero, embracing him with his arms and telling him 'Be not so. Stay in silence and peace.' And having pacified the mighty-armed one with eyes red in wrath, the king approached his uncle Dhritarashtra, with hands joined in entreaty.

SECTION LXXII

"Yudhishthira said,--'O king, thou art our master. Command us as to what we shall do. O Bharata, we desire to remain always in obedience to thee.'

"Dhritarashtra replied.--'O Ajatasatru, blest be thou. Go thou in peace and safety. Commanded by me, go, rule thy own kingdom with thy wealth. And, O child, take to heart this command of an old man, this wholesome advice that I give, and which is even a nutritive regimen. O Yudhishthira, O child, thou knowest the subtle path of morality. Possessed of great wisdom, thou art also humble, and thou waitest also upon the old. Where there is intelligence, there is forbearance. Therefore, O Bharata, follow thou counsels of peace. The axe falleth upon wood, not upon stone. (Thou art open to advice, not Duryodhana). They are the best of men that remember not the acts of hostility of their foes; that behold only the merits, not the faults, of their enemies; and that never enter into hostilities themselves. They that are good remember only the good deeds of their foes and not the hostile acts their foes might have done unto them. The good, besides, do good unto others without expectation of any good, in return. O Yudhishthira, it is only the worst of men that utter harsh words in quarrelling; while they that are indifferent reply to such when spoken by others. But they that are good and wise never think of or recapitulate such harsh words, little caring whether these may or may not have been uttered by their foes. They that are good, having regard to the state of their own feelings, can understand the feelings of others, and therefore remember only the good deeds and not the acts of hostility of their foes. Thou hast acted even as good men of prepossessing countenance do, who transgress not the limits of virtue, wealth, pleasure and salvation. O child, remember not the harsh words of Duryodhana. Look at thy mother Gandhari and myself also, if thou desirest to remember only what is good. O Bharata, look at me, who am thy father unto you and am old and blind, and still alive. It was for seeing our friends and examining also the strength and weakness of my children, that I had, from motives of policy, suffered this match at dice to proceed. O king those amongst the Kurus that have thee for their ruler, and the intelligent Vidura conversant with every branch of learning for their counsellor, have, indeed, nothing to grieve for. In thee is virtue, in Arjuna is patience, in Bhimasena is prowess, and the twins, those foremost of men, is pure reverence for superiors. Blest be thou, O Ajatasatru. Return to Khandavaprastha, and let there be brotherly love between thee and thy cousins. Let thy heart also be ever fixed on virtue.'"

Vaisampayana continued,--"That foremost of the Bharatas--king Yudhishthira the just--then, thus addressed by his uncle, having gone through every ceremony of politeness, set out with his brothers for Khandavaprastha. And accompanied by Draupadi and ascending their cars which were all of the hue of the clouds, with cheerful hearts they all set out for that best of cities called Indraprastha."

SECTION LXXIII

Janamejaya said,--"How did the sons of Dhritarashtra feel, when they came to know that the Pandavas had, with Dhritarashtra's leave, left Hastinapore with all their wealth and jewels?"

Vaisampayana said,--"O king, learning that the Pandavas had been commanded by the wise Dhritarashtra to return to their capital, Dussasana went without loss of time unto his brother. And, O bull of the Bharata race, having arrived before Duryodhana with his counsellor, the prince, afflicted with grief, began to say,--'Ye mighty warriors, that which we had won after so much trouble, the old man (our father) hath thrown away. Know ye that he hath made over the whole of that wealth to the foes.' At these words, Duryodhana and Karna and Sakuni, the son of Suvala, all of whom were guided by vanity, united together, and desirous of counteracting the sons of Pandu, approaching in haste saw privately the wise king Dhritarashtra--the son of Vichitravirya and spake unto him these pleasing and artful words. Duryodhana said,--

"'Hast thou not heard, O king, what the learned Vrihaspati the preceptor of the celestials, said in course of counselling Sakra about mortals and politics? Even these, O slayer of foes, were the words of Vrihaspati, "Those enemies that always do wrong by stratagem or force, should be slain by every means." If, therefore, with the wealth of the Pandavas, we gratify the kings of the earth and then fight with the sons of Pandu, what reverses can overtake us? When one hath placed on the neck and back of venomous snakes full of wrath for encompassing his destruction, is it possible for him to take them off? Equipped with weapon and seated on their cars, the angry sons of Pandu like wrathful and venomous snakes will assuredly annihilate us, O father. Even now Arjuna proceedeth, encased in mail and furnished with his couple of quivers, frequently taking up the Gandiva and breathing hard and casting angry glances around. It hath (also) been heard by us that Vrikodara, hastily ordering his car to be made ready and riding on it, is proceeding along, frequently whirling his heavy mace. Nakula also is going along, with the sword in his grasp and the semi-circular shield in his hand. And Sahadeva and the king (Yudhishthira) have made signs clearly testifying to their intentions. Having ascended their cars that are full of all kinds of arms, they are whipping their horses (for going to Khandava soon) and assembling their forces. Persecuted thus by us they are incapable of forgiving us those injuries. Who is there among them that will forgive that insult to Draupadi? Blest be thou. We will again gamble with the son of Pandu for sending them to exile. O bull among men, we are competent to bring them thus under our sway. Dressed in skins, either we or they defeated at dice, shall repair to the woods for twelve years. The thirteenth year shall have to be spent in some inhabited country unrecognised; and, if recognised, an exile for another twelve years shall be the consequence. Either we or they shall live so. Let the play begin, casting the dice, let the sons of Pandu once more play. O bull of the Bharata race, O king, even this is our highest duty. This Sakuni knoweth well the whole science of dice. Even if they succeed in observing this vow for thirteen years, we shall be in the meantime firmly rooted in the kingdom and making alliances, assemble a vast invincible host and keep them content, so that we shall, O king, defeat the sons of Pandu if they reappear. Let this plan recommend itself to thee, O slayer of foes.'

"Dhritarashtra said,--'Bring back the Pandavas then, indeed, even if they have gone a great way. Let them come at once again to cast dice.'"

Vaisampayana continued,--"Then Drona, Somadatta and Valhika, Gautama, Vidura, the son of Drona, and the mighty son of Dhritarashtra by his Vaisya wife, Bhurisravas, and Bhishma, and that mighty warrior Vikarna,-- all said, 'Let not the play commence. Let there be peace.' But Dhritarashtra, partial to his sons, disregarding the counsels of all his wise friends and relatives, summoned the sons of Pandu."

SECTION LXXIV

Vaisampayana said,--"O monarch, it was then that the virtuous Gandhari, afflicted with grief on account of her affection for her sons, addressed king Dhritarashtra and said, 'When Duryodhana was born, Vidura of great intelligence had said, "It is well to send this disgrace of the race to the other world. He cried repeatedly and dissonantly like a jackal. It is certain he will prove the destruction of our race." Take this to heart, O king of the Kurus. O Bharata, sink not, for thy own fault, into an ocean of calamity. O lord, accord not thy approbation to the counsels of the wicked ones of immature years. Be not thou the cause of the terrible destruction of this race. Who is there that will break an embankment which hath been completed, or re-kindle a conflagration which hath been extinguished? O bull of the Bharata race, who is there that will provoke the peaceful sons of Pritha? Thou rememberest, O Ajamida, everything, but still I will call thy attention to this. The scriptures can never control the wicked-minded for good or evil. And, O king, a person of immature understanding will never act as one of mature years. Let thy sons follow thee as their leader. Let them not be separated from thee for ever (by losing their lives). Therefore, at my word, O king, abandon this wretch of our race. Thou couldst not, O king, from parental affection, do it before. Know that the time hath come for the destruction of race through him. Err not, O king. Let thy mind, guided by counsels of peace, virtue, and true policy, be what it naturally is. That prosperity which is acquired by the aid of wicked acts, is soon destroyed; while that which is won by mild means taketh root and descendeth from generation to generation.'

"The king, thus addressed by Gandhari who pointed out to him in such language the path of virtue, replied unto her, saying,--'If the destruction of our race is come, let it take place freely. I am ill able to prevent it. Let it be as they (these my sons) desire. Let the Pandavas return. And let my sons again gamble with the sons of Pandu.'"

SECTION LXXV

Vaisampayana said,--"The royal messenger, agreeably to the commands of the intelligent king Dhritarashtra, coming upon Yudhishthira, the son of Pritha who had by that time gone a great way, addressed the monarch and said,--'Even these are the words of thy father-like uncle, O Bharata, spoken unto thee, "The assembly is ready. O son of Pandu, O king Yudhisthira, come and cast the dice."'

"Yudhishthira said,--'Creatures obtain fruits good and ill according to the dispensation of the Ordainer of the creation. Those fruits are inevitable whether I play or not. This is a summons to dice; it is, besides the command of the old king. Although I know that it will prove destructive to me, yet I cannot refuse.'"

Vaisampayana continued,--"Although (a living) animal made of gold was an impossibility, yet Rama suffered himself to be tempted by a (golden) deer. Indeed, the minds of men over whom calamities hang, became deranged and out of order. Yudhishthira, therefore, having said these words, retraced his steps along with his brothers. And knowing full well the deception practised by Sakuni, the son of Pritha came back to sit at dice with him again. These mighty warriors again entered that assembly, afflicting the hearts of all their friends. And compelled by Fate they once more sat down at ease for gambling for the destruction of themselves.

"Sakuni then said,--'The old king hath given ye back all your wealth. That is well. But, O bull of the Bharata race, listen to me, there is a stake of great value. Either defeated by ye at dice, dressed in deer skins we shall enter the great forest and live there for twelve years passing the whole of the thirteenth year in some inhabited region, unrecognised, and if recognised return to an exile of another twelve years; or vanquished by us, dressed in deer skins ye shall, with Krishna, live for twelve years in the woods passing the whole of the thirteenth year unrecognised, in some inhabited region. If recognised, an exile of another twelve years is to be the consequence. On the expiry of the thirteenth year, each is to have his kingdom surrendered by the other. O Yudhishthira, with this resolution, play with us, O Bharata, casting the dice.'

"At these words, they that were in that assembly, raising up their arms said in great anxiety of mind, and from the strength of their feelings these words,--'Alas, fie on the friends of Duryodhana that they do not apprise him of his great danger. Whether he, O bull among the Bharatas, (Dhritarashtra) understandeth or not, of his own sense, it is thy duty to tell him plainly.'"

Vaisampayana continued,--"King Yudhishthira, even hearing these various remarks, from shame and a sense of virtue again sat at dice. And though possessed of great intelligence and fully knowing the consequences, he again began to play, as if knowing that the destruction of the Kurus was at hand.

"And Yudhishthira said,--'How can, O Sakuni, a king like me, always observant of the uses of his own order, refuse, when summoned to dice? Therefore I play with thee.'

"Sakuni answered,--'We have many kine and horses, and milch cows, and an infinite number of goats and sheep; and elephants and treasures and gold and slaves both male and female. All these were staked by us before but now let this be our one stake, viz., exile into the woods,--being defeated either ye or we will dwell in the woods (for twelve years) and the thirteenth year, unrecognised, in some inhabited place. Ye bulls among men, with this determination, will we play.'

"O Bharata, this proposal about a stay in the woods was uttered but once. The son of Pritha, however, accepted it and Sakuni took up the dice. And casting them he said unto Yudhishthira,--'Lo, I have won.'"

SECTION LXXVI

Vaisampayana said,--"Then the vanquished sons of Pritha prepared for their exile into the woods. And they, one after another, in due order, casting off their royal robes, attired themselves in deer-skins. And Dussasana, beholding those chastisers of foes, dressed in deer-skins and deprived of their kingdom and ready to go into exile, exclaimed 'The absolute sovereignty of the illustrious king Duryodhana hath commenced. The sons of Pandu have been vanquished, and plunged into great affliction. Now have we attained the goal either by broad or narrow paths. For today becoming superior to our foes in point of prosperity as also of duration of rule have we become praiseworthy of men. The sons of Pritha have all been plunged by us into everlasting hell. They have been deprived of happiness and kingdom for ever and ever. They who, proud of their wealth, laughed in derision at the son of Dhritarashtra, will now have to go into the woods, defeated and deprived by us of all their wealth. Let them now put off their variegated coats of mail, their resplendent robes of celestial make, and let them all attire themselves in deer-skins according to the stake they had accepted of the son of Suvala. They who always used to boast that they had no equals in all the world, will now know and regard themselves in this their calamity as grains of sesame without the kernel. Although in this dress of theirs the Pandavas seem like unto wise and powerful persons installed in a sacrifice, yet they look like persons not entitled to perform sacrifices, wearing such a guise. The wise Yajnasena of the Somake race, having bestowed his daughter--the princess of Panchala--on the sons of Pandu, acted most unfortunately for the husbands of Yajnaseni--these sons of Pritha are as eunuchs. And O Yajnaseni, what joy will be thine upon beholding in the woods these thy husbands dressed in skins and thread- bare rags, deprived of their wealth and possessions. Elect thou a husband, whomsoever thou likest, from among all these present here. These Kurus assembled here, are all forbearing and self-controlled, and possessed of great wealth. Elect thou one amongst these as thy lord, so that these great calamity may not drag thee to wretchedness. The sons of Pandu now are even like grains of sesame without the kernel, or like show-animals encased in skins, or like grains of rice without the kernel. Why shouldst thou then longer wait upon the fallen sons of Pandu? Vain is the labour used upon pressing the sesame grain devoid of the kernel!'

"Thus did Dussasana, the son of Dhritarashtra, utter in the hearing of the Pandavas, harsh words of the most cruel import. And hearing them, the unforbearing Bhima, in wrath suddenly approaching that prince like a Himalayan lion upon a jackal, loudly and chastisingly rebuked him in these words,--'Wicked-minded villain, ravest thou so in words that are uttered alone by the sinful? Boastest thou thus in the midst of the kings, advanced as thou art by the skill of the king of Gandhara. As thou piercest our hearts here with these thy arrowy words, so shall I pierce thy heart in battle, recalling all this to thy mind. And they also who from anger or covetousness are walking behind thee as thy protectors,-- them also shall I send to the abode of Yama with their descendants and relatives.'"

Vaisampayana continued,--"Unto Bhima dressed in deer-skins and uttering these words of wrath without doing any thing, for he could not deviate from the path of virtue, Dussasana abandoning all sense of shame, dancing around the Kurus, loudly said, 'O cow! O cow!'

"Bhima at this once more said,--'Wretch darest thou, O Dussasana, use harsh words as these? Whom doth it behove to boast, thus having won wealth by foul means? I tell thee that if Vrikodara, the son of Pritha, drinketh not thy life-blood, piercing open thy breast in battle, let him not attain to regions of blessedness, I tell thee truly that by slaying the sons of Dhritarashtra in battle, before the very eyes of all the warriors, I shall pacify this wrath of mine soon enough.'"

Vaisampayana continued,--"And as the Pandavas were going away from the assembly, the wicked king Duryodhana from excess of joy mimiced by his own steps the playful leonine trade of Bhima. Then Vrikodara, half turning towards the king said, 'Think not ye fool that by this thou gainest any ascendency over me; slay thee shall I soon with all thy followers, and answer thee, recalling all this to thy mind.' And beholding this insult offered to him, the mighty and proud Bhima, suppressing his rising rage and following the steps of Yudhishthira, also spake these words while going out of the Kaurava court, 'I will slay Duryodhana, and Dhananjaya will slay Karna, and Sahadeva will slay Sakuni that gambler with dice. I also repeat in this assembly these proud words which the gods will assuredly make good, if ever we engage in battle with the Kurus, I will slay this wretched Duryodhana in battle with my mace, and prostrating him on the ground I will place my foot on his head. And as regards this (other) wicked person-- Dussasana who is audacious in speech, I will drink his blood like a lion.'

"And Arjuna said,--'O Bhima, the resolutions of superior men are not known in words only. On the fourteenth year from this day, they shall see what happeneth.'

"And Bhima again said,--'The earth shall drink the blood of Duryodhana, and Karna, and the wicked Sakuni, and Dussasana that maketh the fourth.'

"And Arjuna said,--'O Bhima, I will, as thou directest, slay in battle this Karna so malicious and jealous and harsh-speeched and vain. For doing what is agreeable to Bhima, Arjuna voweth that he will slay in battle with his arrows this Karna with all his followers. And I will send unto the regions of Yama also all those other kings that will from foolishness fight against me. The mountains of Himavat might be removed from where they are, the maker of the day lose his brightness, the moon his coldness, but this vow of mine will ever be cherished. And all this shall assuredly happen if on the fourteenth year from this, Duryodhana doth not, with proper respect, return us our kingdom.'"

Vaisampayana continued,--"After Arjuna had said this, Sahadeva the handsome son of Madri, endued with great energy, desirous of slaying Sakuni, waving his mighty arms and sighing like snake, exclaimed, with eyes red with anger--'Thou disgrace of the Gandhara kings, those whom thou thinkest as defeated are not really so. Those are even sharp-pointed arrows from whose wounds thou hast run the risk in battle. I shall certainly accomplish all which Bhima hath said adverting to thee with all thy followers. If therefore thou hast anything to do, do it before that day cometh. I shall assuredly slay thee in battle with all thy followers soon enough, it thou, O son of Suvala, stayest in the light pursuant to the Kshatriya usage.'

"Then, O monarch hearing these words of Sahadeva, Nakula the handsomest of men spake these words,--'I shall certainly send unto the abode of Yama all those wicked sons of Dhritarashtra, who desirous of death and impelled by Fate, and moved also by the wish of doing what is agreeable to Duryodhana, have used harsh and insulting speeches towards this daughter of Yajnasena at the gambling match. Soon enough shall I, at the command of Yudhishthira and remembering the wrongs to Draupadi, make the earth destitute of the sons of Dhritarashtra.'"

Vaisampayana continued,--"And those tigers among men, all endued with long arms, having thus pledged themselves to virtuous promises approached king Dhritarashtra.

SECTION LXXVII

"Yudhishthira said,--'I bid farewell unto all the Bharatas, unto my old grand-sire (Bhishma), king Somadatta, the great king Vahlika, Drona, Kripa, all the other kings, Aswathaman, Vidura, Dhritarashtra, all the sons of Dhritarashtra, Yayutsu, Sanjaya, and all the courtiers, I bid fare well, all of ye and returning again I shall see you.""

Vaisampayana continued,--"Overcome with shame none of those that were present there, could tell Yudhishthira anything. Within their hearts, however, they prayed for the welfare of that intelligent prince.

"Vidura then said,--'The reverend Pritha is a princess by birth. It behoveth her not to go into the woods. Delicate and old and ever known to happiness the blessed one will live, respected by me, in my abode. Known this, ye sons of Pandu. And let safety be always yours.'"

Vaisampayana continued,--"The Pandavas thereupon said,--'O sinless one, let it be as thou sayest. Thou art our uncle, and, therefore like as our father. We also are all obedient to thee. Thou art, O learned one, our most respected superior. We should always obey what thou choosest to command. And, O high-souled one, order thou whatever else there is that remaineth to be done.'

"Vidura replied,--'O Yudhishthira, O bull of the Bharata race, know this to be my opinion, that one that is vanquished by sinful means need not be pained by such defeat. Thou knowest every rule of morality; Dhananjaya is ever victorious in battle; Bhimasena is the slayer of foes; Nakula is the gatherer of wealth; Sahadeva hath administrative talents, Dhaumya is the foremost of all conversant with the vedas; and the well-behaved Draupadi is conversant with virtue and economy. Ye are attached to one another and feel delight at one another's sight and enemies can not separate you from one another, and ye are contented. Therefore, who is there that will not envy ye? O Bharata, this patient abstraction from the possession of the world will be of great benefit to thee. No foe, even if he were equal to sakra himself, will be able to stand it. Formerly thou wert instructed on the mountains of Himavat by Meru Savarni; in the town of Varanavata by Krishna Dwaipayana; on the cliff of Bhrigu by Rama; and on the banks of the Dhrishadwati by Sambhu himself. Thou hast also listened to the instruction of the great Rishi Asita on the hills of Anjana; and thou becamest a disciple of Bhrigu on the banks of the Kalmashi. Narada and this thy priest Dhaumya will now become thy instructors. In the matter of the next world, abandon not these excellent lessons thou hast obtained from the Rishis. O son of Pandu, thou surpassest in intelligence even Pururavas, the son of Ila; in strength, all other monarchs; and in virtue, even the Rishis. Therefore, resolve thou earnestly to win victory, which belongeth to Indra; to control thy wrath, which belongeth to Yama; to give in charity, which belongeth to Kuvera; and to control all passions, which belongeth to Varuna. And, O Bharata, obtain thou the power of gladdening from the moon, the power of sustaining all from water; forbearance from the earth; energy from the entire solar disc; strength from the winds, and affluence from the other elements. Welfare and immunity from ailment be thine; I hope to see thee return. And, O Yudhishthira, act properly and duly in all seasons,--in those of distress--in those of difficulty,-- indeed, in respect of everything, O son of Kunti, with our leave go hence. O Bharata, blessing be thine. No one can say that ye have done anything sinful before. We hope to see thee, therefore, return in safety and crowned with success.'"

Vaisampayana continued,--"Thus addressed by Vidura, Yudhishthira the son of Pandu, of prowess incapable of being baffled, saying, 'So be it,' bowing low unto Bhishma and Drona, went away."

SECTION LXXVIII

Vaisampayana said,--"Then when Draupadi was about to set out she went unto the illustrious Pritha and solicited her leave. And she also asked leave of the other ladies of the household who had all been plunged into grief. And saluting and embracing every one of them as each deserved, she desired to go away. Then there arose within the inner apartments of the Pandavas a loud wail of woe. And Kunti, terribly afflicted upon beholding Draupadi on the eve of her journey, uttered these words in a voice choked with grief,--

"'O child, grieve not that this great calamity hath overtaken thee. Thou art well conversant with the duties of the female sex, and thy behaviour and conduct also are as they should be. It behoveth me not, O thou of sweet smiles, to instruct thee as to thy duties towards thy lords. Thou art chaste and accomplished, and thy qualities have adorned the race of thy birth as also the race into which thou hast been admitted by marriage. Fortunate are the Kauravas that they have not been burnt by thy wrath. O child, safely go thou blest by my prayers. Good women never suffer their hearts to the unstung at what is inevitable. Protected by virtue that is superior to everything, soon shalt thou obtain good fortune. While living in the woods, keep thy eye on my child Sahadeva. See that his heart sinketh not under this great calamity.'

"Saying 'So be it!' the princess Draupadi bathed in tears, and clad in one piece of cloth, stained with blood, and with hair dishevelled left her mother-in-law. And as she went away weeping and wailing Pritha herself in grief followed her. She had not gone far when she saw her sons shorn of their ornaments and robes, their bodies clad in deerskins, and their heads down with shame. And she beheld them surrounded by rejoicing foes and pitied by friends. Endued with excess of parental affection, Kunti approached her sons in that state, and embracing them all, and in accents choked by woe, She said these words,--

"'Ye are virtuous and good-mannered, and adorned with all excellent qualities and respectful behaviour. Ye are all high-minded, and engaged in the service of your superiors. And ye are also devoted to the gods and the performance of sacrifices. Why, then, hath this calamity overtaken you. Whence is this reverse of fortune? I do not see by whose wickedness this sin hath overtaken you. Alas I have brought you forth. All this must be due to my ill fortune. It is for this that ye have been overtaken by this calamity, though ye all are endued with excellent virtues. In energy and prowess and strength and firmness and might, ye are not wanting. How shall ye now, losing your wealth and possessions, live poor in the pathless woods? If I had known before that ye were destined to live in the woods, I would not have on Pandu's death come from the mountains of Satasringa to Hastinapore. Fortunate was your father, as I now regard, for he truly reaped the fruit of his asceticism, and he was gifted with foresight, as he entertained the wish of ascending heaven, without having to feel any pain on account of his sons. Fortunate also was the virtuous Madri, as I regard her today, who had, it seems, a fore-knowledge of what would happen and who on that account, obtained the high path of emancipation and every blessing therewith. Ah, Madri looked upon me as her stay, and her mind and her affections were ever fixed on me. Oh, fie on my desire of life, owing to which suffer all this woe. Ye children, ye are all excellent and dear unto me. I have obtained you after much suffering. I cannot leave you. Even I will go with you. Alas, O Krishna, (Draupadi), why dost thou leave me so? Everything endued with life is sure to perish. Hath Dhata (Brahma) himself forgotten to ordain my death? Perhaps, it is so, and, therefore, life doth not quit me. O Krishna, O thou who dwellest in Dwaraka, O younger brother of Sankarshana, where art thou? Why dost thou not deliver me and these best of men also from such woe? They say that thou who art without beginning and without end deliverest those that think of thee. Why doth this saying become untrue. These my sons are ever attached to virtue and nobility and good fame and prowess. They deserve not to suffer affliction. Oh, show them mercy. Alas, when there are such elders amongst our race as Bhishma and Drona and Kripa, all conversant with morality and the science of worldly concerns, how could such calamity at all come? O Pandu, O king, where art thou? Why sufferest thou quietly thy good children to be thus sent into exile, defeated at dice? O Sahadeva, desist from going. Thou art my dearest child, dearer, O son of Madri, than my body itself. Forsake me not. It behoveth thee to have some kindness for me. Bound by the ties of virtue, let these thy brothers go. But then, earn thou that virtue which springeth from waiting upon me.'"

Vaisampayana continued,--"The Pandavas then consoled their weeping mother and with hearts plunged in grief set out for the woods. And Vidura himself also much afflicted, consoling the distressed Kunti with reasons, and led her slowly to his house. And the ladies of Dhritarashtra's house, hearing everything as it happened, viz., the exile (of the Pandavas) and the dragging of Krishna into the assembly where the princes had gambled, loudly wept censuring the Kauravas. And the ladies of the royal household also sat silent for a long time, covering their lotus-like faces with their fair hands. And king Dhritarashtra also thinking of the dangers that threatened his sons, became a prey to anxiety and could not enjoy peace of mind. And anxiously meditating on everything, and with mind deprived of its equanimity through grief, he sent a messenger unto Vidura, saying, 'Let Kshatta come to me without a moment's delay.'

"At this summons, Vidura quickly came to Dhritarashtra's palace. And as soon as he came, the monarch asked him with great anxiety how the Pandavas had left Hastinapore."

SECTION LXXIX

Vaisampayana said,--"As soon as Vidura endued with great foresight came unto him king Dhritarashtra, the son of Amvika, timidly asked his brother,--'How doth Yudhishthira, the son of Dharma, proceed along? And how Arjuna? And how the twin sons of Madri? And how, O Kshatta, doth Dhaumya proceed along? And how the illustrious Draupadi? I desire to hear everything, O Kshatta; describe to me all their acts.'

"Vidura replied,--'Yudhishthira, the son of Kunti, hath gone away covering his face with his cloth. And Bhima, O king, hath gone away looking at his own mighty arms. And Jishnu (Arjuna) hath gone away, following the king spreading sand-grains around. And Sahadeva, the son of Madri, hath gone away besmearing his face, and Nakula, the handsomest of men, O king, hath gone away, staining himself with dust and his heart in great affliction. And the large-eyed and beautiful Krishna hath gone away, covering her face with her dishevelled hair following in the wake of the king, weeping and in tears. And O monarch, Dhaumya goeth along the road, with kusa grass in hand,

and uttering the aweful mantras of Sama Veda that relate to Yama.'

"Dhritarashtra asked,--'Tell me, O Vidura, why is it that the Pandavas are leaving Hastinapore in such varied guise.'

"Vidura replied,--'Though persecuted by thy sons and robbed of his kingdom and wealth the mind of the wise king Yudhishthira the just hath not yet deviated from the path of virtue. King Yudhishthira is always kind, O Bharata, to thy children. Though deprived (of his kingdom and possessions) by foul means, filled with wrath as he is, he doth not open eyes. "I should not burn the people by looking at them with angry eyes,"--thinking so, the royal son of Pandu goeth covering his face. Listen to me as I tell thee, O bull of the Bharata race, why Bhima goeth so. "There is none equal to me in strength of arms," thinking so Bhima goeth repeatedly stretching forth his mighty arms. And, O king, proud of the strength of his arms, Vrikodara goeth, exhibiting them and desiring to do unto his enemies deeds worthy of those arms. And Arjuna the son of Kunti, capable of using both his arms (in wielding the Gandiva) followeth the footsteps of Yudhishthira, scattering sand-grains emblematical of the arrows he would shower in battle. O Bharata, he indicateth that as the sand-grains are scattered by him with ease, so will he rain arrows with perfect ease on the foe (in time of battle). And Sahadeva goeth besmearing his face, thinking "None may recognise me in this day of trouble." And, O exalted one, Nakula goeth staining himself with dust thinking, "Lest otherwise I steal the hearts of the ladies that may look at me." And Draupadi goeth, attired in one piece of stained cloth, her hair dishevelled, and weeping, signifying--"The wives of those for whom I have been reduced to such a plight, shall on the fourteenth year hence be deprived of husbands, sons and relatives and dear ones and smeared all over with blood, with hair dishevelled and all in their feminine seasons enter Hastinapore having offered oblations of water (unto the manes of those they will have lost)." And O Bharata, the learned Dhaumya with passions under full control, holding the kusa grass in his hand and pointing the same towards the south-west, walketh before, singing the mantras of the Sama Veda that relate to Yama. And, O monarch, that learned Brahamana goeth, also signifying, "When the Bharatas shall be slain in battle, the priests of the Kurus will thus sing the Soma mantras (for the benefit of the deceased)." And the citizens, afflicted with great grief, are repeatedly crying out, "Alas, alas, behold our masters are going away! O fie on the Kuru elders that have acted like foolish children in thus banishing heirs of Pandu from covetousness alone. Alas, separated from the son of Pandu we all shall become masterless. What love can we bear to the wicked and avaricious Kurus?" Thus O king, have the sons of Kunti, endued with great energy of mind, gone away,--indicating, by manner and signs, the resolutions that are in their hearts. And as those foremost of men had gone away from Hastinapore, flashes of lightning appeared in the sky though without clouds and the earth itself began to tremble. And Rahu came to devour the Sun, although it was not the day of conjunction. And meteors began to fall, keeping the city to their right. And jackals and vultures and ravens and other carnivorous beasts and birds began to shriek and cry aloud from the temples of the gods and the tops of sacred trees and walls and house-tops. And these extraordinary calamitous portents, O king, were seen and heard, indicating the destruction of the Bharatas as the consequence of thy evil counsels.'"

Vaisampayana continued,--"And, O monarch, while king Dhritarashtra and the wise Vidura were thus talking with each other, there appeared in that assembly of the Kauravas and before the eyes of all, the best of the celestial Rishis. And appearing before them all, he uttered these terrible words, On the fourteenth year hence, the Kauravas, in consequence of Duryodhana's fault, will all be destroyed by the might of Bhima and Arjuna. And having said this, that best of celestial Rishis, adorned with surpassing Vedic grace, passing through the skies, disappeared from the scene. Then Duryodhana and Karna and Sakuni, the son of Suvala regarding Drona as their sole refuge, offered the kingdom to him. Drona then, addressing the envious and wrathful Duryodhana and Dussasana and Karna and all the Bharata, said, 'The Brahamanas have said that the Pandavas being of celestial origin are incapable of being slain. The sons of Dhritarashtra, however, having, with all the kings, heartily and with reverence sought my protection, I shall look after them to the best of my power. Destiny is supreme, I cannot abandon them. The sons of Pandu, defeated at dice, are going into exile in pursuance of their promise. They will live in the woods for twelve years. Practising the Brahmacharyya mode of life for this period, they will return in anger and to our great grief take the amplest vengeance on their foes. I had formerly deprived Drupada of his kingdom in a friendly dispute. Robbed of his kingdom by me, O Bharata, the king performed a sacrifice for obtaining a son (that should slay me). Aided by the ascetic power of Yaja and Upayaja, Drupada obtained from the (sacrificial) fire a son named Dhrishtadyumna and a daughter, viz., the faultless Krishna, both risen from the sacrificial platform. That Dhrishtadyumna is the brother-in-law of the sons of Pandu by marriage, and dear unto them. It is for him, therefore that I have much fear. Of celestial origin and resplendent as the fire, he was born with bow, arrows, and encased in mail. I am a being that is mortal. Therefore it is for him that I have great fear. That slayer of all foes, the son of Parshatta, hath taken the side of the Pandavas. I shall have to lose my life, if he and I ever encounter each other in battle. What grief can be greater to me in this world than this, ye Kauravas that Dhrishtadyumna is the destined slayer of Drona--this belief is general. That he hath been born for slaying me hath been heard by me and is widely known also in the world. For thy sake, O Duryodhana, that terrible season of destruction is almost come. Do without loss of time, what may be beneficial unto thee. Think not that everything hath been accomplished by sending the Pandavas into exile. This thy happiness will last for but a moment, even as in winter the shadow of the top of the palm tree resteth (for a short time) at its base. Perform various kinds of sacrifices, and enjoy, and give O Bharata, everything thou likest. On the fourteenth year hence, a great calamity will overwhelm thee.'"

Vaisampayana continued,--"Hearing these words of Drona, Dhritarashtra said,--'O Kshatta, the preceptor hath uttered what is true. Go thou and bring back the Pandavas. If they do not come back, let them go treated with respect and affection. Let those my sons go with weapons, and cars, and infantry, and enjoying every other good thing.'"

SECTION LXXX

Vaisampayana said,--"defeated at dice, after the Pandavas had gone to the woods, Dhritarashtra, O king, was overcome with anxiety. And while he was seated restless with anxiety and sighing in grief, Sanjaya approaching him said, 'O lord of the earth having now obtained the whole earth with all its wealth and sent away the sons of Pandu into exile, why is it, O king, that thou grievest so?'

"Dhritarashtra said,--'What have they not to grieve for who will have to encounter in battle those bulls among warriors--the sons of Pandu-- fighting on great cars and aided by allies?'

"Sanjaya said,--'O king, all this great hostility is inevitable on account of thy mistaken action, and this will assuredly bring about the wholesale destruction of the whole world. Forbidden by Bhishma, by Drona, and by Vidura, thy wicked-minded and shameless son Duryodhana sent his Suta messenger commanding him to bring into court the beloved and virtuous wife of the Pandavas. The gods first deprive that man of his reason unto whom they send defeat and disgrace. It is for this that such a person seeth things in a strange light. When destruction is at hand, evil appeareth as good unto the understanding polluted by sin, and the man adhereth to it firmly. That which is improper appeareth as proper, and that which is proper appeareth as improper unto the man about to be overwhelmed by destruction, and evil and impropriety are what he liketh. The time that bringeth on destruction doth not come with upraised club and smash one's head. On the other hand the peculiarity of such a time is that it maketh a man behold evil in good and good in evil. The wretches have brought on themselves this terrible, wholesale, and horrible destruction by dragging the helpless princess of Panchala into the court. Who else than Duryodhana--that false player of dice could bring into the assembly, with insults, the daughter of Drupada, endued with beauty and intelligence, and conversant with every rule of morality and duty, and sprung not from any woman's womb but from the sacred fire? The handsome Krishna, then in her season, attired in one piece of stained cloth when brought into the court cast her eyes upon the

Pandavas. She beheld them, however, robbed of their wealth, of their kingdom, of even their attire, of their beauty, of every enjoyment, and plunged into a state of bondage. Bound by the tie of virtue, they were then unable to exert their prowess. And before all the assembled kings Duryodhana and Karna spake cruel and harsh words unto the distressed and enraged Krishna undeserving of such treatment. O monarch, all this appeareth to me as foreboding fearful consequences.'

"Dhritarashtra said,--'O Sanjaya, the glances of the distressed daughter of Drupada might consume the whole earth. Can it be possible that even a single son of mine will live? The wives of the Bharatas, uniting with Gandhari upon beholding virtuous Krishna, the wedded wife of the Pandavas, endued with beauty and youth, dragged into the court, set up frightful wail. Even now, along with all my subjects, they weep every day. Enraged at the ill treatment of Draupadi, the Brahmanas in a body did not perform that evening their Agnihotra ceremony. The winds blew mightily as they did at the time of the universal dissolution. There was a terrible thunder- storm also. Meteors fell from the sky, and Rahu by swallowing the Sun unseasonably alarmed the people terribly. Our war-chariots were suddenly ablaze, and all their flagstaffs fell down foreboding evil unto the Bharatas. Jackals began to cry frightfully from within the sacred fire- chamber of Duryodhana, and asses from all directions began to bray in response. Then Bhishma and Drona, and Kripa, and Somadatta and the high- souled Vahlika, all left the assembly. It was then that at the advice of Vidura I addressed Krishna and said, "I will grant thee boons, O Krishna, indeed, whatever thou wouldst ask?" The princess of the Panchala there begged of me the liberation of the Pandavas. Out of my own motion I then set free the Pandavas, commanding them to return (to their capital) on their cars and with their bows and arrows. It was then that Vidura told me, "Even this will prove the destruction of the Bharata race, viz., this dragging of Krishna into the court. This daughter of the King of Panchala is the faultless Sree herself. Of celestial origin, she is the wedded wife of the Pandavas. The wrathful sons of Pandu will never forgive this insult offered unto her. Nor will the mighty bowmen of the Vrishni race, nor the mighty warriors amongst the Panchalas suffer this in silence. Supported by Vasudeva of unbaffled prowess, Arjuna will assuredly come back, surrounded by the Panchala host. And that mighty warrior amongst them, Bhimasena endued with surpassing strength, will also come back, whirling his mace like Yama himself with his club. These kings will scarcely be able to bear the force of Bhima's mace. Therefore, O king, not hostility but peace for ever with the sons of Pandu is what seemeth to me to be the best. The sons of Pandu are always stronger than the Kurus. Thou knowest, O king, that the illustrious and mighty king Jarasandha was slain in battle by Bhima with his bare arms alone. Therefore, O bull of the Bharata race, it behoveth thee to make peace with the sons of Pandu. Without scruples of any kind, unite the two parties, O king. And if thou actest in this way, thou art sure to obtain good luck, O king." It was thus, O son of Gavalgani, that Vidura addressed me in words of both virtue and profit. And I did not accept this counsel, moved by affection for my son.'"

The End of Sabha Parva

24518761R00110

Made in the USA
Middletown, DE
27 September 2015